To Rescue A Witch

Lisa A. Traugott

Rose Castle Media

Copyright © 2024 by Lisa A. Traugott

All rights reserved.

No part of this publication may be reproduced, distributed, or transmitted in any form or by any means, including photocopying, recording, or other electronic or mechanical methods, without the prior written permission of the publisher, except as permitted by U.S. copyright law. For permission requests, contact Rose Castle Media at lisatraugott.com.

The story, all names, characters, and incidents portrayed in this production are fictitious. No identification with actual persons (living or deceased), places, buildings, and products is intended or should be inferred.

Thank You!

Thanks for reading my book! Looking for fun book club content? Head over to my website, lisatraugott.com, to sign up for my newsletter to take the quiz to see if YOU would have been convicted for witchcraft!

Chapter One

ANNALIESE

Virginia Colony, 1734

Rob Birch bought Annaliese as a wedding gift.

Sitting in her shift on the hearth, Annaliese played with her doll as he held the mantle and swayed. Wind whistled eerily through the chinks in the cabin logs as he stabbed the tinder with a fire poker, making sparks fly up the wattle and daub chimney.

"Did you stop at the tavern?" Ma asked softly, wrapping her worn plaid shawl over her thin shoulders. She scratched her belly, big with the new baby.

Flexing his fingers on the poker handle, he spit tobacco juice into the flames before setting the poker against the wall.

Annaliese whispered with her doll and giggled.

A shock of greasy hair fell over his tanned face. "What'd yer doll say?"

Annaliese covered her mouth and looked to Ma, who shook her head 'no.' *Stupid Annaliese.* Swallowing hard, she said, "Nuthin', Pa."

Pa's crooked smile faded. "Nuthin', huh? Don't lie to me, Red." His nostrils flared and his breathing got noisy.

Ma moved closer, keeping her voice light. "The wean was just playing, Rob."

Pa snapped, "Ain't no one talking to you, Eleanor. You think I'm gonna deal with slave bullshit all day then come home to sass from your five-year-old?" Rolling up his sleeves, his fingers moved to his buckle.

Pa's belt scared Annaliese. Her mouth went dry, and she wished she could hide under the table, but he was standing over her. Not even heat from the fire could stop her from inching back from his sweaty face. *Look down, be respectful.* Annaliese lowered her eyes to his mud-crusted boots, but he snatched her doll anyway. "No!"

"Whatdyer doll say?" His bloodshot eyes narrowed, and she knew what he was gonna say next. "Little bastard."

Before she could think, Annaliese spat out, "She called you a witch's tit."

Pa hurled her baby doll into the fire. She reached for it, but he grabbed her wrist and held it against the chimney, thrusting the poker in the blaze with his other hand.

Ma yelled, "Rob, no!"

Annaliese twisted in terror when she understood what was coming. He pressed the red-tipped iron into the back of her hand, making her writhe and shriek as it hissed and sizzled her skin.

Ma pulled his arm and the poker clanked on the floor, as she yelled, "Why do you torture her?"

Annaliese buried her face in Ma's blonde hair, sobbing onto her neck, wishing they could run hard and fast away from him forever.

Pa growled, "You always butt in and then wonder why she's a spoiled brat. My pa beat me and I'm fine. Let me handle your bastard." He yanked her from Ma's arms. "You hush your mouth, girl before I sell you."

Annaliese gulped back her tears, afraid of what he'd do next, and wiped her runny nose on her arm. He grabbed her shaking hand and smiled at the branding. Already bright red, it throbbed like all Ma's pins and needles stabbing her at once. Squeezing her eyes shut, she turned from him, wishing him away.

Pa pressed his lips to her ear and whispered, "Now everyone will know how bad you is."

Later that night, when Pa was passed out on the bed with an empty bottle of corn whiskey next to him, Annaliese watched Ma sneak out her book from its hiding spot, rip out a page and scratch something with her old quill pen. Blowing on the clumpy ink, Ma quickly folded the paper and hid it in her pocket.

Ma made the sign of the cross and whispered, "Please, God, let Lord Hallewell save us."

Chapter Two

WILLIAM MACLEOD

London, 1739

William MacLeod didna plan on cleaving Viscount Percy's hand off, but he didna regret it, either.

Earlier, MacLeod had strode the harbor, inhaling the salty air. Even though he dressed in the English manner of breeches, coat and tricorn hat, he carried his Scottish Highlander claymore purely for the fear it instilled in the hearts of any of Lord Hallewell's perceived enemies.

Seagulls scattered as he met the petty officer on the bustling dock.

MacLeod said, "This better be important. If I dinna get to the Highlands in time for my son's wedding, Fiona will have my bollocks."

"Aye, sir, it's bad. See that ship, the *Icarus*? Viscount Percy Monroe owns it, stupid blunderbuss. He's registered to sell wine, but we found smuggled slaves instead."

"What's this to do with me?"

"Viscount Percy claimed Lord Hallewell is his silent partner. HM Customs' agent is harassing me, wondering why I haven't arrested anyone; eighty emaciated Africans are rotting in makeshift pens; and the damned reporters from Fleet Street keep asking questions about Lord Hallewell's connection. It's been a right dung pile."

MacLeod pressed cash into the petty officer's palm. "You were right to call. Where's the cargo?"

The stench of suffering hit him before his hulking frame cast a shadow over a wooden barracoon crammed with Africans in loincloths.

"I think Lord Hallewell's son is the real partner. I've seen Alexander drinking and whoring with Viscount Percy. We've already sold these slaves to the colonies. They're boarding the next floating coffin soon."

A dying child with sores around her mouth wheezed a death rattle in the arms of a man with a deep scar over his left eye.

"Wretched business. Give them water, for God's sake."

"Thank you," the African said.

It startled MacLeod that he knew English words and manners. MacLeod nodded.

"Be careful of him," said an old salt, rambling over, the bone buttons of his dark overcoat straining to cover his belly. "I dursen't, but I think he cursed the ship, the double-poxed hound. Now we don't even get to keep our profit."

"You are ...?"

"I'm ship's master, Mr. Grubb. You're MacLeod? You don't look like a barrister. You're even taller than Alexander said. I knew Lord Hallewell would come to reclaim our cargo. Didn't I say he would protect his investment, Turner? I put half my life savings in this lot."

MacLeod put his bear claw around the squat man's shoulders, leading him away. "I'm going to give you free legal advice. Keep your gob shut around authorities, aye? Why didna you register the cargo properly?"

"Why pay the agent? The crown ain't need it none," Mr. Grubb said, standing at his full five feet two inches. Cheap rum scented his breath.

Bloody edijits. "The viscount's on board?"

"With a lady friend." Mr. Grubb gave an oily grin. "You'll get me my money back, aye?" the old salt called, as MacLeod walked the gangplank and boarded the *Icarus*, its gleaming polished wood masking the rotting enterprise below.

MacLeod descended the narrow steps and hunted for the captain's quarters.

Viscount Percy Monroe, naked save for his double pigtail peruke, was rutting a pretty brunette between candlesticks and peacock quills on the map table. His yellow silks lay rumpled on the floor between a grandfather clock and a gilded birdcage lodging a parrot.

It was already noon. *Of all days to deal with this jingle brain.* MacLeod had already sent his coachman ahead to collect his younger sons from school and send them to Scotland alone.

MacLeod cleared his throat. "My client isna happy with you."

Gasping, the woman tugged her petticoats to cover herself, but Viscount Percy pressed his forearm into her back. "What, you're shy?" Holding MacLeod's gaze, the noble continued thrusting. "I'll tell you the same I told everyone else. If you think you're getting a refund for the confiscated slaves, you can suck my cock. Now bugger off, I'm busy."

The parrot fluttered its emerald wings. "*Caw.* Bugger off. *Caw.*"

Viscount Percy thrust harder, as if to make a point by making the woman grunt in obvious pain. MacLeod grimaced at that. He tapped Viscount Percy's shoulder. The noble spun around in annoyance. MacLeod cracked his forehead against Percy's nose, dropping the aristocrat to his knees. Percy squealed like a piglet as snot and blood rolled through his fingers.

MacLeod handed the woman her cloak. "All right, lass?"

"All in a day's work," she said, lifting a small coin bag on her way out.

MacLeod leaned against the desk, arms crossed. "Did anyone ever teach you how to act like a decent human, you entitled piece of shite?"

Viscount Percy moaned. "You broke my nose. My father's the fifth Earl of Cheshire. He shall destroy you." His veins bulged down his thick neck.

"My client is Lord George Hallewell."

Understanding inched across Viscount Percy's reddened face. "Oh. You must be Mr. MacLeod? Why didn't you tell me sooner who you were? I'm friends with his son, Alexander."

"What are you, twenty-five? You're friends with a sixteen-year-old boy? More like taking advantage of him with your asinine business ideas. Why on earth would you bring slaves anywhere but the colonies?"

"Alexander said his mother wanted them."

Damned Lady Margaret. What's her game? Time to scare the lad. "Ack, liar. You thought you'd traffic and get away with it. I'm sorting this out for Alexander, but I'm not helping you. Put on your breeches. Time to visit the Old Bailey."

"Prison? It's not my fault the agents raided. Lady Margaret said she'd bribe them." MacLeod frowned at this news.

Viscount Percy became all smiles and courtesy. "Mr. MacLeod, I shall endeavor to make things right. I certainly don't desire to be enemies with Lord Hallewell and his notorious enforcer."

MacLeod's shoulders relaxed. *I might make it to the wedding after all.* "Fine. I'll need a full refund for Alexander's share, and then I'll make this situation disappear."

"Right." Cupping his cods in one hand while pinching his bloody nose in the other, the suddenly modest young aristocrat did his best to negotiate with a straight face. "Here's the trouble. I'm not flush right now, but perhaps a note of terms?"

MacLeod snorted. "Your note's as worthless as a declaration of virginity from a whore."

"Then let me sign over a ten percent stake in my ship to cover the fines and losses, and we'll call it done and done."

"Is it your ship, laddie, or your father's?"

"Mine," Viscount Percy said through gritted teeth.

MacLeod made a quick assessment. Beyond the stench, the *Icarus* was well appointed, and a ship would expand options for future commerce. "Fifty percent. Where's the deed? Dinna bleed where you sign."

Viscount Percy wiped his nose on his arm, extracting the papers from a drawer. He signed with one of the peacock quills scattered on the desk. As MacLeod read it, Viscount Percy bashed his skull with a candlestick.

"Agh." MacLeod clasped the back of his head, blinking in shock as his vision momentarily blurred.

Viscount Percy grabbed his rapier from the wall and pointed it at MacLeod's throat. "Lord Hallewell should talk to his wife before he sends his Scottish bitch after me. Alexander owes *me* money because his mother's too stupid to bribe an agent. I'm going to cut off your head, shove your bollocks in your mouth and send it to the whole damned family as a message."

MacLeod's head throbbed. *Stay calm. Dead nobles cause more headaches than they're worth.* "Lower your sword, lad, or you'll regret it."

Viscount Percy's hand trembled. *The worst kind of opponent*, MacLeod thought. *Scared amateurs do dangerous things.*

"Like you regret leaving your witch wife alone with Colonel Wilkes? I hear she's exceptional at enchanting men." As Viscount Percy laughed, his wavering rapier moved out of range.

In a flash, MacLeod pulled his claymore from its sheath and cleaved off the viscount's hand. The sword clinked as it landed, with Percy's long fingers still wrapped around the handle as blood splattered everywhere. MacLeod put his sword in his sheath, grabbed the severed hand, and the viscount by the neck, and dragged him up the stairs and onto the deck.

Outside, the Africans shuffled in groups of twenty toward the long, pointed boats taking them to the slave ship. Heavy chains linked one person's neck to another's.

"Mercy!" Viscount Percy yelped, as MacLeod lobbed him naked and flailing overboard. Percy's severed hand soon splashed beside him.

"Viscount Percy!" shouted Mr. Grubb, racing to throw him a line of rope.

Ankle chains scraped the boardwalk as the enslaved rushed to the dock's edge for a glimpse. A slow laugh rippled through the crowd as they gawked at their former captor's twist of fortune. MacLeod noted the little girl the African had been holding slumped in the cage corner, unmoving.

Boldness overtook the African with the scar, and he pissed on Viscount Percy's bobbing head to hoots and cheers. MacLeod wiped the blood from his claymore with a nearby rag, revealing the inscription, *Justice*. MacLeod connected eyes with the African. They gave each other a nod of respect.

That didna go as I planned. Viscount Percy's father, the earl, was a prickly old bastard. Would he be angrier about the hand, or his son being made a fool of? There'd be consequences. Still. MacLeod was happy he did it. But why did Viscount Percy mention Colonel Wilkes or call his wife a witch? It had been fifteen years since the salt circle. What had Lady Margaret been saying to this little weasel, and why?

Standing with palm in palm behind his back, the afternoon sun cast an amber glow over Lord Hallewell's eclectically decorated study at Astwick House. *If I leave by coach first thing tomorrow, I'll be able to make it home just before James' wedding. Come on, come on. Where's Lord Hallewell?*

Lady Margaret's narcissus perfume spread like a noxious cloud as she entered with her errant son, Alexander. She couldn't be called beautiful, her features were too strong, but what she lacked in bearing, her first husband's fortune more than made up for. It was the sole reason MacLeod had arranged for Lord Hallewell to marry her. Her signature red gown was like a matador's cape flashing before his raging bull. Something seemed different about her, a subtle fury in her cold eyes. *Hold fast, MacLeod. You've already done one stupid thing today.*

Lord Hallewell sauntered in, impeccably dressed as always, in a black coat with white embroidery. His powdered peruke's ponytail was tied inside a black taffeta bag with a rosette of white ribbon. He sat beneath a giant portrait of a lie—himself appearing young and happy. Perched on a high-backed armchair behind his carved walnut desk, he purposefully kept no chairs for visitors, thus everyone had to stand before him, king on the throne.

What must it be like to sit in his chair? To be of noble blood?

"It's lucky you're still in town, MacLeod," Lord Hallewell said.

Lucky me.

Alexander, Lady Margaret's son from her first marriage, squirmed before his stepfather, knotting the black curls on both sides of his head and tying them together in the back. "How was I to know Viscount Percy's a scoundrel?" Alex carried his mother's dark features, which suited him better. "Can't Mr. MacLeod fix it?"

"The fixer," Lady Margaret sneered, exposing rotten teeth. "Too bad you never *prevent* problems." She massaged her lower jaw.

MacLeod ignored her. "My lord, I bribed the officials and journalists, snuffing the scandal. You ken, preventing things," he said cheerfully.

"You're now the proud owner of the ship, the *Icarus*. Technically, Viscount Percy has partial ownership, but I took full possession."

"You stole the ship?" Lord Hallewell smirked.

"Which more than covers Alexander's losses. To avoid trouble, perhaps young Master Alexander should tell me his plans, not his mistakes."

Lord Hallewell laughed. "Just like in our Oxford days. I'd think everything was hopeless, and you'd find solutions, old friend. I'm very pleased indeed. But not with you, Alexander. Where did you meet this merchant?"

"He's not a merchant. His father's the fifth Earl of Cheshire. We met at the club."

MacLeod said, "He winnae be playing cards any time soon. His hand's fish food."

Alexander whined, "How can I go to the club now?"

Lady Margaret turned as pale as the lace fan she fluttered. "How barbaric."

"Self-defense. He breathes." MacLeod twisted the knife. "My lord, Viscount Percy said you should've consulted your wife before sending me."

Her blush betrayed surprise. *Bet you need to fan yourself now, Margaret.*

His lordship's eyes pierced his wife's. "It seems you like to keep secrets." Something in Lord Hallewell's tone was different, more accusatory. She seemed to notice, too. *What the hell is going on?*

"Forgive me, my lord, but I didn't want to bother you with insignificant matters. In five years, the trust dissolves and Alexander comes into his inheritance. He needs to learn how to manage it. Slave smuggling's quite profitable."

"To the West Indies perhaps, but London?" quipped MacLeod.

"How dare you let him speak to me thus?" she appealed to her husband, ruby earrings dangling like blood drops.

Shite. MacLeod bowed. "Apologies, my lord, my lady."

Lord Hallewell exhaled through his nose. "Well, why did you smuggle them here?"

Lady Margaret held her head high. "It's fashionable to have a Negro footman. Why not profit on the trend? Control the market? We had advanced sales to the finest families."

"Aye, my lady," MacLeod said, barely containing his annoyance. "Now they're demanding full refunds or threatening to sue. It'll take me days to negotiate settlements to avoid court. You never smuggle in London. That's why God created western Wales."

Lord Hallewell slammed his fist on the desk, surprising them. "I decide, not you, Margaret. I'm cutting off both your and Alexander's allowances until further notice."

Panic swept her features. "My lord, I aimed to be a dutiful mother."

"Try being a dutiful wife, madam," Lord Hallewell said.

Freezing momentarily at the rebuke, she gave a dignified nod. "I shall strive to please you better in the future." Pivoting abruptly, she stabbed MacLeod with an icy glare, massaging her jaw as she left with her son in tow.

Lord Hallewell rang a bell as MacLeod swatted away her lingering perfume. A servant in blue livery arrived with port. "Leave the bottle." Lord Hallewell raised his glass. "To the king."

"The king." MacLeod drank. "You should speak with Viscount Percy's father, the earl, as a courtesy. They're estranged apparently, but why tempt a duel?"

"I don't care about such trifles."

Then why did I waste my whole day on this?

Lord Hallewell opened his top desk drawer and handed over a well-worn letter, its ink scratched across the page with urgency. "Margaret doesn't realize I found this in her bedchamber."

Blast it, what needs fixing now? I'll never get home in time. His stomach sank at the address. *Please dinna be who I think it is.*

March 1, 1734
Williamsburg, Virginia Colony

My Dearest George,
I know I'm not supposed to write to you, but I must. You

have a daughter, Annaliese. I fear my husband will kill us. I beg your mercy and forgiveness. If you ever loved me, please save our daughter.

Yours,

Eleanor

MacLeod digested its contents. "A daughter? Are they safe? This letter's nearly five years old."

"How should I know?" Lord Hallewell paced the room, his heeled shoes echoing on the hardwood floor. "Notice how worn it is? Margaret not only hid it, she clearly draws happiness envisioning my mistress and natural daughter getting bludgeoned." He tapped the letter to his lips. "All this time I wondered where Eleanor went, what I did so wrong she'd leave me."

Distract him. "How did Lady Margaret get the letter? Were there any others?"

"You think I'm going to ask my wife anything about a former mistress? Are you mad?"

The din of London pressed outside the window. MacLeod shifted on his feet, itching to leave. "I'll send inquiries on the way out of town. Dinna fash, I'll arrange for their safety."

"How could you have let this happen?"

"Me? Beg pardon, my lord, but I cannae deal with your bastards unless I ken they exist."

"She's not supposed to write to me? Says whom?" Lord Hallewell drained his glass, then poured another. "What in heavens is Eleanor doing in the colonies?"

"Eleanor buggered off with an actor, aye?" MacLeod ken this to be a sore spot and pressed. "If she hasna written since 1734, matters must have resolved themselves with her man."

"Happy with a brute? She begged me to save them. You must travel at once."

MacLeod almost spit out his port. "Me? To Virginia?"

"Leave tomorrow, and they'll be here by summer's end."

"A trip to the colonies takes two months going, six weeks back, assuming good weather and immediate passage, and I'd still have to find them. I'd be gone for months."

"Make Fiona happy and pack a kilt. I hear it's warm there and the fresh air might do your bollocks some good."

"The last thing I want is to return to Highlander garb."

"Coat and breeches then. Don't worry about booking passage. Apparently, I own a ship now." A boyish smile spread across Lord Hallewell's face.

"My lord, dinna be impulsive."

"Why are you fighting me?" Lord Hallewell's eyes narrowed.

"I have other clients with court cases, and my tenants to collect rent from. Besides, I cannae leave before harvest. Fiona will already be furious that I'm late to the wedding. Fiona—"

"Is lucky you haven't abandoned her, considering."

MacLeod lowered his drink. "You're threatening me?"

Lord Hallewell stared up, unflinching. "When the time came, I fixed your problem, despite the risk to my reputation. I expect, no, demand, your loyalty. You are loyal, aren't you?"

"You have to ask?"

"Do I?"

"She's just a mistress, George. What good comes from bringing them here? You really want to expose yourself to scandal for some servant you fucked a decade ago? Think on it."

Lord Hallewell touched his arm. "William, you don't understand what it's like to lose someone and then—find them again. I don't care about our roles in society. Aristocrat. Servant. It's just a construct, not who we are."

Only a rich man with noble blood could say something as stupid as that.

Lord Hallewell said, "I don't even mind learning the truth behind why she left. We must face our past, even if it's uncomfortable, if we want any hope for a better tomorrow."

"The only way to reach tomorrow at all is to keep our past sins buried," snorted MacLeod.

"I love her." Lord Hallewell's eyes welled.

They locked stares. Rare to see his lordship vulnerable, like when they were truly friends. But now George was his lord to serve. "Yes, my lord."

Forcing a smile, Lord Hallewell said, "Forgive me, William. I'm not myself today. I meant no disrespect to you or Fiona. I adore that lovely sprite." He punched MacLeod's arm playfully. "I know you're loyal. Other solicitors can fix Alex's indiscretions. You're the only one I trust to protect the people most dear to me."

MacLeod sighed. Yet another thing Fiona would complain about, but considering Lord Hallewell now considered this trip a loyalty test, his wife would need to grin and bear it. "I'll get my household in order, and set sail by the end of the month, my lord."

Lord Hallewell beamed, heartily patted MacLeod's back and poured another glass, giddy with the future. "God save the king. And grant you safe travels." He drank.

MacLeod skimmed the worn letter. *Why would Lady Margaret keep the evidence? Daft cow.* "I need Eleanor's letter to prove paternity. What'll you tell Lady Margaret when she discovers it's missing?"

"I think she already suspects, but we'll never broach that subject. We always dance around failures big and small in our marriage." He sipped. "Why do you think Eleanor named my daughter Annaliese? Was she trying to make the girl sound Dutch? Her name should be Anna or Elizabeth, not a combination. Eleanor's adorably silly. God, I love her."

MacLeod grimaced. "Who kens if they're still in Virginia? Or alive? Disease runs rampant in the colonies." *Let's hope. Bloody Eleanor. Even now, she's a pain in the arse.*

"You can't ruin my mood, MacLeod. My favorite mistress shall return. God, she must have thought I left her to die."

"This is a fool's errand."

"Lord Hallewell's no fool. No one keeps secrets from me. I always find out."

Not always. "Yes, my lord. I'm off to the inn. I'll sail the *Icarus* from Glasgow."

"When you find that wife-beating brute ... Rough, MacLeod. Make him hurt."

He nodded. *Jesus, Joseph and Mary. It'll take at least three days to finish the preparations. Bloody former mistresses and their spoiled brats. The nerve to name her Annaliese. She's going to pay for that letter.*

Chapter Three

FIONA

Scotland

I shouldnae be here. William forbids it. Fiona pursued the source of the bewitching sound, never quite making out more than a blur of a girl with tangled red curls, until she came upon a dozen waterfalls rumbling from the mountains. An electric current charged the darkening sky.

Fiona panted, catching her breath. "What did you want me to see, child?"

The girl stared with eyes blue as the Fairy Pools she stood beside.

"Are you a changeling?" Fiona called.

Spinning abruptly, the lass waded into the water. Cold spray from the waterfalls dampened Fiona's skin. Suddenly, William appeared on the opposite side of the stream, tall and strong by the craggy rocks, his tartan wrapped loosely over his shoulder. How odd—how wonderful—to see him in Highlander plaid again.

Fiona felt separated from her body, like she was watching a play unfold about a forsaken witch, able to predict but never alter the future. Here, in her husband's clan lands, she felt acutely aware of the distance between them. No matter how close he stood, they were apart—and aching.

Pointing to a magnificent red stag with regal antlers descending the hills, the girl said, "Look." It stopped at the water's edge.

Fiona touched her fingers to her parted lips, staring. The beast held her gaze an instant before dashing through and troubling the water, transforming crystal blue to muddy confusion. Fiona glanced to William, feeling the hairs on her arms stand on end.

Sparks of lightning revealed the fairy girl getting swept away in a white whirlwind. Fiona clapped her hands over her mouth, frozen as she watched the child reach out for help with spindly arms covered in bleeding scratches. William dove deep to rescue the girl.

With a growing tingling in her chest, Fiona hunted the surface of the water for signs of their reemergence, but a thick mist rolled in.

"William?"

Fiona's fists clenched and unclenched. *Is he lost for good?*

She opened her eyes back in Kirkhaven, pressing her palm against her chest, rattled by her vision. Fiona never asked for this gift, 'twas more a curse. What good had second sight done for Auntie Matilda but char her bones?

I shouldnae be doing this.

Like a child waiting to be caught, Fiona glanced over her shoulder. Thankfully, the castle ruins shielded her sins. No one would spy on her salt circle here. Mugwort leaves smoldered nearby. Taking deep, controlled breaths, she inhaled the earthly scent mixing with the salt of the sea. Dried seaweed crunched in her fist as she pulled it from her satchel and sprinkled it along with limpet shells in the smoldering leaves to cast the spell.

"*Eisd rium a Dhia.* Auntie Matilda, hear me. It's been fifteen years since my last vision. Why now? Help me understand the warning you've sent. Bestow enchantments with harm to none."

Her pulse raced as she quickly swept the salt anticlockwise from west to north in a pile, placing it along with the ashes and candle in a burlap sack, and flinging it into the Firth of Clyde. Nothing made her feel more grounded, more powerful, more alive than magic. Fiona clapped her hands clean, noticing her emerald and diamond bracelet. Like her marriage, its sparkle had dimmed. *Hurry, lest he finds you again.*

Dashing up the pockmarked steps beneath the water gate archway, she found her horse near the collapsed stables in the Upper Bailey and mounted it. They cantered past the hills of blooming redshank, and her thoughts shifted to her son's wedding, mere days away. *James was a wee bairn just a moment ago, how can he be getting married?*

Just beyond the birch and alder trees, her three-story manor rose from the glen. Dismounting, she handed the reins to a stable boy who brought the horse into the large, detached barn. Her husband's coach approached past the stone fence. *Perfect timing.*

Servants stood at attention in a line on the left as she joined James, their eldest, on the right. He draped his arm over the petite shoulders of his blonde fiancée, Nelly. Fiona bounced on tiptoe in anticipation, as her black cat, Pooka, curled around her legs.

Her two youngest bairns emerged, still wearing their school clothes. "My boys, how I've missed you," she said, pulling them into a bear hug.

Hamish, a flame-haired seven-year-old, and the spitting image of William, ran in circles around her like a puppy. "What's stinky, Mam?"

Her eyes popped open. *Mugwort leaves.* "I've been gardening," she said, keeping her tone light. *William willnae recognize the scent's purpose, will he?*

"What's for dinner?" Lachlan called, sauntering inside. A masculine version of Fiona, he shared her honey-tresses and cat-colored eyes. At thirteen, he was a year younger and a head taller than Broderick, still slumped in the post-chaise.

Fiona inspected inside, as though it would make her husband appear. James followed, equally confused. Fiona marked her quiet fourteen-year-old, Broderick. Dark hair, dark eyes, face hidden behind his hand.

"Where's your father?" she asked.

Broderick shrugged. "Where else? Lord Hallewell has an urgent matter he must attend."

James exploded, "The wedding is Wednesday!"

"I'm sure he's on the way," Fiona said. *He'd never intentionally miss James' nuptials.*

Broderick rushed out of the coach with his head bowed, but James stopped him. "What's wrong with your face?" James pulled Broderick's hand away, exposing a black eye and a swollen lip.

Broderick said, "You think it'll heal before Da returns? I dinna want him to ken."

Oh, no. William will lose his mind when he sees this. "The same lad as before?" Fiona touched Broderick's cut, and he winced. "Sorry. There's still salt on my fingers."

James arched his eyebrow, and she averted her gaze.

Where is my husband?

Chapter Four

WILLIAM MACLEOD

William MacLeod had barely fallen asleep when the knock came saying he had a visitor, and it was urgent. A mousy serving girl piloted him through pipe smoke clouds to the back of the tavern, then scurried away.

Lady Margaret, already seated and drinking claret, lowered her hooded cloak.

"Ale," he called to the bartender, eyeing Lady Margaret warily. "Why so clandestine, my lady?"

"I assume you've got my allowance flowing again."

He let slip a smile. "Who am I to tell a husband how to discipline his wife?"

"You must be an expert from constant practice. Fiona casts quite a spell over men, doesn't she?"

A cool breeze passed them as the door opened. Travelers shook rain from their coats.

MacLeod said, "Your veiled barbs are offensive and unjustified. Haven't I resolved every mess your family's gotten into, my lady? But let's be frank. Why did Viscount Percy mention Colonel Wilkes dancing with my wife? He wasnae at the wedding, and Wilkes is long gone."

Lady Margaret smiled, sipping her wine. "People talk."

"No, *you* talk."

"How brave to speak with such impudence when my husband isn't near." She sipped her wine. "Things are about to change dramatically between us. You're about to lose your proximity to power, your money, your stupid wife's love."

Candlelight flickered as a wench deposited a mug of ale, which he drank from. "Oh?"

Digging into her cloak, Lady Margaret untangled Fiona's tartan shawl, stained from blood and dirt. Out dropped an emblem of Saint George.

Oh, shite.

Was Lord Hallewell keeping this for blackmail all along? After all his talk of loyalty? Hold fast. Lady Margaret didna ken anything. "This means nothing to me."

"No? My gardeners unearthed this last week. The last time anyone saw Colonel Wilkes alive, he wore that emblem, and your wife was reading his palm. What an odd coincidence someone would bury those two items together in my courtyard."

Lady Margaret fingered the brass medal with an aching expression. Colonel Wilkes was her former lover, after all.

"There's no proof it's Fiona's shawl," he said, drinking casually. Lifting the emblem, he rolled the cold metal in his hand, then tossed it on the table with a clank. "And Wilkes isna the only man to receive the Order of the Garter."

Rain pounded harder on the rooftop and against the windowpanes. Another coachful of travelers came in and dripped near the fireplace.

Lady Margaret rubbed her jaw as she leaned in. "Seems like evidence to me. Be a shame if rumors were to spread about a murderous social-climbing barrister and his witch wife luring the poor colonel into a trap. What a gruesome twosome. The reporters on Fleet Street would eat it up."

Shattering glass from a dropped beer tray made him jump. Patrons slipped on the spill.

MacLeod said, "I'll tell those same reporters about Alexander's paternity. Your first husband's relatives would be fascinated to learn the 'heir' is but one of Colonel Wilkes' wee bastards. We both have leverage, dinna we?"

"You're too honorable a man to condemn my innocent son for my sins. Besides, exposing Alexander's true paternity renders everyone penniless. Is that something you want to risk as trustee? The skeletons in my closet have reduced to dust, but yours keep piling up, don't they? Not even Fiona's protective charms will save you from the hangman's noose."

Accusations, scandal—all over again. The smoky tavern closed in as he realized in that harrowing, incomprehensible moment that Lady Margaret had outmaneuvered him. The bitch had the power to utterly destroy his life. Slumping on the bench in defeat, he said, "What do you want, my lady?"

She hid the evidence beneath her cloak. After another sip of her drink, she licked her lips. "Two thousand pounds, plus a third of your trustee fees, would make a good start," she said, her tone considerably brightening.

"I need time. His lordship is sending me on a trip, and my money is bound in barley. You'll have to wait until I return, and my harvest is sold."

"You'll find my money before you set sail to Virginia."

Finishing his ale, he frowned at the bitter aftertaste. "Done." *Is that it?*

"And I want her dead."

"Who?" he asked, bewildered.

"Eleanor. I know the purpose of your trip. Dead mistresses cause no trouble. Kill the bastard, too."

Goddamn this insufferable woman. "I'm not a murderer," he said, shifting in his creaky seat. Boisterous youths sang "The Gelding of the Devil" between gulps of their pints.

"Oh, but we both know you are."

MacLeod muttered into his ale, "Eleanor cannae cause problems exiled to the colonies."

"Do tell her that when you reach Williamsburg." Sipping her claret, thoughts seemed to roll about her skull. "Exiled? How do you know she's exiled?"

Blast it. "Why else would she be in the colonies?" He shook his head. "You had to keep the letter as your little prize, didna you? Eleanor's suffering wasna enough?"

"No. But envisioning her violent demise by a cruel husband while making her believe Lord Hallewell had abandoned her? That tickled me." Stained red lips spread over her mouth, exposing brown holes across her yellowed incisors. "I always suspected my husband had you kill my lover. It's only fair I have you kill his."

"Your soul's as rotten as your teeth."

She frowned. "Spare me your false pity for servants who climb into their lords' beds. It's tedious."

"My lady, what is it you think I've done?"

"You blackmailed me into a loveless marriage to your idiot friend so you could grow rich off my fortune as trustee for my son. Colonel Wilkes was the most honorable, brilliant man I've ever met. You knew he'd protect my son's interests and that's why you needed him gone. A duel would have at least been honorable, but both you and George knew Wilkes would win. No, you had to be insidious. You tricked Fiona, with all her ridiculous talk of fairies and magic, into reading his palm to lure him from the crowd so you could murder him. You greedy, ambitious, heartless men think you can get away with everything, don't you? Well, now that I know the truth, you'll be the one to pay. Do as I command, or I'll tell everyone your wife is a witch and will blame Wilkes' murder on her. It's more than fair, MacLeod. Kill the mistress and child, or watch your wife burn at the stake."

It took every ounce of restraint not to strangle the wee bitch in the middle of the tavern. *Hold fast, MacLeod.* Beads of sweat dotted his hairline as he mulled over how to handle this. "Eleanor will never set foot in London, but I want assurances you'll stop spreading poison about Fiona."

Lady Margaret's expressionless manner betrayed no commitment. "I've waited years to watch panic seep into your arrogant face as your world collapses." Sliding from the bench, she whispered in his ear, "Mr. MacLeod, you treated your scandals carelessly, and you underestimated me." She raised her cloak hood. "Send Fiona my love."

I'll never escape the Hallewells' clutch. Hopefully I'll be lucky, and Eleanor's husband already killed her and the bastard.

Chapter Five

ANNALIESE

Virginia Colony

Pa owned Annaliese's bastard ass and he never let her forget it, neither. In the setting sun, Annaliese fled past Ma's grave, overgrown with five years of weeds.

"Keep up, Sam," she whispered, holding her little brother's hand. He got winded quick.

Branches tugged threads from her ratty, fingerless gloves, while twigs broke beneath her grimy, bare feet.

Daniel Crowan had dressed extra dandy today, wearing a powdered wig beneath his tricorn hat. If only she could punch his gap-toothed mouth. *How long before they notice we's gone?*

"Annaliese," Pa hollered.

Slapping her sweaty neck, she squished a mosquito and squinted down a path lit by lightning bugs. *Schneider farm? No, the father will send us home again.*

"W-where we g-going?" Sam asked.

"Shh." *No time to explain.* She yanked him forward.

Pa yelled, "Annaliese, come back now and I ain't gonna whip you for running."

Liar. They reached the old oak. Left took them to town, right led to the York River.

"S-stop," Sam huffed.

Mr. Daniel called, "This way. I found a thread from her glove."

Sam climbed on her back, and she picked through the thorns toward the river. Her feet sank in the sand, spongy with pine needles.

Pa called, "Sam, you ain't helping your sister none. You making me mad. Stop hiding."

A hint of Mr. Daniel's dark green waistcoat caught her eye. "There," he called.

Sprinting blind through hot puddles, low-hanging branches snapped at her face, stinging her cheek. Twisting to check behind, she tripped hard over a snarled tree root. Sam rolled into the undergrowth. Scrambling up, he helped free her foot. Sam gaped at her ankle, already turning purple.

"P-pa, h-help!" Sam shouted.

Her mouth dropped. Gripping the rough, cracked ridges of tree bark to help her up, she ignored the sharp pain and limped toward the river.

Sam chased after her, grabbing her hand. "S-stop. Y-you're h-hurt."

She shoved him. *He ain't understand.*

"Halt there," the gentleman commanded from ten yards back.

Annaliese struggled to see the path, losing them again in a curve. Crawling under an upturned oak stump, dirt rained down her shift. She pulled Sam under and covered his mouth with her hand, not trusting him to keep quiet. Less than a minute later, the gentleman's buckled shoes stopped beside their hiding spot.

"Where's their trail?" Mr. Daniel panted. "I'm not dressed for running through a forest." He sounded annoyed.

"She here," Pa said softly.

A murder of crows cawed as they flew over the treetops. It was hard to get a lungful in the muggy trapped heat.

"Annaliese," Pa sang in his gravelly voice. "I known you here, girl."

Please leave. Just leave.

"Sam," he sang, "I'm gonna remember this."

Sam's nails dug into her arm, making half-moons. The wind blew stronger.

"This wasn't the deal, Rob."

"Ain't nuthin' like a hunt. Ain't used to working for something, is you?" Pa laughed nervously. "Sorry she's causing trouble. Never could make Eleanor's bastard behave."

Please, please leave. Sam's sweaty body pressed against her, overheating her.

"I certainly don't have all night," complained Mr. Daniel. "Why am I chasing children through the forest? We can resolve this in court."

"Ain't no need for anyone to go to prison. She just scared after last time." Pa's heavy boots walked past the opening. "She's like Eleanor was. Needs a firm hand, is all."

In the shadows, she watched Sam's small chest rise and fall, and felt the wetness of his nose running over her fingers. Lightning fell scattershot into their hiding spot.

"Annaliese," Pa continued to sing, soft and sweet, just yards away. Thunder rumbled in the distance. "Ain't got all night, girl."

Snap.

Only a mouse. Her ankle throbbed. A tinkling confused her until she realized it was Sam's warm piss. "Damn it, Sam," she mouthed. He cried. Hugging him tighter, she hoped Pa wouldn't smell it. She felt sick.

Crack. A branch broke in the distance. "This way." Their footsteps chased after the noise until their voices grew distant. Keeping her hand tight against Sam's mouth, Annaliese strained to hear. It was suffocating under the rotting oak. She pulled her mother's torn shift away from her sticky skin. *Did they leave for good?*

After what felt like hours, she let out a huge breath and leaned against Sam, taking her hand off his mouth. She rubbed her temples to smooth out her jumbled thoughts. *We'll go to the river and find a boat.*

A long breeze rustled through the trees.

We did it. A soft drizzle fell outside.

A giddy sigh left her mouth. *We got away.*

Pa's calloused hands tore into the roots. "Gotcha."

"No." She twisted, her fingernails clawing the ground. Dirt poured on the back of her neck as he dragged her out by the arms. Sam held her legs, but his strength was no match.

"Oh, you in a heap of trouble now," Pa said. The men laughed.

"You're a naughty little girl, aren't you? Thought we'd never find you," Mr. Daniel said with his gap-toothed grin.

"Told you she's bad. That's why she wears gloves." Pa peeled one off. "Ain't want no one to see your branding, huh?"

Warm raindrops fell, wetting her ugly hand. Her skin felt prickly as she broke into a cold sweat knowing what would come next.

Mr. Daniel said, "Feel free to play cards with me any time, Birch."

The men had a good laugh.

Stop laughing.

Stop laughing.

Stop laughing.

After, Annaliese limped home as steady rain fell on her lowered head.

"Quit your cryin'," Pa said, yanking her arm. "You hush your mouth, now."

Swallowing her sobs, she stood in the front yard between discarded chicken bones and broken whiskey bottles. Pa jangled a key and locked her swollen ankle to a chain connected to a heavy metal ball.

"You selfish piece of shit. I feed you, give you a place to sleep. You ain't even mine. You want me in debtors' prison? You cain't lie still for five damn minutes while Daniel Crowan do his business? You wanna run wild? Spend a night with the witches." Pa heaved Sam inside the cabin and slammed the door.

He ain't gonna break me. Pounding rain dripped off her nose.

Annaliese tried to escape the sound of Sam's screams as Pa beat him, but the ball and chain only allowed five feet of movement. *This is all my fault.* Her stomach hurt with guilt.

The rain stopped as the moon climbed above the pine trees. Her teeth chattered as she stared into the dark forest. Pa told her once that the middle of the night was the Devil's Hour. Yellow eyes glared from the forest.

"Who's there?"

Terrified of being mauled or choked by witches, she stayed awake, flinching at every noise. Her skin itched powerful fierce, and her breath caught in her throat until everything went black.

At daybreak, she woke with ants crawling on her and paw prints nearby. *Everyone known witches can change themselves into animals. Wish I could be a witch—make myself into a cat and run away.*

She slapped off the insects as the door opened. Pa shoved Sam next to her and headed to the shack to milk the cow and feed the horse Mr. Daniel had loaned him.

Annaliese hugged Sam, rubbing away the sting from the belt welts along his neck, but he punched her arm. *He blames me for his whipping, is all.*

Her mouth tasted sticky. "Sneak me some water." He shook no. *Pa scared him good.*

Pa came with the bucket and squatted. His eyes were bloodshot and his breath stunk like corn whiskey. "*Mm.* Sure looks tasty." He drank the foamy milk and the fat stuck to his whiskers. "Sam, who's that?"

One of his games.

"M-my s-sister."

"She's my indentured. She a person?"

Sam glanced at Annaliese with those big brown eyes. "N-no."

He ain't really mean it.

Pa talked slow, like he was teaching Sam. "She ain't no better than a dog, or a pig. Pig tells you to run, you gonna run?"

"N-no."

"Stay away from her. She needs to learn. Drink you some milk."

Sam drank, leaving a little at the bottom.

Pa eyeballed her. "Animals can be trained. You gonna be my pussycat when I'm through. Any pussycats want some milk?"

Shit. That's not what I meant when I wished to be a cat. A pounding throb hurt her head and she licked her cracked lips. Lower your eyes. Beg. That's his game—shame me.

"What do you say?"

Do what he wants. "Meow."

Pa elbowed Sam's ribs. "Here kitty, kitty, crawl if you want some milk. Meow."

Sam giggled nervously.

Annaliese crawled with the chain lagging behind. "Meow."

Pa dumped the milk just outside her reach and laughed. The cloudy puddle seeped into the ground.

"I hate you," she said, throwing a fistful of dirt at him. Pa stomped his boot, and she curled up expecting his kick.

"Catch us some fish for dinner," he told Sam.

Pa went inside to drink. Sam left with his pole, ducking her eyes.

What good did running do? No. Shouldn't think like that. Just gotta plan it better. Her tongue brushed over her slimy teeth. *Pa will let me go soon. I known it.*

She wrung the bottom of her dress, sucking dampness from last night's rain. Mid-morning sun burned her skin as chimney swifts flew over the garden. *Pa will let me go any minute. He'll want me to weed.*

Late afternoon, Pa tossed his empty bottle in the yard and snapped his short whip he kept on the wood pile. Even chained, she tried to escape. Pa's whip moved faster than sound. Never sure where it would land, it bit like a snake until she screeched, and her tears streamed.

"You better hush your mouth, or I'll whip you harder," he warned, looping his whip.

That was his way. Beat her until she cried, then tell her to stop cryin'. Long after Pa left, she lay in the muck with a familiar lump in her throat. Blood from her welted skin seeped through the thin fabric, staining her shift again. Shadows from the pine trees shifted across the ground. Every inch of her stung, but nuthin' stung worse than his words. *You ain't no better than a pig.*

Sam came back with three catfish but ignored her. Buttered fish frying in the spider pan soon scented the air, making her hands shake with hunger.

Hours passed.

Pa's gonna starve me. She felt nauseous and heaved. Nuthin' came up but the moon.

Night vermin scratched for food. Or was it a witch? She listened to the animal noises to keep her mind off things. Barred owl. Black vulture. A low growl pricked her ear. *Witch?*

"Who's out there?!" she yelled. "Pa? Let me in. I'm sorry."

Dragging the ball and chain toward the cabin, she made a valley in the mud. A sharp calf cramp buckled her just steps from the door.

"Pa, please. I ain't never gonna run again. Pa," she cried until her voice went hoarse and the world went dark.

Hot breath on her neck woke her. *Click-clack.* Pa's musket pointed at her face.

Bang.

A wolf yelped behind her. Blood drained from the bullet hole over its white-gray fur.

Pa knelt inches from her face. "Only thing between you and death is me. When Daniel Crowan comes to collect a debt, you gonna run again?"

"No, sir."

He jostled out a key and unlocked the shackle, and she rubbed her ankle, purple and thick as her thigh.

"Why cain't you be good? You think I like chaining you? I do this 'cause I love you."

"I known it," she said, keeping her burning stare on her bad hand, wishing she could hide it with her glove.

Pa stood and cracked his back. "Gotta break in a new crop of slaves today. Them collard greens better be weeded when I come home Saturday." He dropped a knife. "Skin the wolf. I can sell the pelt."

Sam slinked from inside the cabin. "Y-you b-behave or else, b-bastard."

Pa winked proudly at his boy, then rode off.

Annaliese slashed open the lone wolf's throat, drinking the hot, thick blood, tasting copper on her tongue. Her first drink in two days.

Annaliese saw how guilty Sam felt, how his eyes begged forgiveness, but she ignored him. Sam acted extra nice while she rested her ankle. He found her glove to cover her branded hand, even did all the chores. By the end of the week, it got easier to walk and harder to stay mad at him.

"Fish be in a feeding frenzy with the storm coming," she said. Sam's face exploded in a relieved smile. That was their way. The Birch family never apologized, they moved on.

Sam grabbed the poles and dug some worms from the garden, dropping them in a pail. They walked to the docks off the tidal marsh in Taskinas Creek. A path divided the creek from the York River where the bigger fish swam. A blue heron craned its neck over the green water to watch them trek down the steep hill.

"B-boats!" Sam shrieked, like he always did, like it was a surprise to watch them move cargo up and down the river. He waded in.

Annaliese set the fishing poles a few yards from the dock, where abandoned flat-bottomed boats bounced in the choppy water. "Not past your knees. You ain't a good swimmer."

"Ahoy, beautiful."

An older boy, maybe fourteen, with black hair tied in a ponytail, rowed up. Tattoos of mermaids swimming through skulls covered his forearm. His crystal-blue eyes stopped her breath. But older boys meant trouble.

"I know you," he said. "I watch you behind taverns. You always eat from pigpens?"

Heat rose to her cheeks. *He wants to shame me, too.* "We ain't eat nuthin'."

"You don't have to lie. I've eaten trash before. Hey, you hungry? Pretty girl like you shouldn't eat scraps."

Glancing around, she weighed the danger level. "This a trick?"

A few warm raindrops fell through the steamy air.

"No trick," he said, offering bacon from his pail.

Rumbles came from her stomach. Snatching the bacon greedily, she shoved it in her mouth, enjoying the mix of crunchy and fatty on her tongue. The boy held one for Sam.

She called, "Sam, come here."

Sam's breeches were wet past his thighs, and sand stuck to his feet. He hid behind Annaliese 'cause he didn't like new peoples, but smiled after eating a strip.

"I got an apple, too." Taking a bone-handle knife from his pocket, the older boy sliced the fruit. "Thank you," he said, offering a chunk to her.

"For what?" Annaliese licked the grease off each finger before taking the slice.

"No, you're supposed to say it. Didn't your parents teach you nuthin'?"

Her cheeks flamed. "Thank you."

"I'm Jack."

"Annaliese. This here's Sam."

"It's a little warm for gloves," Jack said, as the sky cracked open, pelting rain hard enough to hurt. "Follow me to the warehouse." He raced toward a rickety shack fifty feet back.

Sam tugged on her skirt. "L-let's s-swim."

"In the rain? I'm stayin' dry. Not too deep, hear? Riptide's strong."

Joining Jack in the warehouse, she shivered at the temperature drop inside. Rain pinged on the roof and drips fell through the rotting beams. Her eyes adjusted to the dark. Yellowed tobacco leaves hung from the ceiling to dry, their edges beginning to curl. Hogshead barrels lined the walls.

"You're more like his mother than a sister."

Annaliese shrugged, not sure if it was a compliment or he was only noticing. Jumping over a puddle forming beneath the beam, she sat inside a rowboat resting on the floor, wondering what it would be like to sail away to a place where no one knew her.

Jack said, "You orphans?"

"Ma died a long time ago. She told me once my real father was some fancy lord, and he was gonna buy me a doll, but he ain't never come. Pa says I look like her."

"Then your ma must have been pretty."

Tingles traveled up and down her body. Leaving the rowboat, she skimmed past Jack and hovered near the door, just in case. Rain poured like a waterfall over the opening and seeped through the dirty glazed windows. "You said you seen me before?"

He nodded. "I deliver to all the taverns. That's how come I saw you."

"Pa sends us into town on auction days." She smirked.

"What happens auction days?"

Annaliese chewed her thumbnail. *Should I tell him?* "Check your breeches."

Jack tapped his pockets. "Where's my knife?"

Unclenching her fingers, she grinned.

"You little thief." He strode past wheat sacks toward her.

Stepping back, she readied to dash into the rain. "I was only playing. You gonna hit me?"

"Me? Nah." Jack laughed, taking his knife. He glanced at her neck. "Your pa do that?"

Fixing her shift, she covered the welt marks. "Reckon I had it comin'." Shifting away from him, she jumped barrel to barrel, her toes spreading on the wood as she landed. "You like rowing boats? You could become a pirate," she said, sounding more excited than she wanted.

Jack smiled. "How old are you?"

"Fourteen," she said, sitting on a barrel, inhaling the sweet tobacco fumes.

He laughed out loud. "Liar. You eight? Nine?"

"I'm nine *and a half*."

"You could run away, if you plan it right. You have a place to stay? A job?"

"Well, not yet, but we was already planning on running when the time's right," she said, trying to sound tough but feeling heavy. *Pa ain't never gonna let me leave.* She swung her legs a little, picking at a scab on her knee.

"There're ways a pretty girl like you could make some money. Good money, too." Jack puffed out his chest. "I can help you, Annaliese. Pretty name for a pretty girl."

Her face felt impossibly hot as she squirmed. Tugging the glove over her scar, she said, "You the liar now. I ain't pretty."

A tear slipped down her cheek, and he wiped it with his rough thumb. The room got smaller, and she shivered. No one had ever dried her tears before. Lifting her chin, she wanted to be closer to him. Jack stroked his thumb back and forth over her bottom lip and she felt a need to touch him, please him. Annaliese sucked on his thumb, searching his crystal eyes for approval.

A crooked smile answered. "Where'd you learn a thing like that?"

Panicked shouting interrupted them. "Sam?"

Bolting into the pouring rain, she waded waist-deep into the cold river. Weeds tangled around her feet as the tide pulled. Sam flailed wildly as he floated further into the river. No boat was close enough to help.

Jack pulled her back. "Don't both drown." Jack dove against the riptide.

"Kick your feet out. Float on your back," she hollered.

Jack put his arm under Sam's armpits, kicking strong against the tide. Breaking a long branch, she held it out to reel them in. Jack grabbed it. Digging in her heels, her ankle ached with their weight, but she dragged them in.

Annaliese hugged Sam tight, rocking his shivering body. Sam spit up water on the bank and coughed, his blue lips quivering.

"Ain't I tell you not too deep?" she yelled, hitting him hard.

"Easy, beautiful. He's fine." Jack wasn't mad or nuthin'.

Annaliese touched Jack's forearm, cold from the river. "Thank you."

A middle-aged man in a wagon stopped on the road. Rain dripped off his wide-brimmed hat. "You got my shipment, or are you too busy swimming in the rain with beggars?"

"Aye, coming, sir," Jack called. Facing Annaliese, his crystal blue eyes sparkled. "Next time you're hungry, leave your brother and come to the warehouse near Black Swan Tavern off Nicholson Street. See you around, beautiful."

Chapter Six

Fiona

Scotland, 1716

Fiona felt heat on her face and a fluttery, empty feeling in her stomach as villagers walked their cattle between two bonfires to ward off bad spirits. She didna fear the spirits, just her vision of the future. Auntie Matilda had confirmed long ago this was the night her life would change.

William MacLeod smirked as he sauntered over, parting a sea of envious village girls eager for the young laird's attentions. "Tisk tisk! A bonny lass standing alone on Samhain? Witches are wandering."

"I've no fear of witches," she said.

"I suppose Ewan will protect you," he offered, glancing toward Ewan standing with her brother, Malcolm. She noted more than a wee hint of jealousy in his voice.

"If Malcolm likes him so much, he can marry him."

A confident grin tugged at William's lips, making a dimple in his left cheek. "Would you like a slice of Hallowe'en cake, Fiona?"

She nodded. Ushering her to the harvest table decorated with carved, candlelit turnips, a stout matron gave them a knowing smile and two slices of barmbrack. They made their way to sit on large stones.

"Are you sure your very proper English grandfather would approve of you sitting with your lowly Scottish tenants, my laird?"

"Considering he's dead, he hasna much say in the matter. Grandsire didna approve of my Scottish father, and Da's family didna like that my mam was English and French. Honestly, my family has always been at war with each other."

"You're Scottish, English and French? Why, Mr. MacLeod, you're a walking contradiction," she said, shivering.

"I huvnae mentioned that before? I thought I told you everything." He draped his tartan over her shoulders and a flooding sensation of warmth came over her not remotely related to the plaid. After taking a bite of sweetbread, he started laughing, pulling a silver threepenny bit from his mouth.

"You're going to be rich." Fiona pricked the sweetbread, hoping desperately for a ring and not a thimble. A ring meant first to be wed, a thimble meant you'd be a spinster. Most slices held nothing.

"I ken that without the coin, but validation's nice," he said, thrusting out his chest as though he needed to. William MacLeod looked like a giant among men.

"Such humility," she said, rolling her eyes. Tracing her finger over his open hand, she began to study its textures.

"Perhaps with a proper wife, I'd behave better. Do you see your name in the lines of my palm?"

Yes, she wanted to scream. Fiona frowned, dropping his hand. "Stop teasing me, Mr. MacLeod."

"Call me William," he said in a low voice, inching ever closer beside her.

"You have crumbs on your beard, William."

A blush came to his cheeks, and he rushed to clean it, missing the mark. "Well, come Monday my beard winnae be a problem. One of the stipulations of my inheritance is that I attend Oxford to get my law degree. My grandfather desired I get a 'proper English education.' On Monday, it's a clean-shaven face and breeches for me."

"You're leaving me?" Fiona wiped the crumbs for him, their eyes connecting. Perhaps she let her fingers linger over his lips a wee bit too long. "I mean, you're leaving the village? When will you return?"

"When it's time to collect the rents, I suppose. Unless you'd like me to come home earlier for a proper church wedding? My brother, Cam, will be thrilled to meet you. He was convinced I'd pursue a rich English widow."

Fiona didna want to love him. Auntie Matilda warned her a rich man from Skye would try to take her magic away. Aching to touch William's face, she forced herself to break her gaze. "Ambitious men dinna marry crofters' daughters. Just because we've had a few interesting conversations since you've arrived dinna mean we should wed. You'd grow bored. Marry an English duchess. That's the life you crave. I cannae even read."

The skirl of bagpipes rang through the evening air and villagers began to dance. William glanced between his new tenants enjoying the festivities and his grandfather's mansion high on the hill above the castle ruins.

"First to wed!" called a petite blonde lifting a ring from her slice of cake to cheers.

"Aye. I suppose you're right. I winnae marry someone who cannae read. My grandfather would roll in his grave."

A sour taste filled her mouth. *My vision was just a magical fantasy all along. Auntie Matilda was wrong to think I had her gift of second sight.*

"So, I'll have to teach you to read before we wed," he whispered. "If you'll have me."

Fiona's mind raced, searching his face to see if he was serious. His finger lifted her chin and her breath quickened.

"You're witty, bonny and you dabble in magic. That's a lass who can hold a man's attention. To hell with my grandfather's notions. I love you, Fiona, and no brute will keep me from you."

When did it get so warm outside? Her hands shook as she cut into the barmbrack to give her time to process what he had said. A ring dangled from her fork. "But the other lass found the wedding ring in her slice."

William shrugged. "I had my own ring snuck in. I dinna take chances with important matters."

Throwing her head back, she laughed, and he hugged her, right there for the whole village to witness. Her brother, Malcolm, crossed his arms over his chest, with Ewan scowling next to him. "Let's take a jaunter," she said, slinging her satchel over her shoulder.

"Come. Let me show you my castle ruins."

Thistles and thorns ensnared her skirts, but she pressed on. Twenty feet high, the door had been bolted long ago. William clasped her hand as they crossed through a break in the stone wall into the decrepit castle. Dark and drafty, she sensed ghosts whispering.

William leaned in, smelling like lumber. She swallowed, unsure what to do. His lips brushed hers. He parted them, and she felt the shock of exploring a forbidden mouth with her tongue. Her chilled fingertips touched his dark red beard.

"I've never been kissed before," she said.

"Never? But you'll kiss me?" A slow smile grew and spread.

"I take no chances with important matters. A husband should kiss well," she said, tracing her fingers over his soft lips.

Weaving his fingers through her honey-brown hair, he kissed her again. Electricity passed between them. His other hand leisurely traced over her breasts, releasing one from her bodice, feeling its weight in his palm. Her skin tingled with his touch, and her breath hitched.

William took a step back. "I'm sorry. I shouldnae. Your brother hasnae given permission yet. I winnae dishonor you."

They stared at each other.

"You ken, we could handfast," she said, biting her thumbnail. "Or we could wait."

William pulled down the tartan draped over his shoulder. Seizing her palm, he tied their hands together with his plaid. "Handfast. I never thought I'd marry a witch," he said with a grin that showed his dimple. "Sorry, a wise woman." He kissed her knuckles.

Her chin dropped to her chest. "You joke, but I smelled my aunt's skin char, saw our neighbors turn on our family. Your own grandfather led the charge with the reverend." She unwrapped the tartan. "William, marry someone else. I never want to bring shame on you."

He pulled her into his arms. "I shouldnae have teased. I'm an edijit. Fiona, I'm making an oath to protect you, till death do us part, aye?"

A falcon flew from the moonlit sky into its nest, tucked behind the partially collapsed roof, clearly a good omen. "I ken you will. I've seen it."

"Is it true what they say? You have second sight, like Matilda?"

"Aye. I've been having visions about the Fairy Pools in Skye since I was a bairn, even though I've never been beyond the village. When you arrived, it all made sense."

William's eyes gleamed and he paced, unable to stay still. "Think of it—to be able to see the future. Will I become part of the nobility? Or become the King's Attorney? How many sons will we have?"

"Five."

His mouth dropped, but then he cocked his chin. "How accurate are these predictions?"

"That's just from reading your palm as anyone would. If you want a true prediction, I'll have to make a salt circle and sain the air with mugwort first. Auntie Matilda taught me all the spells to interpret visions."

William rapped his fingers against his thigh, checking over her shoulder to make sure they were alone. "Look, I dinna have to study at Oxford to ken witchcraft is illegal. We need to be careful."

Fiona lowered her head. "It was foolish for me to suggest we do anything magical. You're laird, after all. Besides, I've spent my whole life hiding my gift."

Stroking her face, he said, "You never need to hide your powers from me. I was raised on tales of giants and fairies. Magic dinna frighten me; priests do." William nuzzled her neck behind her ear. "Anyway, I'm going to be a barrister. I'd get you off any witch trial."

"You're quite sure of yourself," she chuckled.

"I'm very persuasive."

The heat of his breath intensified on her skin until her head rolled with a sigh. "Happy wedding day. And Samhain. And my birthday, too," she said.

Tugging off his shirt, he exposed his muscled torso, steaming in the raw November air. Trailing kisses down his chest, she gave his nipple a little nip, making him blink in surprise. "Fiona Nesbitt," he said in mock disapproval.

She grinned.

Gripping the nape of her neck, he kissed harder. "Let's see your birthday suit, Mrs. MacLeod."

"It's Mrs. Fiona Nesbitt MacLeod, thank you."

His nimble fingers untied the strings of her stays and wrenched her petticoat free until she stood naked before his receptive gaze. Fiona felt powerful beyond measure.

"God, you're beautiful. You have citrine irises, like a cat."

"Aye. I scratch like one, too."
"I enjoy that in a wife."

Scotland, 1739

Inside the church, William's aristocratic English clients sporting powdered hair mingled with his Highlander relatives in belted tartan plaids and linen shirts. Absolutely everyone from the village attended the wedding ... Except one.

"Where is your husband?" Reverend MacDonald asked, as his wrinkled hand squeezed Fiona's.

"Only an urgent matter would keep him this long." *Oh, I could kill William and bloody Lord Hallewell for forcing me to face the reverend alone.* Fiona avoided the preacher's gaze, as she had fifteen years earlier, kneeling at his buckled shoes in the burlap sack he forced her to wear.

I confess before you, God, and my husband, I've performed the sin of witchcraft. The Lord Jesus Christ chastens me for my excessive pride, for ignoring the truth of the Church and His light alone.

Bagpipes interrupted her shame. Their second son, David, led the congregation from the church to their manor for the reception. David had Fiona's light coloring and temperament, but William's dimple. This was his first visit home in months from studying the pipes at Agegdun Castle. As he passed, she straightened his glasses and kissed his cheek, much to his embarrassment.

Villagers kept a healthy distance from Fiona as they traveled the road, suspicious Matilda's powers had passed down to her. If ever a crop became infested with insects, or a storm crashed a ship, or a newlywed didna conceive a child, they whispered Fiona caused the trouble.

And yet. When a dying relative needed herbs to pass peacefully to the other side, or a husbandless woman needed a pregnancy to end, or someone needed their dream interpreted, or future told, they would always end up on her doorstep. Or they used to a long time ago.

Mary, her sister, approached and looped her arm through Fiona's. "Poor thing. Such circles under your eyes. How could Lord Hallewell keep your husband away?"

The castle ruins at the edge of their land looked stunning in the distance, with the loch's shimmering waters creating a mirror effect of the tower and sky.

Mary said, "Malcolm's still offended you didna ask his permission and got handfast there instead of a proper church wedding."

"Ancient gods foretold our vows and they dinna need anyone's permission. Auntie Matilda was right when she told me to trust my visions."

Mary's smile faded as she scanned over her shoulder. "Wheest. Dinna say such things."

Fiona's lips pressed together in a frown. They walked quietly until Mary scraped her hand through her hair. "Why are you mentioning Auntie Matilda at all?"

Fiona avoided her eyes and whispered, "I've had a vision."

Mary froze. Fiona's brother, Malcolm, joined them, ending the conversation. "Where's the great William MacLeod?"

"He's coming."

Wildflowers scented the air, and their manor at the top of the hill came into view. Still no sign of William.

"Tell us a charm," a village boy taunted, barely loud enough for Fiona to hear as the other children watched in mischievous anticipation.

"Dinna fash, laddie, I'm sure you'll stop being afraid of the dark without a charm from my wife."

The lad blushed and ran off with the other children, laughing.

"William," she said, relieved.

Dust covered his long coat and tricorn hat, and he stank like a horse, but he had arrived, thank God. Servants scrambled outside to greet him, and a stable boy took the reins of his horse.

William sheepishly pecked Fiona's cheek. *At least he has the good sense to look guilty.*

Hamish was already climbing him like a tree. "Da, I lost my tooth at school."

"Aye, you did. You're quite an armful now. Soon you'll be taller than me," he laughed, peering into his son's mouth.

Lachlan lifted his chest. "He winnae, but I will."

"You'll never get a wife talking that way," he said, tussling Lachlan's honey hair. "Women dinna like braggarts. At least, the good ones dinna." He winked at Fiona, trying to get back in her graces, no doubt.

"What kept you so busy you neglected your own family?" Fiona asked quietly. She wanted to keep the peace, but he owed an explanation, and it'd better be a damned good one.

James stepped forward. "You missed our wedding ceremony, Da."

William lowered Hamish to the ground. "Ack, I'm here for the good part. What a bonny bride you make, Nelly. I thought you were such a smart lass, but you married my son anyway."

Nelly smirked.

William said, "Lord Hallewell sends his regards, and these silver candlesticks." He handed them to James, who grinned at the value. David came out with his bagpipes, nodded to his da, then serenaded James and Nelly back to the reception.

"I'm glad you're home, Da," James called over the music.

William's older brother, Cam, wasn't as forgiving. Standing with his arms crossed over his barrel chest, he adjusted the tartan over his shoulder. "Lord Hallewell kept you in London during your firstborn's wedding? You gave up your clan, nay, your soul, in exchange for land and money, and how has it served you, lad?"

"This is neither the time nor the place." William glanced at his aristocratic clients. "I'm here, aren't I? It wasnae my choice to be delayed."

Cam scowled at William's attire. "It was your choice to chase after English nobles. Does your Highlander family embarrass you?"

William's jaw clenched and then his vision fell on Broderick, hiding behind Lachlan. "Your face." William lifted the boy's chin to the sun. Broderick's lip had healed during the week, but his eye still sported a faded bruise.

Fiona's stomach churned. *Please dinna. Broderick's already ashamed.*

Broderick feigned bravado. "Bit of a scrape. You should see the other lad."

"Aye, he got quite winded, chasing Broderick before pulping his face," teased Lachlan.

"You ran?" William asked slowly.

Fiona squeezed William's arm, glancing at the guests mingling in the yard. "Not now, love," she whispered. He shook off her hand.

"'Twas three to one, Da," he said, voice cracking.

William snapped, "Even if it's three hundred to one, MacLeods dinna run."

Cam took Broderick under his arm and tapped the silver brooch on his shoulder. He said quietly, "What's the MacLeod motto?"

Broderick said, "Hold fast."

"Aye. What animal is on our crest?" asked Cam.

"A bull, sir."

William rolled his eyes, sneering, "Perhaps Broderick's crest should have a mouse."

Broderick stood in humiliated agony, doing his damnedest not to cry ... He failed.

William grabbed Broderick's arm. "Jesus, Joseph and Mary, stop crying like a wee lassie." He leaned within an inch of the boy's cowering face and barked, "What are you going to do if someone comes to harm our family? You need to protect—" He caught Fiona's eye, releasing Broderick in disgust. "You dinna deserve my surname."

"William, *stop!*"

Everyone froze to gawk at her brazenness to publicly chide her husband. One of his clients, an English duke, said, "Get your family in order, MacLeod."

William's face reddened. Forcing a smile, he addressed the guests. "It appears my wife forgets her place." The help shifted on their feet and stared forward. "Dismissed. Broderick, wait in the barn with the belt. Since you like crying."

The lad's face drained all color. Just once, she wished William would treat Broderick like their other sons. The noble gave a satisfied nod and went inside, but Cam remained, scowling.

"What happened to you?" Unclasping his brooch, Cam pressed it into William's hand. "I think you need a reminder of our ways more than your son does."

Fiona stood beside her unsmiling husband. The guests returned to chatting and laughing, but she recognized there would be no celebration until they had words.

"Fiona, let's take a jaunter."

She'd rather argue with William privately than feign happiness publicly. They walked in silence until they passed the sheep grazing in the pasture as the clouds grew dark as his mood.

"You're going to scold me in front of my noble clients?"

"I should not have done, but how dare you tell Broderick he dinna deserve your name?"

"This is the conversation you want to have? I've done my duty for your sins."

Her cheeks burned. They walked untouching through the forest and over the flat stones to the creek. "Where were you?" she asked.

Picking up a rock, he skipped it over the water. "Cutting off the hand of a swindler, throwing him overboard and taking his ship, if you must ken."

"Is that a joke? The man I married despised brutes, yet it's what you've become."

William looked hit from the blind side. "I'm a brute? I was defending your honor."

Glimpsing to the heavens for patience, she said, "My honor? What am I accused of now?"

He tossed another stone. "Even after all these years, it follows us. Lady Margaret's gardeners dug up your shawl and Wilkes' emblem."

"Oh, my God." Both hands covered her mouth.

"She's blackmailing me. That's why I was late."

Fiona's mind raced. "Have you spoken to Lord Hallewell? He'd never allow his wife to extort you. I'm sure he'll put her in check."

William stared at the stones in his fist. "I dinna want to involve him."

Fiona put her hands on her hips. "Why not?"

He returned to skipping stones while she fumed. One stone rippled the water, and it jarred the memory of her vision. *Is the red stag troubling the water, Lady Margaret?* "What does she want?"

"Revenge, mostly—against Lord Hallewell's mistress, Eleanor—but money, too, which I'll send. We still have tenant rents and fees from my law firm. We'll tighten our belts and be fine."

"But she's rich."

"He cut off her allowance. I dinna ken what to do. Lord Hallewell tasked me with bringing the mistress and his by-blow home safely, and Lady Margaret wants them dead, or she'll stir up trouble for us. How do I keep everyone content?"

"Dead?" Fiona shook her head and frowned. "Well, where is this mistress now?"

He spun to face her, a pained expression on his face. "I must travel to the colonies."

"The colonies? You've scarcely arrived. Why cannae Lord Hallewell go?"

"You ken he cannae." Heading back to the road, he inspected the sky. "Smells like rain."

Fiona lifted her petticoats, catching up to him. "Cannae this mistress—Eleanor— and her bastard board a ship on their own? They were capable enough to get to the colonies without your help."

William flushed red. A few raindrops fell as he walked past rows of green barley almost glowing against the dark soil. "Lord Hallewell directed me to escort them. He trusts me." Breaking eye contact he knelt, checking the soil's dampness, then touching the texture of the leaves. "The crops seem promising this year." Thunder rumbled in the distance as he wiped the dirt from his hands. "Three and a half months is nothing."

She pinched her forehead. "Is this why you stole a ship? William MacLeod, what the devil are you involved in?" A mist rolled in, like in her vision.

"The ship was a coincidence."

"There are no coincidences." Fiona grabbed his forearm, quite serious. "You cannae go. I had a premonition about your voyage and a storm—"

William yanked her arm off, piercing her with angry eyes. "Enough with your second sight." Drawing in a breath, he paused before speaking. "Does anyone ken about this vision?"

Toying with her emerald bracelet, she darted glances at him, then away. "I might have mentioned something to Mary."

His jaw tightened. "The reverend has finally stopped treating you with suspicion, and you want to flaunt your spectral powers? Right as I'm leaving? What if Lady Margaret caught wind? Are you mad?"

"I didna ken you were leaving until half a minute ago."

"Jesus, Joseph and Mary, this isn't a damned joke. Lady Margaret found your shawl and Wilkes' pendant. I think I met her demands, but what if she tells the newspapers rubbish about you enchanting him?" Pointing a finger in her face, he said, "Dinna be the servant of the Devil then wonder why your arse gets burned. No talk of visions to anyone. Do you understand me?"

Slanting away from him, tension grew in her jaw. "I'm a servant of the Devil? Is that what you think of me?"

His eyes softened. "No ... I winnae be here to defend you."

"Defend me," she snorted.

William's body went rigid as adder leaves rustled in the breeze.

"I wish it never happened," she whispered. "You wouldna hate me and blame Broderick."

"Hate you? Everything I do is for love." He sounded confused. At himself? At her?

Fiona said, "These secrets and lies poison us; they turn us into different people."

"Would you rather tell the world the truth and wear a hangman's noose?"

They stood in silence, the tension growing. "She'll pull you into a storm, William—"

"Stop this—"

Bagpipes and laughter carried over the air. Fiona put her hand on his chest. "Stay."

He kissed her knuckles. "I have to go. I dinna have a choice."

That's when she realized she didna have a choice, either. The only way to protect her family was to practice magic again.

Chapter Seven

Annaliese

Freedom ended three weeks ago when Pa got too drunk in the fields and lost his job. Since then, he'd spent his days drinking until there weren't any bottles left. She tried not to bother him.

Annaliese and Sam sat on the dirt floor with their fingers laced behind their necks while he slept. If she made a sound, he'd beat her from one end of the room to the other.

Sometimes she pretended Jack was talking to her. *Come run to me, beautiful.* How many times did he tell her to run in her mind? Why couldn't she run for real?

A sunbeam sneaked through a chink in the wall and flashed on Pa's knife beneath his bed. His dirty fingers dangled over the blade.

Jack whispered, *If you slit his throat, you'll be free.*

Noiseless as a wolf, she crept toward the knife, willing the flies to stop buzzing as she knelt a foot away from Pa. Sam watched.

Put the ball and chain around his foot this time. Watch his dead body sink to the river bottom. Touching the knife's edge, it spun, slicing her fingertip.

Pa's bloodshot eye opened. Annaliese pulled back her hand, sucking the iron taste from her fingertip as Uncle Hal swung open the door, streaming sunlight into the dark cabin. Pa rubbed his eyes.

"Git up, Rob." Uncle Hal's coat fringe swung as he kicked Pa's mud-caked boot. "Your old boss has a runaway. Been missing for over a week now. Maybe if we catch him, you can git your job back," he said, scratching his wiry gray hair.

As Pa left the bed, Annaliese handed him his knife, which he put in its holster, none the wiser about her attempted escape.

Pa stretched, cracking his neck. "See? Crowan needs me. I ain't been gone barely a month, and they run. How much reward he payin'?"

"Ten pounds. That should clear some debt. How much you owe now?"

Pa went outside to piss. "I'm handling it, Uncle Hal, doing installments. I owe a few peoples, though. They coming Thursday for payment."

They? How many men is coming'? Nausea spread. *I have to run today. Jack said to come alone, but I cain't leave Sam. He wouldn't know how to feed hisself.*

Sam went to pet the hounds waiting by Uncle Hal's horse. One licked his face and Sam's grin was sweeter than honey. "W-what t-they c-called again?"

"*Attemous*," she said.

"What am I called?" asked Uncle Hal.

"*Nimatew*," she said.

"Stop learning her them Indian words. She's already savage enough." Pa splashed his face with well water to sober up. "Pack my musket, Red."

Scowling at the nickname, she stood on tiptoes to reach the gun from the pegs. "Uncle Hal, how come the reward's that big?"

"Mr. Crowan caught wind the slave had a counterfeit pass. He's wantin' to set an example since he trying to be the next governor. The runaway stole a canoe, got ahold of a map. I heard Crowan's yellow girl helped him escape. It's bad," Uncle Hal said.

Pa said, "Crowan likes humping his blackbirds. I told him he cain't trust them." Pa focused on the picture on the flier. "That's Moses, one of the new ones. Yep. I knew that Bite would be a pain in my ass the day I met him."

"When you gonna git back?" she asked Uncle Hal.

"Few days. The hounds are pretty good at finding an old scent. Rob, move. We're already the last ones in on it. Farmer few miles east saw him a day ago."

Annaliese bit her lip from smiling. *I'll be long gone by the time Pa comes home. Jack will steal a boat and row us up the James River. Lots of abandoned shacks line the banks.*

"Why ain't you done?" Pa asked, his voice raw.

Annaliese lowered her eyes and pounded the powder with the ramrod, pretending it was Pa's face. "It's packed."

"Give it here." Pa grabbed it, then tossed all his knives in the cartridge bag. Pa and Uncle Hal mounted their horses and left. Sam chased the dogs until they were nuthin' but a dust trail.

Annaliese grabbed Sam's hand and walked.

"W-where w-we goin'?"

"We gonna run away with Jack."

Sam shook his head no.

"Stop fussing. Jack's gonna git me a job."

"P-pa be m-mad."

"Fine. Stay here." Halfway down the path, she spun to face him. "Samuel Birch, you git a move on."

He pouted, then ran to catch up. They trudged the dusty trail on the hour-long walk, pausing only to rub the sweat from their foreheads. Ox carts passed them over the bridge and Williamsburg's church steeple appeared on the horizon. Her chest raised with anticipation, and she squeezed Sam's hand. *We're running for good this time.* They snaked the narrow alleys between houses and shops until they found the warehouse off Nicholson Street and peeked inside, scanning the men's faces as they stacked barrels in the corner.

"Jack."

Smiling, he stopped working and joined them. His shirt was damp with sweat. "Ahoy, beautiful. I was wondering if you forgot about me." He frowned when he saw Sam, then led them out the back door opening to an alley paved with red bricks leading to a small creek. "Why's he here?"

"He gets scared if I leave him."

Jack put his arms across his chest and frowned.

This isn't going like I planned it. She traced her finger over Jack's mermaid and skull tattoo. "Don't be mad."

Whipping his arm away, he said, "I am mad, though. I'm not gonna waste my time taking you to the lady with puddin' head standing next to you."

"People think Sam's dumb, but he ain't. He's a nervous talker, is all. But he can work. He's real good at collecting buckets of dog shit to sell to the tanner."

Jack shook his head and turned. "I gotta get back."

Annaliese blocked him. "Jack, please don't be mad. Pa's gonna be gone for a few days to catch a runaway and we have to be gone before Thursday."

"What happens then?"

"Some peoples coming to collect a debt. Maybe Mr. Daniel, too."

Jack's eyebrows raised. "Daniel *Crowan?*"

"You known him?"

Jack grinned. "Don't everyone? His daddy's gonna be the governor."

Annaliese spit. "Gap-toothed bastard."

Sam tugged her arm. "C-can I p-play in the c-creek?"

She waved him off and he scrambled away. *If I leave Sam home, would Pa use him for payment, too?* "Please let him come with me."

Jack rubbed his mouth. "All right, but only because you're my girl."

She clapped for joy.

Jack checked behind him. No one from the warehouse seemed to be paying them no mind. "I'll let you make it up to me." He led her past Sam to a sandy part of the creek shaded by maple trees. Dogs barked in the distance.

"On your knees," Jack said, lowering his brown woolen breeches.

Annaliese knelt, feeling the cool sand on her knees. "You're all I think about. Wishin' you'd marry me one day."

"Marry you?" He laughed.

Stupid, Annaliese. "I was just joking—"

Sam's cold, wet hand shook her shoulder.

"Go away." She brushed him off. The barking grew louder. Sam faced the road, tightening his grip.

Jack pulled up his breeches. "Y-you s-s-stupid? L-l-leave." Jack shoved Sam.

Sam pulled her arm and pointed to the road. "P-pa."

"I'll be goddamned," Pa said, sitting on his horse. Uncle Hal held a slave by a rope leash around his neck. Pa hollered, "Annaliese Birch, git yer ass over here. Now."

Pa's forehead had a gash above his eye, and his knuckles looked swollen from fighting dirty. Bad as Pa was, the runaway looked worse. Dusty and bloody with his hands tied in front, all the spirit was beat from him.

Jack's face drained to white. "I better get back to work." He ran in the opposite direction right quick.

The long walk to Pa seemed to last forever. Her skin felt clammy, and her hands shook.

Dismounting, Pa wrenched her arm till it bruised. "What was you doing with that boy?"

Covering her face, she whimpered, "Nuthin', Pa."

"Lie to me again," Pa said, slapping her hard enough to make her ear ring as she stumbled to the ground. A silent instant of pitiful understanding passed between Annaliese and the slave before her gaze shifted back to Pa. His hand moved to his belt buckle, ready to unleash hell on her.

"P-pa," Sam shouted.

The slave looped his slack rope over Pa's neck, pulling it taut to strangle him. Pa dug his fingers into the rope, trying to pry it off.

Uncle Hal called, "Sic 'em."

Snarling bloodhounds bit the runaway's legs, tearing his flesh as he shrieked, dropping the rope. Knocking him over, their fangs clamped onto him. He kicked and punched at their drooling jaws as best he could with his hands still tied.

Pa rubbed his neck, gasping for air, then went crazy kicking the slave's ribs as the dogs yelped.

"Stop. You killing him," Annaliese shouted.

Uncle Hal whistled his dogs off and pulled Pa away, an arm across his chest. "He ain't worth as much dead. You need the money."

Pa panted hard, rubbing his rope-burned neck. A bloody puddle stained the dirt beneath the runaway.

"He dead?" Sam asked in a whisper.

Uncle Hal said, "He breathin', just unconscious." Uncle Hal tied the runaway like a hog then pitched him over Pa's saddle. Sam backed away from the dogs.

"You gonna let some blackbird kill me?" Pa's voice wheezed.

Uncle Hal scowled at her. "What the hell's wrong with you?" He shook his head at Pa. "I'd have sold her years ago."

Pa rubbed his neck. "I think I will. Some men is coming Thursday. Can you take her home? Make sure she don't run?"

Annaliese scratched the itch spreading like wildfire on her neck and chest.

Uncle Hal sighed. "Bring me back my share of the reward." To Annaliese. "Come on before I stick the dogs on you, too."

Chapter Eight

Lady Margaret

London

Lady Margaret sauntered past the impoverished souls lined up outside the barber-surgeon's shop. Her red silk heels clicked on the cobblestones as she stopped beside each wretch to inspect their teeth. Her son, Alexander, lagged with a disgusted scowl and a handkerchief covering his nose.

"Smile," Lady Margaret commanded. Standing at attention, the crowd desperately pulled back their lips. "It's unfair white teeth are wasted on the poor," she sighed.

Examining the choppers of a bone-thin woman in her early twenties, Alexander grimaced at the woman's loose dress speckled with coarsely sewn patches.

"How about this one?" Lady Margaret asked Alexander.

The woman appealed to the handsome youth with her eyes, seeming to live out a romance novel in her very stare.

"Why, she's hideous," he said.

In a split second, the woman's face darkened with the shame that comes from allowing oneself to dream.

"Not the pauper. Her teeth."

"Oh. Open," he ordered dispassionately. The woman did, as though it were an examination her life depended upon. Perhaps it was.

The barber-surgeon, a hefty, disheveled figure, appeared wearing a long leather apron over his navy breeches. "Lady Hallewell, let's get you past this riffraff." Rolling his shirt sleeves above hairy arms, he yelled to the crowd, "Back off."

"This one will do, Mr. Skinner," Lady Margaret said, pointing to the woman, who nodded enthusiastically.

Let MacLeod call my teeth rotten with these pearls in my mouth. God, I hate that man.

"I've already selected the best ones. They're waiting inside, my lady. These are extras."

Clutching Lady Margaret's elbow with her bony fingers, the haggard young woman pleaded, "Oh, please, m'lady. I need the money for my wean. She's dreadful sick and we need medicine."

Lady Margaret snapped her arm away. "Don't touch me How dare you?"

Mr. Skinner shoved the woman into the street, where she tumbled into a filthy puddle. Alexander snorted as the woman fled, crying.

"I hope she wasn't contagious." Lady Margaret wiped her elbow.

"This is why I keep my clients separate from the wretches. Follow me. I should have come to you at Astwick House."

"Ah, but then my husband would find out," she said, winking at her son.

"Won't your husband notice your new teeth when you talk?"

"We try not to speak." To Alexander, "How is your friend, Viscount Percy Monroe?" she asked casually. "I've written him a letter of apology for Mr. MacLeod's brutality, but he won't reply." *Why is Percy punishing me? Did he abandon me?*

Alexander answered with a shrug.

Inside, a gentleman draped in a towel got a shave while an apprentice swept hair from the floor. "Zounds. Leave some skin on my face next time," the man said, paying his sixpence and walking past the pathetic lot waiting to sell their teeth.

Lady Margaret sat, fluffing her white paduasoy petticoat adorned with large red peonies. "You should invite Viscount Percy over for tea." *With the newfound evidence and Percy by my side, I can finally extract revenge on MacLeod for murdering Wilkes. We should relish this time MacLeod is in the colonies and develop a plan.*

Mr. Skinner teetered on his stool. "Open wide." Selecting an iron hook from a table of instruments worthy of the Spanish Inquisition, he scraped between her swollen gums. "Someone enjoys sugar in her tea."

Lady Margaret shifted uncomfortably. *He didn't have to scold me.*

Alexander wandered around the room, playing with dental hooks as the nervous group watched. "I don't think it's a good idea to invite him over. Father will disapprove."

She groaned. *Damned Lord George Hallewell. Our marriage is as putrid as my teeth.*

"You need your top two incisors and a bottom right molar extracted. I'll insert the new tooth into your empty socket and sew it in place with wire. You'll leave with a winning smile, and it'll cure your ill-smelling breath."

Mortified, she covered her mouth and snapped her fingers. "Alexander."

Her son produced a silver flask from his plum-colored waistcoat.

Mr. Skinner said, "Oh, I have alcohol, my lady."

"Yes, but I doubt it's the caliber of my own." She gulped, then shook her head from its strength. To Alexander, "If you don't want your father to know, invite Viscount Percy to our Oxford estate."

"I don't want to," he whined. "Percy travels with a rogue crew of highway men. What if he sent them after me because MacLeod stole his ship?"

Just do what I want you to do, damned boy. Shifting her annoyance onto the barber-surgeon, she snapped, "Stop dithering. I don't have all day."

"Normally people wait for the alcohol to take effect, but if you're in a rush, I'll accommodate," he said, handing her a towel. "This may hurt a little, my lady," he said with a menacing twist of the lip. "Hold her down," he commanded Alexander.

Mr. Skinner leaned in with what looked like a key. Immediately, she regretted her impatience as he clamped on the right incisor and twisted. Pain ripped from her tooth socket to her skullcap, and she groaned.

Clink. One rotten tooth dropped in the tin pot. Tears streaked down her flamed cheeks. *Clank.* Two rotten teeth with brown holes in the tin pot. Leaning into his work, he rocked back and forth. "Damned molar broke. I'm going to have to pull it out piece by piece with the pliers."

"No. Leave it."

Mr. Skinner yanked the roots with a bull's force. Shrieking in agony, she kicked and writhed in pain. Alexander lay across her chest as she bled on his shoulder.

Dirty hands pressed against the windows as several people outside laughed. The glass barely blocked the sound. "Serves her right, nasty bitch," a woman in servant livery said to another woman. "I ain't giving her my teeth."

Why is everyone miserable to me?

Clink-clunk. The broken molar bits dropped in the tin pot, stinking with rot and drained pus. Lady Margaret sat up, covered in drool. Alexander removed his wet coat with a grimace, then handed her the flask. Spitting on the floor, she wiped her tears and drank a long swig.

"I'm tho embarathed." With three missing teeth and the alcohol, her *s* sounded like *th*.

"Ignore the stupid peasants, Mother." Alexander leaned in with a rictus grin. "I'll bet your moans were insignificant compared to Viscount Percy's squeals when MacLeod threw his bare arse overboard. I heard slaves pissed on his head as he flailed in the water. Witnesses swore he had his mouth open and swallowed some."

Lady Margaret wanted to defend Percy, but would it raise Alexander's suspicions? "How boorith. MacLeod thould be thot."

"Thot? Oh, shot. Yes. MacLeod crossed the line. Percy's a deformed joke at the moment, but what happens when his father finally dies, and he becomes the sixth earl of Cheshire? It will reflect poorly on me at the club."

Mr. Skinner walked the line of peasants. "Ready?" They gave weak nods, one man gripping his tweed cap between his hands. Choosing a woman with wavy ginger hair, Mr. Skinner said, "Open wide."

"Give her thomthing to drink firth," Lady Margaret said, rubbing her mouth.

"Aw, thank you, missus. M'lady." The woman approached, bobbing her head.

"No, not from my flathk. The barber hath thome," Lady Margaret whistled through her missing teeth.

Mr. Skinner snorted and gave the woman gin, then grabbed his dental key and went to work. Moan. *Clink* dropped the white tooth. Groan. *Clank*. Two healthy teeth in the tin pot.

Alexander said, "I find it quite droll MacLeod cut off Percy's hand, but I'm decidedly furious he didn't fix our allowance situation before he buggered off. They denied me entrance to the club last night. Imagine."

Mr. Skinner spun around. The dripping pliers made dark wet spots on his leather apron. "You brought the money, didn't you, madam?"

Now toothless, the woman's eyes opened wide. Irish laborers gaped at each other.

"I have thomthing better than cath."

Sure, she could have used the blackmail money MacLeod had sent her, but she wanted to reserve that for something fun. As far as she was concerned, husbands should pay all medical costs, otherwise, why have a husband at all? She held Lord Hallewell's golden locket containing Eleanor's portrait. *Oh, George, there are a thousand different ways I can hurt you.*

"That will work nicely, I should think." Mr. Skinner said, returning to his task.

Moan. *Clunk* went the tooth. "Next."

"Promith you'll convinth Perthy to come to Oxford. Your father will never know. I'll fix everything." She hiccupped.

"Fine, Mother, but I won't be there."

Even better. Please come, Percy. My freedom depends on it.

Chapter Nine

WILLIAM MACLEOD

Virginia Colony

Did I land in Africa? MacLeod had never seen so many Black faces in his life. They appeared distinctive—so many unique nose shapes, eye colors and skin tones.

Williamsburg made a stunning contrast to London. The main street was ten feet wide and calf-deep in muck, with hardly more than a few dozen houses and shops, and a population of less than a thousand people. The governor's palace, the most significant building, loomed at the end of the green. English colonists butchered pigs in the open market alongside a slave auction.

Tugging his jabot from his sweaty neck, he was surprised to see Shawnee with long braids gallop past him carrying bundles of pelts.

At first, he rolled his eyes when he discovered Fiona had packed one of his kilts for the trip, but it was so bloody hot here, he was seriously considering wearing it. He chuckled. *Maybe Fiona saw the weather forecast in her visions.*

MacLeod hadn't realized his friend, Matthew Crowan, had become a man of significant political stature who owned multiple plantations, but he finally tracked down the correct one. The sun simmered MacLeod's pale cheeks as he rode a rented horse to Sweetwater Plantation, where

Eleanor had served her indentured contract. Dozens of slaves sang in the fields while a white man on a horse wielded a whip.

Coaches manned by Negro men dressed in red livery clogged the path until he rounded a dusty road shaded by oak trees. Ahead loomed a three-story mansion with eight columns.

At Oxford law school, everyone had called Matthew 'Governor' and MacLeod 'King's Attorney,' but only Matthew lived up to the name. Southern society elites rolled through the front yard like waves of cotton. Gentlemen in fine coats drank rum under the oaks while slaves fanned their mistresses. Apparently, MacLeod just invited himself to a party.

MacLeod dismounted, asking the stable boy, "Excuse me, lad. Does Matthew Crowan live here?"

"You get lost, Scotsman?" a nearby gentleman said. "Not many sheep here. *Bah. Bah.*"

Even in the New World, the Old World could nettle him. He patted the drunken fellow's back as he passed. "If I wanted to hear an arsehole make noise, I'd fart."

A Negro butler in a powdered wig greeted him at the open front doors.

"I'm William MacLeod, an old friend of Mr. Crowan's from Oxford."

The butler bowed, disappearing into the crowded parlor bursting with laughter. Little blonde girls with pink bodices and petticoats ran through the house, stopping to take biscuits from a slave holding a silver platter. They chased each other up the grand staircase circling above. MacLeod looked at five-feet-tall family portraits from the 1600s.

The butler reappeared. "This way, sir."

The front parlor overflowed with animated people flirting and talking politics. A door swung to reveal a side room for house slaves. They deposited dirty glasses on a long wooden table in exchange for appetizer platters to be served. A middle-aged Negro woman rocked in a chair with a vacant expression. Her mind seemed severed from her surroundings. Closing the door, the butler hid the scene and kept walking.

MacLeod rubbed his sunburned neck, feeling unsettled, remembering the Africans rotting in cages outside the *Icarus*. He passed the dining room set for fifty into a yellow parlor with an enormous fireplace. Inside, a young man dressed entirely in white slumped against the armchair by the window, sloshing his bourbon in a crystal glass. Finally, they entered a quiet study overlooking the James River and the butler bowed off.

Matthew Crowan stood, punching MacLeod's arm in a throwback to their youth. "Mac, you Scottish bastard. What are you doing here?"

"Quite a plantation, Matthew. Even better than you described at university."

"It's one of four I own," Matthew said. "Are you here to buy land? I knew you'd leave your little piece of dirt near Skye and see how the true land barons live. Mark me, Negroes and land are the best investments a man can make. What are you drinking these days? Whiskey still?" He snapped his fingers. "Thomas."

An older slave with graying hair came in from the hall to pour their drinks, then blended into the background, looking straight ahead.

"Aye, thank you. Unfortunately, this isna a social visit. Lord Hallewell sends me."

"Why on God's green earth are you still working for George Hallewell? I thought you'd be King's Attorney by now."

Ouch.

Matthew lifted his coat-tails before sitting in an armchair. MacLeod sat opposite on the couch, dabbing his sweaty brow with his handkerchief. "Do you remember the convict you purchased about a decade ago? Eleanor Cameron?"

"You mean the Scottish laundress you tricked me into buying without mentioning she was in a delicate condition?"

"I didna realize she was quick."

Matthew Crowan smirked, sipping his drink. "If I'd known George sired the baby, I would have had it shipped off to the church orphanage instead of paying to feed it. Cute girl. Peculiar name, though. Anna something—"

"Annaliese."

"Yes, that's it. Eleanor left years ago when she married Rob. He was just here yesterday."

"What's his name?"

"Rob Birch. Can't hold his liquor worth a damn but knows tobacco. He's the best slave catcher in Virginia, I'd wager."

"What sort of man is Rob Birch? Beyond drunk and good at working the lash?"

MacLeod noticed Thomas shift uncomfortably, staring at his feet.

"Rob can be overzealous, but honestly, these little monkeys are worse than children. They're already bound for life. What's left to motivate but the whip? We had to hang one yesterday. That made my wife happy." He chuckled with a frown. "I'm selling the other runaway to the Deep South to send a message. Didn't even get a full harvest out of him." He shrugged and took a sip. "Such is the cost of business. You know, I did you a huge favor, taking on George's mistress."

"You paid a measly twelve pounds for four years, hardly a favor." MacLeod held his glass for a refill.

Matthew said, "Thirteen pounds, plus ten acres for freedom dues. Although I reclaimed about eight."

"Reclaimed?"

"Rob Birch is always in debt. I took land back as payment." To Thomas, "Fetch Daniel."

"Yes, master."

MacLeod steepled his fingers against his lips, thinking of Eleanor's desperate letter. She could be melodramatic. But it did take a certain personality to be a slave overseer. It wasn't too far a stretch for this Rob Birch fellow to be a wife-beater, too. "Eleanor wrote Lord Hallewell about her husband's cruelty and requested to be rescued."

"That'll be difficult, considering she's dead."

MacLeod blinked. The last time he saw Eleanor, she was dressed in her convict's brown serge and spit in his face. *I deserved it.* "Rob Birch killed her?"

"Gracious, no. She died in childbirth. Her third. The babe died, too. Mm. Very sad." Matthew sipped his drink. "Ah, Daniel, come in. Meet my old friend from Oxford, Mr. William MacLeod."

The young, inebriated man in white from the parlor appeared. "Good afternoon, sir." Daniel bowed slowly, perhaps to keep from falling over.

Matthew said, "You're friends with Rob. MacLeod is trying to locate the daughter."

Daniel swayed, sucking air through the sizable gap in his teeth. "You mean Annaliese? What do you want with her? She's quite naughty."

Matthew shot a look at his son, who fidgeted with his drink. MacLeod narrowed his eyes at the interaction.

Matthew forced a laugh. "Right, right. Eleanor's girl was quite the rascal, wasn't she? Used to climb the sycamore and jump onto the wrap-around porch all the time. At three, no less. I remember Rob gave her quite the whipping."

Daniel leaned on a side table. "Rob solves all sorts of problems, doesn't he? No one likes a governor with a yellow daughter. Right, Daddy?"

Matthew's jaw tightened. "Enough bourbon, son."

Yellow? MacLeod moved to the window, staring at the light-skinned woman bearing a striking resemblance to Matthew dangling like an ornament from the sycamore. Virginia's elite strolled past the dead woman while they sipped mint julep.

"I remember you railing against the moral debauchery of human chattel, saying you wanted to free your father's slaves upon his death."

Thomas glanced up, then lowered his eyes.

Matthew laughed, joining MacLeod at the window. "Morals cost nothing when you're sixteen and it's your father's money. Will I go to hell for owning people and killing some? Possibly. In the colonies, life without slaves would be terribly inconvenient." Swirling his glass, he laughed, like it was self-deprecating humor. "But in the Old World, Lord Hallewell and his ilk have people like you at their beck and call. No need for slaves. I'm sure he has you do all his dirty work."

Laughter and the sound of clinking crystal glasses wafted into the room. MacLeod felt the room shrink and fought the urge to leave.

Matthew said, "I best return to my guests. People believe I'll make an excellent governor if I play my cards right. I have some powerful friends on the council and my title is practically guaranteed. How do you like the sound of it—Sir Matthew Crowan? And then Governor Crowan? Forgive me for going on. You should stay for dinner and enjoy some Southern hospitality."

"Thank you, but I need to find the by-blow. My lord wants me to bring her to London, but I'm not sure taking her across the sea to dump her in a boarding school is the best plan."

Daniel blinked his glazed eyes, squeezing the chair tightly. "Daddy, why don't we bring her here? She could be a laundress at the governor's mansion."

Matthew glared at his son before turning stone-faced. "I don't think ... We already have slaves, Daniel. You don't need my friend's bastard."

MacLeod tilted his head, studying the men. "It's gracious for your son to offer, but I'll figure something out. Oh, where is Mr. Birch's farmstead?"

Matthew said, "About five miles east, not too far from the York River. It's the only cabin out there. Give my regards to Lord Hallewell and your wife. Does she still read palms? She was right about me becoming governor. We'll disregard the other part of the reading," he said with a good-natured smile.

"What did she predict, Daddy?"

Swirling his drink, he said, "At least one of my children would die violently. Absolute rubbish." MacLeod stared through the window at the girl lynched in a sycamore tree. "What was her name again? Fanny?"

MacLeod finished his whiskey. "Fiona."

"What fun to see each other after all these years and see the men we've grown into."

MacLeod forced a smile as Thomas escorted him out. Daniel came to the porch and pulled a little blonde girl onto his lap. An uneasy expression fell on her face.

Sunshine glistened off the serene waves of the James River flowing behind the Big House, while a wave of nausea hit MacLeod. Was it the heat? Fiona's prediction coming true? Or was it facing the nastiest part of the English nobility's underbelly?

He wiped his sweaty forehead beneath his tricorn hat as he rode off, while enslaved people in the fields sang, "God's gonna trouble the water."

Chapter Ten

ANNALIESE

Annaliese slumped against the cabin wall between mouse droppings and empty whiskey bottles sticky with spider webs. Waiting.

Uncle Hal's gray beard hung off his wrinkled face as he pulled an old red rag from his pocket to rub tallow onto his shotgun. The dogs began to yip and howl.

Sam shoved his shoulder against the creaky door to open it. "P-pa's home."

Her stomach clenched. *Today's Thursday. Who's comin' to do their business on me? Is Pa gonna sell me? Will my new masters treat me worse?*

Lacing her hands behind her sweaty neck, she stared at her dirty toenails. Her heart pounded at the thump of Pa's approaching heavy boot.

"Sam, go water my horse." Pa spoke in the careful voice he used to hide how drunk he was. Even so, anyone with a nose could smell Old Stitch on him.

Uncle Hal crammed the oily rag in his pocket. "You had a few at the tavern?"

"Might have celebrated a bit. Crowan hired me back. Start tomorrow."

Annaliese raised her head in relief. *He'll be gone soon.*

TO RESCUE A WITCH

"Full-time overseer?" Uncle Hal smiled.

"Even better. Slave Patrol."

Annaliese flinched as Pa stepped near to unload cornmeal from his canvas onto the shelf.

"Crowan told me all the plantation owners was sayin' they was impressed I paraded the runaway at every courthouse. Said I'm the kind of man they need to keep order. It pays good money, too."

"Heard all about *you*, huh? Not us?"

"Jesus, they heard about us, all right? Cain't you be happy for me? No more tobacco fields and fighting slaves breaking tools. I git to hunt them for quick cash, finally git respect."

"What about her?"

"Oh, we gonna talk," Pa said.

Annaliese hugged her scabbed knees tighter. A mosquito buzzed in her ear.

Uncle Hal said, "That girl's like her mama. Sets on her high horse for an indentured. It's good you selling her. She'll make you some money at least." Uncle Hal put on his cowhide coat.

"I known it," Pa said. "I'll probably keep her. Just hire her out some."

A fluttery feeling rose in her chest.

Uncle Hal leaned on his musket and shook his head. "Well?"

"Well, what?"

"Where's my share of the reward? Five pounds for the runaway plus extra 'cause I brung the hounds."

"I ain't got it. Look, Daniel Crowan tricked me."

Uncle Hal said, "Goddamn it, what's that got to do with me?"

"Daniel lied and said I ain't made payments. His daddy put the money toward my debt."

"Ah, hell, boy, that ain't my problem. Pay me."

"Matthew Crowan just gave me a job. What am I supposed to do? Say his son's a liar, and lose it? I ain't no fool."

"But you think I am? Goddamn it, Rob. I wasted all my time to help you out and ain't got paid shit. Watching your damned girl."

"Ain't my fault."

"Nuthin' ever is. I'm making a claim with the sheriff. That's what I'm gonna do. Add six pounds to your existing debt, boy, and see you in gaol.

I'm sure your whore daughter—servant—whatever the hell she is—will join you soon." Uncle Hal's jacket fringe swayed as he pushed past Sam coming back in.

Pa hollered out the warped doorframe, "You gonna call the law on your own nephew?" He then got real quiet. "Light the fire, Sam."

Annaliese rocked slowly, hands behind her neck. *Pa's gonna take it out on me.* Sam gathered tinder from the woodpile, placing it in the center, stacking kindling on top in a teepee.

Change his mood. "I'm glad you got your job back, Pa."

Ruffling through his canvas, he pulled out a thick brown stick. "Known what this here is?"

She shook no.

Pa put it under her nose. "Smell good? It's called a cigar. Some bigwig from Spain come to the plantation and gave Mr. Crowan a box. Figure it's the least he owes me for cheating me out my money."

Orange flames licked up the sides of the kindling until an air bubble popped, shooting sparks up the chimney. "Out, Sam."

The door slammed shut, creaking on its hinges. Alone with Pa, she watched light filter through the sideboard gaps into the dark, smoky cabin. Pa touched the cigar to the flame, puffing on it. "I coulda sold you when your whore ma died, but didn't. Ain't never left you, like my pa left me."

"I known it." Her eyes focused on the smoldering tip as ash fell.

Sitting on the edge of the lopsided table, he scratched the bruises around his neck where the runaway strangled him. "Come here. I ain't gonna bite."

Stand close enough to be respectful, but not too close. The burning cigar left a trace of ammonia in the air. A painful lump formed in her throat. *Flatter him.* "Slave Patrol sounds good. You real good at catching runaways."

"Guess I better be, since you running off with boys now, like some whore." Pa blew smoke in her face until she blinked. "*Annaliese*," he sang. "Go on now. Tell me his name."

Chewing her bottom lip, she avoided his gaze.

Grabbing her wrist, he peeled off her glove. "You gonna cry real tears. His name."

The cabin shrunk around her as the smoke from the chimney and Pa's cigar stung her eyes. She twisted. "No." A fast, cool-hot pricking pain shot through her forearm as he ground it into her. "Jack!"

"You make everything hard. You think I like burning you?"

He dotted her arm until she screamed in agony, then he finally let go. Annaliese whimpered as she sucked on her arm. Returning the cigar to his mouth, he puffed. "Hush up now before I burn you again. You tell Jack he owes me. I ain't gonna give you out for free, hear?"

Sam ran in, slamming the door. "T-two m-men coming."

"Already? Is Daniel Crowan one of them?"

"N-no. Sh-sheriff."

"Goddamn it." Pa squeezed his eyes shut, then looked at Annaliese with panic. "I ain't here." Sliding under the bed, he left the cigar burning on the table.

Chapter Eleven

WILLIAM MACLEOD

William MacLeod hadna worn a kilt in years. The wool might have felt comfortable on his skin, but he was decidedly uncomfortable being seen in it as he rode alongside the sheriff. Still, it felt good to feel a breeze on his bollocks again.

A few minutes earlier, a wee lad spotted them and fled jerkily into the Virginia backwoods.

Sheriff Brown, a weathered man in a black coat with brass buttons, said, "That was Rob Birch's boy. He's a little slow."

A child's scream interrupted the quiet of the dark pines, and MacLeod instinctively gripped *Justice*'s handle as they cantered through the dark pines to hunt the source. They dismounted in front of a dilapidated cabin. A goat wandered aimlessly past broken whiskey bottles, weeds stabbing through the dirt, and a rusty ball with a long chain next to the garden fence. A coiled whip rested on the log pile.

Stepping in animal shit, the sheriff said, "Exactly as I remembered it."

Eleanor lived here?

Sheriff Brown tapped his staff on the warped door. "Mr. Birch?"

"Who's askin'?" a lass challenged.

"Sheriff Brown. Open the door, girl."

"Pa ain't home. You best leave."

They smirked at each other. Neither was used to being back talked by a child. "We heard the boy call him. We need to speak with your father about you."

A musket emerged from the cracked door, pointing squarely between MacLeod's eyes. He took a startled step back.

"Move an inch closer and I'm gonna blow your brains out, hear? Ain't no debt collections gonna happen today."

"Whoa," Sheriff Brown said. "You know it's a crime to point a gun at a sheriff?"

"Ain't pointed at you." *Click-clack.* She cocked the gun.

Of all the scenarios MacLeod had envisioned for meeting Eleanor's child, this wasna one.

Sheriff Brown called, "Birch, tell your girl to put the gun down. I'm about to tap her shoulder with my staff, and then you'll both go to gaol."

Heavy boots stumbled and a deep, gravelly voice said, "Who sent you? My Uncle Hal find you on the road?" Rob Birch pushed past the girl, sizing them up. A stale mixture of tobacco, sweat and Old Stitch almost knocked MacLeod over. "Daniel Crowan send you? I worked payment out with his daddy. I known my rights."

MacLeod studied the bruises around Rob Birch's neck and face, and the torn Vs on his ears. *Someone's been to the pillory.*

"We're not debt collectors," Sheriff Brown said, calmly fingering his own pistol.

Rob raised his voice. "Put it down, Red."

Keeping her alert eyes on the men, she backed away.

Rob asked, "Why you two here if it ain't for the debt? I ain't done nuthin' wrong. The girl ain't done nuthin'. You ain't git caught stealing, did you?"

"Nah, Pa. I've been here."

"If you let us come in, I'll explain everything," Sheriff Brown said.

Rob's gaze dropped to MacLeod's hilt. "Leave the sword on the wood pile. I ain't known you from Adam."

MacLeod disarmed, propping his sword against the uneven walls sprouting mushrooms between the cracks. Bending under the doorframe, his eyes adjusted to the dimly lit single-room cabin. It felt claustrophobic inside. A table—cluttered with tools, crumpled fliers and a worn deck of cards—had a smoldering cigar ground out in the middle. *Odd for something decidedly expensive to be here.* The cupboard was empty save a sagging bag of oats and some cornmeal. Any remnants of Eleanor had long disappeared.

Hovering near the door, the girl's scrawny arms lifted a musket almost as long as her to hang it on pegs. Her tattered dress, if you could deem it one, must have been Eleanor's old shift and petticoat, now discolored and ripped. No bodice or apron. She was grimy. The dirt made deep lines into her elbows past where her fingerless gloves stopped. The girl kept scratching her arm. *Flea bites?*

Without her weapon, the girl resembled more a scared kitten than mountain lion. MacLeod's brows raised with recognition as light fell across her face. "Eleanor," he gasped. The lass was a near replica, save her red hair.

"Eleanor was my ma."

He kept staring at the shape of her face, the length of her eyelashes. It was like Eleanor's ghost haunting him. Her eyes looked puffy from crying. *Why did she scream?*

Rob Birch spit yellow phlegm. "You known my wife?" Birch looked at him, then the girl, and snorted. "You that fancy lord? This your bastard I been raising all these years?"

"I'm not the girl's father, but I represent him. Dinna fash yourself, lass, I'm not here to hurt you. My name's Mr. MacLeod. I was your mother's friend." *Eleanor's rolling in her grave over that one.*

Looking confused, the girl peered deeply at him now.

"Hold on a minute. I gotta piss." Rob relieved himself outside the door.

Sheriff Brown handed MacLeod a crumpled runaway slave advert from the table. "This is how he makes money."

RAN AWAY FROM HIS MASTER. Mr. Crowan, of Williamsburg, in the colony of Virginia, on September 15, 1739, a Negro man Servant named Moses, about twenty Years of Age, a thick well sat Fellow, has a scar over his left eye; had on homespun blue cloth breeches, white shirt.

Whoever apprehends him and conveys to his master shall have ten pounds Reward and all necessary charges.

The sheriff said, "Got this runaway locked in my gaol right now until the slave traders come next week. Good money in slave catching."

Wasn't the runaway's accomplice hanging from Matthew's tree? MacLeod tucked the flier in his sporran then loosened his jabot in the putrid, roasting air.

A little boy as filthy as the girl darted behind her. Clearly starving, the children stared as flies buzzed around them.

"Who's this wee one?"

"Sam." She picked at a scab on her elbow while the boy's stomach growled with gusto.

"Dinna he talk?"

Cowering behind his sister, the boy blinked large brown eyes with thick lashes. MacLeod's mind flashed to Broderick, around the same age, trembling behind Fiona. *"Dinna you talk, laddie? Or do words scare you, too?" Broderick quivered. "I thought I saw a fox, sir." "So, you ran, coward? You let the chickens get slaughtered?"*

MacLeod felt a pang of guilt. *Does Broderick think I'm a brute, like Fiona said I've become?* "There's no need to fear me," he said to Sam. To the girl, "Your father sends for you."

"What?" Rob leaned against the doorframe, eyeing MacLeod, more sober now.

Annaliese tilted her head. "My pa's right there."

"Mr. Birch, here is a letter from Eleanor requesting Lord Hallewell assume custody, which he has agreed to do. I'm Annaliese's guardian until she's settled."

Rob said, "Your papers ain't mean shit."

MacLeod groaned internally. *Why did Eleanor marry this thorny scoundrel?*

"A letter? Ma's dead goin' on five years."

"Hush up. Ain't no one talking to you," Rob said.

Flinching, Annaliese's shoulders collapsed inward, and she stared at the floor.

MacLeod held out the letter, but Rob barely glanced at it. "Eleanor wrote it just before her death. I ken it must be a shock, Mr. Birch, but this is what Eleanor wanted. I promise Annaliese will be well cared for."

"You sayin' I ain't care for her?"

Is he being serious? "Consider what's best for the girl ... She's not your daughter."

"Goddamned Eleanor. Even dead, the woman's a pain in the ass. This is bullshit." Rob scratched the overgrown whiskers on his neck. "I told her I ain't want no jealous man coming back here. She said that lord ain't want nuthin' to do with children. Why you here now when the girl's old enough to earn her keep? Ain't no one taking my girl. I've got papers, too."

"Papers?"

Rob shifted through the cupboard drawer overflowing with junk. "See her indenture contract? She mine until twenty-one."

A rather important detail Matthew Crowan neglected to mention. Think fast, MacLeod. "You're assuming she was born unclaimed, which would make her indentured, but her father claims her. She is Lord George Hallewell's property."

"Now I ain't understand no fancy lawyer talk. But I do known this: *Partus sequitur ventrem*. It means any child born to an enslaved mother becomes the master's property. Well, Master Crowan sold the girl to me. Unless you ready to pay up, ain't got nuthin' to say."

Figures Rob Birch is the one bumpkin who ken the law. "Mr. Birch, let's come to an understanding, aye? Court is expensive. You seem in debt. Or maybe you're expecting the lass to shoot all your creditors while you hide?"

Rob punched MacLeod dead in the face, catching him off guard. *I probably deserved that.* Rob tackled his waist, knocking him into the table and onto the dirt. A rusty hammer grazed MacLeod's eyebrow as it fell, making him moan. MacLeod shook his head, taking a few seconds to recover. A surge of rage coursed through his veins. He grabbed Rob by his shirt and delivered a satisfying punch.

Bang.

Both men froze. Sheriff Brown stood over them with a smoking pistol. Rob spit blood. "You shot a damned hole in my roof."

"It's in good company with the others. Birch, just sell the girl, pay off your debt and be done. Court's in session this afternoon, and I need to get back."

MacLeod pinched his eyebrow to stop the bleeding. *This was supposed to be a simple meeting with perhaps a few goodbye tears, not a wee lass pointing a musket in my face, and a dirty brawl with a wife beater.*

"What about Sam?" Annaliese held her brother. "You cain't take me and leave him. He'll die. I ain't leaving without him," she said, as though she were in a position to make demands.

Rob pulled himself onto the sole chair. "Sam's *my* boy. You can buy Eleanor's whore daughter, but you cain't steal my boy." Blood flowed from his swollen lip like red mites escaping a hill.

Sheriff Brown said, "He's right about his son. You can't take him."

Annaliese fiercely guarded the wee lad from Rob. "Hey, mister, cain't you buy him, too?"

Her pleading stirred a twinge of pity. He sighed. "You have debts, Mr. Birch? I can fix that. How much do you owe?"

Rob swatted away a fly. "Twenty pounds about."

"I'll give you forty, and the boy comes with me, too."

"No, sir, not my boy. He almost old enough to rent out, earn me some cash."

"You're sure? You don't want forty pounds all at once today, instead of five per year if you rent him out?" MacLeod laid a stack of cash on the table. Rob ogled the notes.

"One hundred pounds."

MacLeod rolled his eyes.

Rob stood. "Good boy's worth a lot. He a little slow but ain't eat hardly nuthin'. The rest includes ten years' back pay for feeding the brat. Her father's some fancy lord. He owes me."

"Fine. Once you're locked in debtors' prison, I'll sue you for custody, plus damages. You'll lose the few acres of Eleanor's farm you have left."

"You gonna threaten me, Irishman? Fuck you. Daniel Crowan's been hounding me for months to buy her. He's a lying, cheating son of a bitch, but I'd rather sell her to him than you."

Why would Daniel want her? Something seemed suspicious. MacLeod, seal the deal and get her out of here. "I'm Scottish. Fifty. Last offer."

He watched Rob do the calculations, saw the greed filter past his pride.

"Done. They was only worth thirty." Rob grinned and wiped his nose against his arm.

Annaliese held her brother close, blinking rapidly. The boy looked confused. Annaliese said, "The big Scotsman owns us, Sam. You indentured like me now."

"Go outside, children," MacLeod said, extracting papers from his satchel to write the bill of sale. Birch drew an X for his signature and was paid. MacLeod walked into the fresh air, exhaling in relief as the children stared as though he were a giant. For the first time on this trip, he felt good.

A crooked cross half hidden among the patchy grass and weeds caught his eye. No headstone. No flowers. MacLeod's feet rooted to the ground. "Your mother is buried there?"

Annaliese shrugged, scratching her arm. "Her and my sister, Mary. She were a baby."

Seeing her grave felt different. Final. Eleanor's face flashed before him. Such a beauty. Wild and young with the world at her feet. Now she was buried beside a shack in the wilderness. *Forgive me, Eleanor.*

Chapter Twelve

ANNALIESE

"The hell you takin'?" asked Pa, as Annaliese ran back inside, dug through the cupboard and grabbed a book while he counted his money.

Hugging it to her chest, she faced him. "You ain't never gived me nuthin'. I earned this."

"Careful. Might not like what she wrote about you," he said with a smug grin.

Darting past him, Annaliese watched the sheriff plunking Sam on his saddle.

"Whew. These children stink to high heaven. Never took you for a bleeding heart, MacLeod. What are you going to do with the boy?"

"I have to think on it. What have you got there, lass?"

"Ma's book."

His mouth fell open. "It cannae be." Opening it, he brushed a finger over a scribbled-out word on the first page and winced. "I'll put it in the pack for safe keeping."

After setting her side-saddle on the horse, he grabbed the reins and clicked his tongue, making the horse trot. Unsure how to balance, she shifted, but he put his giant forearm across her, pinning her to his solid chest. *Should I feel safe or scared?*

Pa looked through the open door with those steel eyes and mouthed, "You still mine."

Her shoulders tensed. MacLeod said, "Dinna fash. I winnae let you fall."

They rode along the creek spilling into the York River. Rowboats crowded the view, racing to load tobacco on big ships headed to Europe. Sam bounced and pointed, happily. She twisted to study MacLeod.

"You look like you have something to say, lass."

"My father's a lord ... He must be a plantation owner, right? Sam, we rich now."

Sam bounced in the saddle as blue-gray herons flew overhead.

MacLeod said, "Your father's rich. You huvnae got a penny. You're a bastard."

Cringing at the word, she muttered, "So, Ma were a whore, like Pa said."

His head jerked back. "Dinna talk like that about your mother," he said sternly.

Annaliese bit her thumbnail, her cheeks burning.

The creek had flooded, making the wetlands muddy for the horses to walk through. Heat waves danced over the water.

"How come you wearing petticoats instead of breeches?" she asked sharply.

Sheriff Brown chuckled but MacLeod didn't. "It's a kilt. I'm from the Scottish Highlands." He sounded a little mad.

Good. Like Pa, she was good at finding people's sore spots. "How many children you got?"

His hands stayed steady on the reins. "What makes you think I have children?"

"Gold ring on your left hand. You pretty old, so you probably got children."

"Is thirty-nine old these days?" MacLeod shared a chuckle with Sheriff Brown. "I have five living sons. What else have you deduced about me? I see you sizing me up."

There was a twinkle of mischief in his eyes, making her thoughts freeze momentarily. *Is this a trick?* Focusing intently on his entire presence, she used a careful tone to describe what she saw. "You got scars on your knuckles, but not your face. Means you fight a lot and win a lot. You wrote a contract like it weren't nuthin'. Makes you smart. Expensive waistcoat. Got money. But if you working for my father, you ain't that rich. Rich people ain't work none."

A hint of a smile crossed his face as he nodded, and the tension in her neck released a little. They rode in silence until she gathered enough courage to ask the real question. "What happens next?"

"We'll clean you up and find a good apprenticeship for you."

They left the cool forest and entered the open road beneath the blistering sun. "Wait, I ain't living with my new pa?"

"He already has a family. Daniel Crowan offered you an apprenticeship at Sweetwater. His father isna convinced, but I could negotiate it. Perhaps you could be a laundress like your mother. Would you like that?"

Her body tensed at the thought of Mr. Daniel messing with her every night, and she felt MacLeod's eyes study her reaction. *Why would he care what I think of Mr. Daniel? Ain't like I got a say in the matter.* Changing the subject, she asked, "What's on your hip?"

"My sporran."

"Keep money in there, huh?" Petting the circular pouch made of soft leather, she rubbed the sharp little claws of the three rabbit feet hung in front.

Sheriff Brown slapped a mosquito. "Watch out. Her fingers are sticky as molasses."

Annaliese ground her teeth. "I ain't no thief."

"Sure. And I'm not being eaten alive by mosquitos."

"Go to hell," she muttered.

"Whoa." MacLeod stopped the horse and grabbed her chin. "Look at me, you wee backwoods urchin. Your pa might have allowed such talk, but you have a new father now, aye?" MacLeod released her chin. "Tell me all the curse words you ken."

Annaliese blinked in confusion and looked at Sheriff Brown, but he seemed as confused as her. "This a trick?"

"No."

What kind of master is this man? He probably thinks I ain't gonna do it. Fuck him. Let's get this over with. Twisting a loose curl, she said,

"Cods, cock, prick, cunt, bastard, whore-lady, bitch, goddamn." Closing her eyes, she covered her face, and waited for the punch.

"Come on," MacLeod said, "I'm sure you can do better than that."

Opening her eyes, she stared at Sam, who shrugged. Spontaneously laughing, she continued with vigor. "Arsehole, humping, nubbing, prigging, slit, crack, fuck, Eve's box, bum-fiddle, frigging, bollocks, tossing off, doodle sack, cock alley, did I say goddamned already?"

"Aye, you did."

"That would impress pirates watching a hanging," Sheriff Brown said.

Annaliese beamed—until MacLeod's face went serious. She wrapped her arms around her ears, squeezing her eyelids shut. "You gonna whip me?" Her chest pounded.

"You will be whipped if you say any of those words again. You've been warned."

I known it'd be a trick. Her shoulders rolled in. "Yes, master."

"I'm not your master, I'm your guardian. 'Yes, sir' will suffice." MacLeod gave the horse a little kick and went alongside the sheriff. Sam watched nervously.

Damn Sheriff Brown. Why'd he have to say I'm a thief? She scratched her forearm.

"Like I said, she's trouble. The whole family is," the sheriff said, staring her down. "Yeah, you're quiet now." To MacLeod, "Only a matter of time before she ends up in gaol. She'll never amount to anything."

"I thought you were sheriff, not judge and jury. How was this appalling neglect allowed? What about the Poor Laws? Aren't there penalties for Birch not maintaining his children? They're clearly rude and ignorant."

Keep calling me stupid, arsehole. I'll rob you blind and leave you for dead.

"This isn't New England, Mr. MacLeod. Do you know how many orphans, savages and mulattoes I deal with? You think I have time to investigate how well a child knows the Bible? Birch never applied for alms. As long as he feeds them, I have other fish to fry."

"It's good I came for you, Annaliese. You're on a new trajectory."

"What's ajectory?"

"Trajectory. It means you're on a fresh path. Both you children are now."

Horses swatted at the flies as they plodded the road.

Shaking her head, she muttered, "Pa's gonna come git me, hear?"

"No, he winnae. I just paid him more than he'll earn in five years."

Annaliese snorted. *Who's stupid now?* "All the money you gave be gone in a week. You think a piece of paper is gonna stop him? You in for a nasty surprise."

Horseshoes clacked and clopped stepping back onto the dry part of the road.

"I'm not overly concerned." MacLeod gazed ahead. "Do you trust me?"

She scratched her arm. "Known you for twenty minutes."

MacLeod smiled. "Valid point. You can trust I'll protect you."

Yeah, you'll protect me the entire length of the road until you sell me to Daniel Crowan; I'm taking Sam and running once we git to town. Jack will help me run, I known it.

―※―

Annaliese's mouth watered from the roast chicken and gravy smells as they entered Sir Drake's Tavern. Two older gentlemen with powdered hair chatted, walking down a winding staircase and into the dining area.

"Are these two beggars bothering you, Mr. MacLeod?" asked the tavern lady. "Marcus, aren't these the little weasels who steal from my pigpen?"

A large Negro man wiping glasses said, "Yes, ma'am. Chase them all the time."

Sam hid behind her. Annaliese marked the doors in case they needed to run.

Mr. MacLeod said, "This is my ward, Annaliese Cameron. Annaliese, this is Mrs. Otis."

Why is he calling me by a different last name? I'm Annaliese Birch.

Mrs. Otis's face brightened. "Your ward? What a happy change. Anna, you really must learn to curtsy properly if you want to pass yourself off as a gentleman's ward. Dip like a bucket in a well, not some chicken pecking at feed."

Mrs. Otis demonstrated. Everyone looked at Annaliese until she obliged.

"Well, you're not ready for court, but it's a start." Mrs. Otis walked beneath dried herbs hung from the ceiling beams and pointed them toward a square table with mismatched chairs next to the fireplace. Mr. MacLeod and the sheriff sat while Annaliese moved to the floor in the corner, pulling Sam onto her lap.

MacLeod said, "Get over here. Sit at the table."

He sounded mad. *Is this a trick? Pa never lets us sit at the table.* Slowly, they sat opposite the men. Sam dug his nails into her arm.

A stocky Negro woman said, "English tea bread with parsley butter," as she put it on the table alongside four relish plates and four short beers. Mr. MacLeod put a napkin on his lap, nodding for them to follow his lead.

"Eat," he said kindly.

They both tore at the bread, fighting over it, pulling the butter close. Annaliese dug her fingers into the soft stuff, sucking it before anyone took it away. Mr. MacLeod slapped her hand. *I knew it were a trick.* Blood rushed to her cheeks, and she held her breath.

"Keep your dirty fingers from there. Use a knife." Mr. MacLeod sipped his beer. "Your pa had his way and I have mine. You were raised in chaos. I have rules. Are you good at following rules?"

Annaliese bit her lip.

"I didna think so. Behave and you'll have no need to fear me, aye?"

A slave came with steaming hot pies, and a bowl of currant jelly. Annaliese ripped into the pie, burning her fingertips. Mr. MacLeod forced a spoon in her fist. Scooping currant jelly, she dropped it on the pie, gobbled the cured ham and gravy, then dragged her fist against her chin and licked her sticky fingers while Sam guzzled his beer.

"Slow down, or you'll get sick," MacLeod warned.

Sam belched loud enough to make an old man lower his newspaper. Annaliese laughed. Sheriff Brown crinkled his wide nose.

A youth carried in two crates toward the storage room. Annaliese waved wildly once she recognized him. "Jack."

Jack rounded the corner and smiled. "Ahoy, beautiful."

Mr. MacLeod looked none too happy. "Whom are you?"

"Jack Bellum. Who's askin'?" he said, balancing the crates on his knee. Annaliese leaned in, curious how this would play out.

"Sheriff Brown is asking," said the law man, sitting taller in the chair.

"She called *me* over, boss," Jack said with a wicked smile.

"I a-ain't f-feel g-good." Sam stared at the pie crust.

"Jack works on the river," she bragged.

"Best get back to your rowboat," MacLeod said.

"I ain't f-feel g-good." Sam belched then splashed vomit all over the table. Sheriff Brown stood, disgusted. Jack laughed and headed to the root cellar while a slave wiped the table with a wet rag.

"Let's go outside, Sam." She grabbed his wrist.

"Sure you don't want to send them back to Birch?" the sheriff half-joked as they passed.

Out in the midday sun, Sam splattered half-chewed meat onto a fancy shrub with orange flowers. Annaliese whacked the back of his head good and hard. "Why you gotta be greedy and eat fast? Now he ain't gonna feed us again." Sam sobbed between hurls. "You hush your mouth, boy."

A long line of spit ran from Sam's mouth to the dirt. She broke it with her finger and gripped his shoulders. "When I hit you, it's 'cause I love you. When the Scotsman hits us, it's 'cause we ain't nuthin' to him, hear?"

Sam swallowed his tears and stayed on his knees, holding his stomach as little tremors shook up and down his arms. A few minutes later, Jack slid by her side smelling good, like sawdust and beer. *I known he'd come for me.*

"Who's the Scottish prick?"

"My real father's servant, I reckon. Jack, my real pa's rich. The man just paid fifty pounds for us. He had a ton of money in his sporran. I was gonna take it but not with the sheriff right there. I ain't stupid."

Jack's face lit up and he rubbed his lip, like his mind was working real hard. "You stayin' here? We can rob him. I need time to set things up, though."

"But I want to go now. He's talking about sending me back to Sweetwater."

"No, beautiful. Stick with him today. We'll rob him after dark then run away. You're my girl, right?" Kissing her full on the mouth, he stroked her cheek with his ringed fingers.

"Hey. Get away from her," MacLeod hollered, scary enough to make Jack hop the white picket fence and run down the alley. "Annaliese, what the hell are you doing?"

She grinned. "He's gonna marry me."

"You're nine."

"Nine and a half."

"Get inside." MacLeod yanked her arm toward the door. Sheriff Brown stood, laughing.

MacLeod said, "This is why I dinna have daughters."

Chapter Thirteen

FIONA

Scotland

"En garde."

Fiona cringed at the heavy clank of Lachlan's sword smiting Broderick's. Her sons drilled in the yard with her brother, Malcolm, in the final days of summer. Short and solid, Fiona's brother trained her younger boys in the art of war. William's older brother, Cam, trained James and David back on the Isle of Skye when they were about the same age.

Chickens flew to escape the battle. James shook his head, muttering curses at Broderick's shoddy effort while he supervised wee Hamish hitting a staff against the alder tree.

Broderick barely had time to parry against the relentless cuts Lachlan made, forcing him to step back until he stumbled over his own feet, landing hard in the dirt. Lachlan held his sword tip against his brother's throat.

"I yield," Broderick said.

Malcolm said, "Good job, Lachlan. Tomorrow, I'll teach you to use the claymore, if you can lift it."

Lachlan smiled, entrusting his smallsword to James. "I'll dominate with any weapon."

James hit him upside his head. "Braggards beg beheading. Stay humble in your win."

Lachlan rubbed his head and went inside to eat. Broderick dusted his kilt and headed toward the door.

Malcolm stopped him. "You need more practice."

Broderick groaned. "I'm tired. I've been fighting all morning."

"Aye, ducking and running away is tiresome. James, take over. Mind you tell the field hands to salvage what they can of the barley. I have to head home and work on my own harvest. Damn this drought."

Wee Hamish said, "Dinna go. I want to fight with a sword."

Malcolm said, "First sticks, then swords."

"No one ever won a battle with a stick," Hamish complained, leaning against his staff.

"Oh, no?" Malcolm kicked the staff away from Hamish's feet, tripping him to the dirt. Hamish grumbled as he went inside.

Fiona kissed her brother's cheek. "Thank you. I truly appreciate all your help."

"Ack," he grumbled, mounting his horse.

Fiona, James and Broderick watched Malcolm's horse trot down the stone-lined road.

"Uncle Malcolm's done a shite job training you," James said to Broderick.

Fiona agreed, at least internally. *Make a bravery potion with nettle leaves? No. Dinna practice magic. Courage is earned through action, not enchantments.*

James dressed down his brother. "If you're fighting a MacDonald, he winnae stop for you to catch your breath."

"Da says I'm going to be a minister. No one duels God's representative."

"En garde," James said, holding Lachlan's sword.

Broderick's sword drooped.

"Brod, fix your stance. It's not like you're holding *Justice*. Make your move."

Broderick tried a moulinet, swinging the sword full circle, but he faltered. James easily counterattacked, nicking his brother's arm. Broderick winced, pinching the skin beneath his torn sleeve.

"No one uses extravagant moves in battle. It's slash and cut, and if you're lucky, you can kill a redcoat or a Campbell."

"Stop lecturing me. I'm not a bloody warrior." Broderick threw the sword in exasperation, forcing chickens to fly.

"Broderick," Fiona yelled.

"What the hell is wrong with you, boy? That's no' a toy," James shouted.

"Sorry," Broderick said, retrieving the weapon. His face grew ruddy as he gripped the brass hilt, raising then lowering it, on the verge of tears. "I'm never going to be good. Lachlan always beats me. He's bigger, faster, stronger ..."

James wrapped his arm over Broderick's shoulder. "You're smarter. Defense is science, not bashing each other. Stop letting him in your head. Again. En garde. Fix your damned stance. Now scream."

"Scream?"

"A blood-curdling, primal scream. Scares the shite out of your enemy. Like this."

James' shrieks ricocheted around the glen as he charged. Broderick fled, but James blocked him. Right cut, left cut. Broderick thrusted back. Parry. Parry. James advanced until they were both gasping, his sword ready to slice down. Broderick's whole body locked in fear.

"What are you closing your eyes for?!" James shouted.

Broderick knelt on the ground and dry-heaved as tears wet the dust beneath him. James stared at Fiona in frustrated sympathy.

"Get up, Broderick," she said, kneeling beside him.

"I cannae," he said. Tears streamed his face. "Da's right. I dinna deserve his name."

Fiona's heart broke. "Your da only wants you to defend yourself and your family. Come now."

"Da hates me," Broderick said, sobbing.

"This is useless," James said.

Her body tensed, furious with William. Did he comprehend what he'd done to the lad? Broderick loved him, feared him, wanted nothing more than to please him. Before she was even aware, Fiona had cast a silent spell.

LISA A. TRAUGOTT

Eisd rium a Dhia. While William's off in the colonies rescuing some other woman's child, let him reflect on the treatment of his own. With harm to none, so it be done.

Chapter Fourteen

Annaliese

"Why you holding my hand like I'm a baby? Where we goin'?"

MacLeod heel-toed them through the garden paved with crushed oyster shells, past the white picket fence, and into the bustling street. "Church."

Why would we go there? It was only a few blocks away from the tavern, on West Duke of Gloucester. A crowd grew at the courthouse for the sessions. They passed the wig maker's shop window filled with nine blockheads of perukes stinking of goat hair and lavender.

MacLeod said to Sam, "What trade interests you? Gunsmith, nailor, cooper—"

"Blacksmith, sir." It was the first time Sam hadn't stuttered.

Annaliese said, "Really? Or is you saying it because we passin' the blacksmith's now?"

Through the open doors they watched a Negro man in a leather apron step his heavy boots over the singed metal bits covering the floor. Rolling his sleeves above muscular forearms, he directed two young apprentices holding sledgehammers bigger than themselves to hit the metal balanced on a stump. Pounding clanks and flying sparks made her chest tighten. The blacksmith shimmied the spiked poker from the raging fire, its sharp tip glowing red. Her skin felt tingly, and her breath caught in her throat. "You gonna like working near fire all day?"

Sam nodded. "I like h-hammers."

MacLeod seemed pleased. "Blacksmith is an honorable profession. You get to learn to be a man, aye? No more sloth and idleness."

Sam agreed with a firm nod as they entered the brick church. Annaliese hadn't been to church since Ma was alive. Inside, they passed long pews hemmed in by white boxes with a Bible at each end, and she peeked up wooden stairs that led to a box where the preacher spoke.

A man with puffy bags under his eyes and thinning hair combed over a bald spot said, "I'm Reverend Shaw. May I help you?" Pa always said he'd rather pay a fine than sit through Reverend Shaw's bullshit.

"I'd like to set up apprenticeships for these wee ones. The lad wants to be a blacksmith."

After giving them the once over, the reverend said, "Are these the Birch children? I just saw Mr. Birch in town with a runaway a few days ago. Has something happened to him?"

"He's fine. I'm their mother's friend from the Old Country. They became my wards this morning."

"My real father's a rich lord," Annaliese said, raising her chin.

"Wheest," MacLeod said loud enough to reach God. *Ma used to say wheest, too.*

Reverend Shaw gave a knowing look to MacLeod. "I can set up the boy easy enough in town. The girl's got a reputation as a troublemaker, though. I have a milliner's shop in Richmond looking for a girl, but not until the end of the month."

"Wait, I ain't gonna be with Sam?" Her palms grew sweaty as she studied the men's faces.

"Annaliese, a word." MacLeod steered her to the back of the church while Sam sat on a pew. MacLeod spoke in a hush. "It's apparent you love your brother very much. You need to be strong so he dinna get scared when we leave. No tears, aye?"

Annaliese leaned against a pew to steady herself. Her forearm itched something terrible where Pa had burned her, and her brain felt fuzzy. "Well, you could be our new pa." Her words sounded stupid before they even left her mouth. She just wasn't expecting to be split from her brother.

"Richmond isna far." He patted her shoulder. "You'll see each other."

Throwing off his arm, she said, "You think I'm stupid? Richmond is two days away and we'll be apprenticed for years. We ain't never gonna see each other again."

MacLeod crossed his arms over his chest.

Her eyes began to well, but she blinked them back. *Please, God, make this right.* "I cain't leave him." Her voice felt shaky. "They'll laugh at the way he talks and kick him when he cries."

Mr. MacLeod's face softened. "You want the truth? He has a future with the blacksmith. He had nothing with your pa. What's best for Sam?"

Pressing her lips together, she thought things through. *Calm down, Annaliese. Jack said we gonna rob MacLeod tonight and then run away. We'll git Sam soon enough.* Forcing a smile, she exhaled slowly, strode to Sam and said, "You gonna be a blacksmith."

While MacLeod handled the paperwork, she sat on the pew feeling numb. *What if nuthin' works out?* Sam crawled into her lap and sucked his thumb while she wrapped her arms around his shoulders, smelling the dust in his hair. *Jack will help Sam run away after we find an empty cabin, right?*

"Sam," MacLeod called. "Reverend Shaw is going to take you to your new home. I'm going to give you some advice I told my own sons. Use your head before your fists, but if you must fight, punch first. Always do your best. Act as though God were watching because He is." Leaning in, he whispered, "Here's a secret I wish I told my middle son, Broderick. All men cry. Just dinna do it around other boys. Cry at night, aye?"

Sam gave a firm nod.

Annaliese angled away and scratched her forearm. *Why'd MacLeod have to be nice all of a sudden when I want to hate him?* Her stomach felt upset. *Be strong for Sam. No tears, Annaliese. You'll figure this out.* Faking a big smile, she kissed Sam's cheek. "Be good."

Sam skipped away with the reverend, not a care in the world. Did he understand what an apprenticeship meant? As soon as they left the church, MacLeod said, "You did the right thing. See how happy he was? It's better this way, aye?"

"I think it's better for *you* this way, Mr. MacLeod."

∞

Annaliese pressed her dirty fingers against Jane Woollery's mantua shop window, staring at the dolls in the newest fashions, just like when she was five.

She pressed her bandaged hand against the glass. "Them babies is so pretty." "Maybe your father will get one for you," Ma said. "Pa ain't never gonna buy me one." "Not him. Your real father in London."

Annaliese followed MacLeod inside. The store overflowed with women in straw hats holding children's hands. A short man with a mole on his forehead came from behind the counter and snapped at Annaliese, "What did I tell you about coming inside?"

She took a step back, but MacLeod placed his hands on her shoulders.

"Sir, she is my new ward, and needs a full wardrobe."

How the storekeeper's mood changed. "Jane," he called. "My wife, Jane, is the best seamstress in Williamsburg."

A stout woman in a brown and orange plaid dress with a coif on her head emerged holding a pincushion. She puckered her lips at Annaliese, then looked at her husband.

"This gentleman says he needs clothes for the girl."

Mrs. Woollery's scowl faded. "How many dresses, and how soon, sir?"

"Within the week. I'd like one outfit immediately, if you have something. It can be used. I dinna have any daughters. Tell me what a lass needs."

Mrs. Woollery squeezed Annaliese's chin with her cold hand. "A scullery maid should have two dresses, seven aprons and woolen hose. One pair of sensible shoes per year will do."

Mr. MacLeod asked, "What makes you believe she's going to be a scullery maid?"

"The drunk's daughter? What else could she do?" She laughed, releasing her grip. "Be a young lady? Dress for a ball?" Mrs. Woollery flashed her stained teeth.

Normally, Annaliese might square off, but with Sam gone some of her fight had left with him. Dropping her chin to her chest, she slouched, knowing the shopkeeper was right. *I ain't never gonna be nuthin' no matter where I go.*

MacLeod crossed his arms. "My ward will be a young lady."

Annaliese lifted her head. "I'm gonna be a lady?"

Mrs. Woollery fumbled the pincushion. "Gracious, the girl's fortunes have changed, haven't they?" Clearing her throat, Mrs. Woollery scowled at the cut over MacLeod's eye and blood drops on his shirt and seemed suspicious. "It'll cost you a pretty penny. She'll need stays, shifts, petticoats, bodices, cotton hose, silk gowns, a cloak, a straw hat, a dozen handkerchiefs, shoes and gloves." Putting her hands on her hips, she grinned smugly. "A true lady needs many things, sir." Her tone called his bluff.

With a gleam in his eye, he said, "Deliver the lot to Sir Drake's Tavern within three days, and one dress tonight."

"That's an awful lot of work for three days' time. I'd have to hire helpers, a shoemaker, and the tailor is the one who makes the stays. I'd need a significant deposit."

MacLeod tugged a coin bag from his sporran and jingled it. "Here's eighty pounds. Can you accommodate the request, or shall I seek services elsewhere?"

Mrs. Woollery's eyes popped open. A squeal escaped Annaliese as she scanned the room and giggled. Two boys nearby elbowed each other as nosy customers lifted their heads.

"I can start making the dresses right now," the seamstress said, positively giddy. "Come here, dearie." Mrs. Woollery was all smiles now. "Can't make a dress without you." An apprentice came with folds of fabric. "Well, don't stand there, lift your arms out. Whew. Mercy, you need perfume," she said, plugging her nose. "Which fabric, sir? Yellow is good for a redhead."

"I ain't like yellow. I like blue."

"Hush. Blue is for blondes." To MacLeod, "The yellow, sir?"

"Blue." He winked at Annaliese. Her lips curled in a smirk.

Mrs. Woollery scowled like she had whiffed a cheeser in church. "As you wish, sir."

MacLeod casually strolled the shop with his arms behind his back. "I'd like a white dress, too, for church. The pretty one with the long ribbons down the back. Beyond that, I yield to your good judgment, madam."

Annaliese deliberately raised her eyebrows and said, "I'm gonna be a lady."

Once MacLeod moved beyond earshot, Mrs. Woollery leaned in. "You can wear the prettiest frock in the store, but it won't change who you are."

Annaliese glared straight into her beady eyes. "Bullshit. I'm gonna be a lady, and you'll always be ugly."

The apprentice snorted while Mrs. Woollery blushed twelve shades of pink. "Filthy drunkard's daughter. I give it one day before your master realizes the scallywag you really are."

"He ain't my master. He's my guardian."

Mrs. Woollery pricked her with a pin on purpose as she layered the fabric over her. "We're done measuring. Scat."

Wandering to the porch, Annaliese shivered at the late afternoon temperature drop. A crowd gathered at the courthouse across the street to mock the people locked in the pillory and stocks.

"*That's a pillory,*" Ma whispered. "*Wheest.*" She touched her finger to Annaliese's lips to be quiet as they hid in the shadows of the courthouse. Pa screamed as a man hammered his ear to the wood. Ma dragged her away. "*We have to mail the letter. We haven't much time.*"

"Annaliese, come in here, please," MacLeod said. Connected to the mantua shop was a general store, where Mr. MacLeod had sundries piled on the counter.

"Want a pastel?" Mr. Woollery offered a plate. "It's cinnamon sugar candy. Quite the rage with the governor's visiting dignitaries," he gave Mr. MacLeod a nudge, "and my wife."

When I was starving, they ran me off, but now that I have a rich guardian, they give me free candy? She shoved a fistful in her mouth.

"Annaliese, say thank you," Mr. MacLeod scolded.

"Thank you," she garbled. After a few seconds, her tongue burned. "Hot." Fanning her mouth, she spit five sticky pieces into her glove. *I known it were a trick.*

"Serves you right, lass. You're only meant to take one." To Mr. Woollery, "Do you have ledgers, quills and ink?"

"No. There's a print shop and bindery next to the station on Botetourt Street."

Mr. MacLeod settled the accounts for both stores.

"We love it when people come here from the Old Country and pay in sterling instead of tobacco," Mr. Woollery said. "The used dress and a shift will be at the tavern within an hour."

On the way out, Annaliese bumped into an older gentleman as he entered. He raised his cane. "Watch your way, child."

Mr. MacLeod patted the man's shoulder. "Apologies, sir. Annaliese, pay attention. Come along, last stop is the printers."

Annaliese slipped a small apple from a wooden basket into her pocket, for when she ran away with Jack. *When will he tell me the plan?*

MacLeod annoyingly held her hand again as they climbed the brick stairs to McCory's Printing Press. "Ma sent the letter here. How come it took five years for you to come?"

"Wheest. Seen and not heard, Annaliese," MacLeod said, heaving a stack of letters from his satchel.

"May I help you, sir?" the clerk asked. Two journeymen laid blocks in the printing press while a third rubbed ink between two hand paddles.

"*Feasgar math*," Mr. MacLeod said in some foreign tongue.

The clerk smiled. "My mother speaks Gaelic better than me. You a Highlander?" They switched into the other language, as Mr. MacLeod wrote a few more lines at the bottom of each letter with the quill on the counter before sealing them.

This day feels so strange. Did Pa burn me this morning? Feels like a lifetime ago. She scratched her forearm. A shelf displayed books and pamphlets for sale. Annaliese traced a finger over a wooden paddle with letters covered by a thin shellacked horn.

Mr. MacLeod noticed what she was doing and said, "Do you read?"

"Naw. Pa says girls and Negros shouldn't read."

"Take everything your pa says and throw it out the window with the contents of the chamber pot." Mr. MacLeod placed the hornbook on the counter. "Please add this."

"My ma could read and write, you know."

"I do. Who do you think taught her?"

Annaliese cocked her head. *Who is this man?* His smug grin shifted to a frown, like he was mad at himself. "You'll learn to read soon enough when you're apprenticed."

"Wait, you said I was gonna be a lady."

A flush crept across his cheeks red as his hair. "Just a wee white lie. I dinna ken, maybe it was her tone, or her rotten teeth that reminded me of a lady I hate, or the way she shamed you, but the shopkeeper needed to be taken down a peg. I hope you dinna mind being the best dressed apprentice in Richmond."

Just like Pa. Another lie. Another game.

Mr. MacLeod cleared his throat. "Sit on the bench."

She shuffled to the window. A woman in a gray linen gown and cotton fichu tied over her shoulders entered with six blond children. The oldest boy tore off bits of freshly baked bread, still steaming. His sisters wore matching flowered bodices and petticoats. They looked like some plantation owner's English garden, taking delicate bites with their flower bud mouths. Her stomach growled.

One girl pinched her upturned nose. "Mama, the dirty girl smells."

Annaliese hissed at the girl, who hid behind her ma's skirts. Mr. MacLeod didn't notice.

"Children, don't stare," the mother whispered, herding them in a tighter circle. Their buckled shoes made little taps across the swept floor.

Mr. MacLeod was taking forever. The man liked to talk. The warm bread's fresh scent drove her crazy. *What if he don't feed me for another day or two?* Slipping the apple from her pocket, she savored the first bite. Delicious—the perfect balance of sweet and tart. Her second bite made a loud crunch. Mr. MacLeod gave her the once-over, confused. "Where did you get an apple?"

Shit. "I found it."

Mr. MacLeod marched over while the English garden girls watched wide-eyed. He seemed nine feet tall. "Did you take it from the store? What else have you got in those pockets?"

She tried to run, but he caught her arm and pulled her pockets inside out. Loose change, five sticky pastels, a fork from the tavern and a pocket watch clanged on the floor.

"What in God's name?"

Annaliese shrugged, smiling. "Pa says I'm the best pickpocket in Williamsburg." In a blink, MacLeod bent her over his knee. "Let go," she said, squirming.

Children laughed as he spanked her hard enough to make loud cracking noises, then he stood her upright, wagging his finger in her face. "You. Do. Not. Steal."

She felt humiliated. Furious. Confused? Six smacks with his open hand? "That it?"

The garden girls gasped. His eyes popped open and his hand slid to his belt buckle. "Shall I hit you harder? Think before you answer."

Chapter Fifteen

LADY MARGARET

Grimbly Manor, Oxford

"Viscount Percy Monroe," the butler announced before bowing off.

Poor Percy's swagger had evaporated. His nose, once perfect, was now dented slightly left, and he kept his right arm tucked into his chestnut waistcoat. Lady Margaret embraced Percy, kissing both his soft cheeks, savoring his musky scent, even if momentarily. Remaining still during the interaction, he abruptly retreated.

Apologize? No, wait for him to bring it up. Let him feel in control.

Plopping on the ornate armchair, he crossed one leg over his knee and stared past her, out the window, past the balcony. "I almost didn't come, but your son persuaded me we'd have much to discuss."

Stroking her neck, she hoped he'd notice that she wore his favorite perfume and her most sensual dress. Every strand of hair on her head was meticulously styled with Percy in mind. "I'm glad you came."

She smiled.

He didn't.

A servant entered with the tea service on a silver platter. The viscount flicked his left hand, and the servant bowed and left. Percy crinkled his brows. "Something's different about you."

Lady Margaret grinned. When he didn't respond, she said, "I have new teeth."

"How smashing for you. I have no right hand."

Standing quickly, her crimson petticoat flared. "Let's explore the garden. Lord Hallewell is in London, but these estates' walls have ears, don't they?"

Outside, they passed the enormous statue of her first husband, General Winston. Her fingers traced the bronze base. "I'm convinced my marriages are farces where the leading men are badly cast."

She laughed.

He didn't.

They trudged untouching through the maze of English yews, trimmed to perfection. At a break in the shrubs, he pulled her into a shady area overlooking a stand-alone structure with Corinthian columns. Now hidden from view, she beamed at the thought he might kiss her.

Viscount Percy slapped her hard with his left hand and she stumbled in shock, tripping on the gardening tools and assorted pots at the hill's base. Pressing her tongue against her new molar, she was thankful it remained in place.

Percy erupted, "You bitch. You were supposed to bribe the agents—"

"I did." Leaning against a marble bench, she brushed off the sting from her cheek.

"No, you clearly didn't. Were you trying to get me killed?"

Nervous to be spotted by groundskeepers, she scouted around before speaking. "No, my love—"

"You dare call me your love? You betrayed me for what? A ship? Was everything a lie?"

"I bribed the agent," she said, rising, "but he got the pox and a new one took over."

"Why didn't you tell MacLeod about our arrangement? You set me up, telling me about his wife dancing with Colonel Wilkes, which I stupidly mentioned. He cut through my wrist like he wished it were my neck. The man humiliated me, Margaret. Slaves pissed on my head. I'm a bloody punchline now." Percy flushed beet red. "Fuck!" he screamed, grabbing a ceramic pot with his left hand and smashing it against the folly column, spewing dirt and broken clay. He folded on the marble bench, bawling.

His bouts of rage were seismic but brief. Now that he shifted into victimhood, she knew he'd be more malleable. Perching next to him, her dress spread like pooled blood. "You act as though I control my own life. Lord Hallewell is glad enough to take my money, but he assumes anyone with a womb lacks intellect, thus I kept my involvement anonymous. You have to believe I'd *never* purposefully put you in harm's way." Stroking his cheek, she wiped away his tears and penetrated his eyes. "I promise we shall avenge all who wronged you." Her voice dripped in venom.

Viscount Percy nodded, wiping his nose on his sleeve, exposing his stump.

Refusing to cringe at his deformity, she instead stared at his plump lips, his strong but broken nose, his bright green eyes now cleansed from weeping.

Rising from the bench, he stared at the structure, then trekked up the hill with Lady Margaret close behind, entering the open-air temple. "What is this thing, anyway?"

"It's a folly. My first husband, the general, salved it from a Scottish estate he burned down during the War of the Three Kingdoms. He meant it to be admired from the manor as a reminder to fear the crown. Whenever MacLeod comes, I point it out to irritate him."

"I long for such trivial irritations." His entire body went flaccid—rounded shoulders, downcast eyes trained on his amputation. "I can't hold a sword, I can't hold a quill, I can't hold my own cock."

"Then let me."

Digging into his breeches, she knew sex was the simplest tool to regain her power. Percy avoided her gaze but didn't reject her hand. As she stroked and massaged him, she tried to kiss his mouth, but he resisted. Nibbling his neck, she inhaled the citrus from his natural wig falling behind his shoulders in tapering chestnut ringlets. His erection grew in her hand.

"You lost your pride, but you never lost your manhood."

Percy sighed. His smooth silk waistcoat tickled her lips as her kisses trailed his muscled chest. She knelt and stared up at him, waiting. His almost imperceptible nod was all she needed as she shimmied his breeches down, exposing a hardness meant only for her.

Bugger. Lady Margaret ran her tongue over her new teeth, praying the wire would cement them. Tentatively, she took him in her mouth, savoring his skin's salty tang, wrapping her hands around his hips to grip him fully. *All will be well. Keep things gentle.*

Percy thrust into her mouth, knocking her over, and she scrambled back in place.

"What's wrong with you today?" he asked, annoyed.

"Sorry." Squeezing his arse again, she opened wide, knowing she must be gallant in this.

"Never mind. Lie back lest I go soft."

Thank God. Scrutinizing the veiled windows of Grimbly Manor, she wished she hadn't worn red. Lifting her panniers at a diagonal angle, she slid on the stone floor, doing her best to stay behind the columns, hiding in the shrubbery's shadows.

Viscount Percy straddled her, penetrating with youthful drive. He was ten years her junior. Her parents raised her to believe older men were wiser. Life improved when she realized all men are immature fools; bed a young one.

Her hips rose to meet his, starving to take him deeper. Lady Margaret hated to crave him, but she did. She felt grateful he let her back into his world, for God's sake.

Percy grunted his release then rolled off, relaxed. Thrilling as it was to frolic with him, she knew his true lust was for her money, but in the warmth of his attention, she tricked herself into believing he might love her, as Colonel Wilkes once had.

Struggling to lift his breeches one-handed, Percy never asked for help—and she didn't offer, either. Emphasizing his weakness wouldn't serve anyone. After adjusting her gown, they rejoined the path, strolling over an arched bridge above a serpentine lake.

"I like your new teeth. They make you look younger."

How novel to be noticed. Her husband looked for his missing locket of Eleanor more than he ever gazed at her.

Glassy water mirrored the gathering gray clouds. Deep in thought, Percy said, "Is Alexander a good shot? Maybe he can duel on my behalf?"

"Duel whom? His own stepfather? Hardly. And MacLeod's gone."

They crested the bridge as a breeze rippled the waters. Leaning against the rail, she watched an elm tree shed.

"Gone where?" he asked.

A baby bird fallen from its nest flapped its tiny wings and squeaked. "My husband has a mistress and bastard in the colonies. MacLeod is retrieving them."

"The colonies? That's why he stole the *Icarus*? Good luck not getting shipwrecked. The African who pissed on me cursed it. It worked, didn't it?"

"I have no faith in curses. I believe in revenge." A few sprinkles dropped as she flicked the bird into the lake with the point of her silky shoe. "I'm actually quite good at it. I study men's weaknesses. I knew if I strategically placed a former mistress' love letter out in the open, the butler would find it and make sure it ended up in my husband's hands. I knew my husband would never travel to the colonies himself; he'd send MacLeod to fix things. This gives me months to plot."

"My god, I love a woman who's devious." Percy stroked his bottom lip, deep in thought. "I'll destroy both MacLeod and Lord Hallewell, but I can't kill a soul until I hire someone to teach me to fight left-handed. Can you loan me a little money, love? Help me make you a widow—then make you my bride?"

Lady Margaret glanced up, startled. Murdering her husband had never been a consideration—until now. Percy's scheming was amateurish, but she fantasized about having a husband like him. He was handsome and genuinely respected her intellect. More importantly, he would eventually come into his own inheritance, and not need her money. Her whole life, men had treated her like a pawn in their games and she obeyed out of duty to her father, or to protect her son's inheritance. Why should a woman like Eleanor—a nobody—a servant—get to have her husband's love? What must that be like? To be loved purely for yourself?

"You're lucky I find you amusing, Percy," she said, tapping his nose. "It tickles me to loan you MacLeod's own money so you can train to kill him, but once it's gone, my well runs dry. George cut off my allowance and isn't inclined to reinstate my funds any time soon. Can't your father help you?"

"We are estranged," he fumed. His expression grew sour. "I wish he'd die already. I'd get my inheritance, kill our enemies and marry you."

Sunshine cracked through the clouds, spilling golden rays into the water. They headed back toward the manor, nodding politely at the pruning gardeners. Lady Margaret trailed her fingers down his arm. "Leave your father to me."

Chapter Sixteen

WILLIAM MACLEOD

William MacLeod deposited the wee nyaff before the store owners, a firm grip on her arm. "Tell them."

"I stoled this," she muttered, dumping the contraband on the counter.

"Wicked child. He bought half the store for you," Mr. Woollery said.

The old gentleman they passed earlier gandered over, then patted himself down. "That's my watch. She took my watch." Lifting his cane at her, she covered her face with her arms.

Mrs. Woollery put her hands on her wide hips. "*Hmpf.* You stared your nose down on me when I tried to warn you."

His jaw clenched. *The lass is just like her mother. Give her everything and it still isna enough.* MacLeod nodded. "Aye. I apologize. It appears you ken her better than me."

"I want her arrested," the old man said. "The court is in session across the street."

MacLeod was about to intervene and fix things, but then he had a revelation. *This is my opportunity. They'll convict her of pickpocketing, and she'll become an indentured convict. Besides, Lord Hallewell dinna care about the child, really, just Eleanor, and she's dead. Lady Margaret will be appeased, and I need to protect my family more than Eleanor's thief daughter.* "Divine providence. Let's take a jaunter to the courthouse, lass."

Annaliese tried to break free, but he clenched her arm. Mrs. Woollery and the old man followed them to the long brick building with white shutters flanking the narrow windows. An imposing white dome capped the top. A leaf with the first hint of autumn blew past two men locked in the pillory. MacLeod said, "Ah, look, babes in the wood. You might be there later today."

"That ain't funny," she said, touching her ears.

"It's not supposed to be."

Sheriff Brown led a man to the platform. "Hear ye, hear ye. This robber was sentenced to hang, but through the benefit of the clergy has been branded and will be whipped instead." He lifted the man's hand, seared with a T for thief, and the crowd pressed forward to gawk. "He now will receive thirty-nine lashes."

"Please, sir," Annaliese begged the old man. "I'm sorry. I won't never steal again. Please don't arrest me."

Two bailiffs stood on the platform holding whips. Ripping the convict's shirt off his back, the right-handed bailiff struck first, making the thief cry in agony while boys threw pebbles at him.

"Dinna shy away, lass. Stare at your fate if you keep acting as your mother did. Watch the man pay his debt to society."

Tugging on his arm, Annaliese spoke with more desperation. "I ain't want to be branded again. Oh, please let me go to London. I'll be good, I'll be so good, I promise." Annaliese looked pathetic, pulling at her filthy dress, scratching her skin, then begging the old man for mercy. "Please, sir …" Her breath hitched. "I want to meet my real pa in London."

Mrs. Woollery said, "London? The only trip you'll take is to the gallows."

Lightly tapping MacLeod with his cane, the old man said, "What's she carrying on about?"

MacLeod sighed. "Her father lives in England, but I doubt he'd welcome a thief into his family."

Twenty lashes later, the criminal barely stood, held only by the ropes on the whipping post. His back dripped blood like flayed venison. A left-handed bailiff took over and snapped his cowhide, forming bloody crosses athwart the convict's back.

Mrs. Woollery said, "You'll be next. You deserve every lash you get, and then some."

MacLeod glanced at the girl. *Is this the brutal fate I want to assign the lass?*

Tapping MacLeod's shoulder again, the old man whispered, "The pocket watch is older than me, and I have it back now. Let her start over in London. Children deserve a second chance. Mercy is a powerful lesson, too."

MacLeod blinked. *How is it a stranger shows more grace than me? I betrayed Eleanor. Will I betray her daughter, too?* Annaliese cried harder, her breath growing shallow, and he felt guilty for throwing her to the wolves. *How will I get her out of this mess?*

Annaliese's entire face broke out in a rash like nothing he'd ever seen. Her dirty fingernails raked her cheeks as she sank to the ground.

"Are you all right?" He knelt. Welts grew large and pink, spreading down her neck the more she scratched. "What are you scratching at? Were you stung by a bee? You're going to draw blood." Prying her fingers from her face, he had visions of her dying in front of him as she wheezed. "Annaliese, breathe."

Flocking around them, the townsfolk grew more interested in her gasps than the thief's cries. Annaliese's eyes rolled back, and she collapsed.

A woman in pink crossed herself and said, "I've never seen the like."

"Annaliese? Can you hear me?"

He drew her onto his lap, lightly tapping her cheeks. Thank God, she opened her eyes. A skinny woman in a striped silk dress fanned her. Annaliese tried to lift her head but looked shaky as dozens gawked.

Mrs. Woollery said, "It's like she's bewitched. Look at her face."

MacLeod rolled his eyes. The last thing he needed was accusations of witchcraft. Hadn't he already dealt with enough of that in relation to his wife? "It's a rash, not marks of the Devil."

"I'm not quite sure about that one," Mrs. Woollery said.

"Breathe, lass," he said softly.

Sheriff Brown sauntered over and joked, "Mr. MacLeod, are you following me?" He frowned at the girl. "She all right?"

MacLeod laughed it off. "Just shocked to witness justice."

Someone handed her a dip spoonful of water as the late afternoon sun sank. MacLeod said to the crowd, "Thank you all, kindly. She's fine. We should go."

"Go? What about the things she stole?" Mrs. Woollery demanded.

"We've returned them. I think she learned her lesson."

"Lesson, my foot. I want to press charges against the little witch."

MacLeod forced a smile. "Aye. But then we wouldn't need any new clothes, would we? And I'd require a full refund."

They stared each other down. "You mark me, Mr. MacLeod, she has the Devil in her. You best send her to church to get the demons removed before going to England, or she'll sink the ship." Mrs. Woollery left in a huff for her store.

"Pleasant woman." MacLeod winked at the sheriff.

Sheriff Brown said, "We're about to start the last trial—a misdemeanor for skipping church. I best go." He bowed, and the good citizens of Williamsburg followed him inside to judge their neighbors.

Annalise sat. Her eyebrows squished together. "You ain't sending me to gaol?"

"I'm giving you a second chance. There winnae be a third, understood?"

Lowering her eyes, she nodded.

"Do you often have fits?" MacLeod asked quietly.

Annaliese mumbled, "Why do you care? Am I going to London? Or is that a lie, too?"

"I dinna ken yet," he said, rubbing his temples. *God, I need a drink.* "You, my dear, have had a very long day." He picked her up by the armpits and she winced as his forearm supported her tender backside.

"Ain't no one carried me since I was five," she grumbled.

"You huvnae had a bath since you were five, either."

A wagon across the street caught his attention. The lad Jack smirked as he unloaded deliveries to a waiting slave. MacLeod glanced in a storefront window and saw the reflection of Annaliese mouthing, "Tonight?"

"Tomorrow," Jack mouthed.

What are these two plotting? As MacLeod entered the tavern, Mrs. Otis joked, "You lost a child. Is the poor boy still sick?"

He glared. *Shut up. Dinna remind the bairn.*

Mrs. Otis was savvy enough to read his face. "Did you want a bath for the girl? It'll cost seven shillings to wash her in the kitchen, twelve for privacy in your room."

"The kitchen is fine," he said, dropping Annaliese.

"I have to git naked in front of everyone?" she asked, crossing her arms over herself.

MacLeod rolled his eyes. "Fine, take her to my room and clean the wee nyaff there. I'll be at the bar. Did they send over clean clothes yet?"

"A few things arrived. I've put them in your room. We'll clean her pretty as a princess." Mrs. Otis passed the girl off to a slave.

As dusk approached, the tavern grew crowded. Farmers with manure on their feet stood next to joiners stinking of sweat.

"Do you have whiskey? It's been a fair awful day."

Mrs. Otis flitted by. "I always keep my shelves stocked for special guests. It'll cost you extra, though."

That woman would upsell anything. "Keep them coming."

He rubbed the scab over his eyebrow. *I'm not going to risk my neck any further taking this delinquent to London. She'd probably get arrested the first week and shipped back on a convict ship. What a bloody waste of time this trip is.* Tomorrow, he'd dump her at the church, set her up with an apprenticeship and leave this wretched colony.

Mrs. Otis rushed to him, flustered. "Excuse me, Mr. MacLeod, but there's a problem."

"Jesus, Joseph and Mary, what did the lass do now?" he asked with an impatient snort.

"Ah ... You might already know, but in case you didn't ..."

Draining the whiskey, he followed her upstairs into the bedroom. A yellow haze from the setting sun cast over Annaliese, as she stared out the window. Mrs. Otis stripped off the towel.

"Oh, my God."

His chest tightened as he swallowed, staring at the shivering girl's raised scars on her whipped back, scabbed cuts, belt welts, puckered skin from a decade of burns, and his own hand's imprint on her bottom.

His darkest fear in the pit of his stomach was bitterly confirmed when Mrs. Otis spun her around, revealing the raw purple bruises around Annaliese's groin. Pulling her into a hug, the girl's arms stayed at her sides. Her gaze seemed a million miles away.

"What did that man do to you?"

Chapter Seventeen

Annaliese

Annaliese felt outside her body again, like she was watching from above. In her mind, Jack stood beside her. *Just one more night, beautiful. We'll row to the cabin in the morning.*

A slave emptied the tub water out the window, then carried the barrel out of the room. Loud music played downstairs as people stomped.

"Can I git dressed now?" Her voice sounded strange to her.

The adults blinked like they were startled. Mrs. Otis put a new shift over her.

Mr. MacLeod looked shaky. "Have a seat."

Annaliese dragged her feet, not wanting to be near anyone. The music changed to a slow drumbeat. Sitting on the bed, she hugged her knees under her chin. The bed felt soft, not like Pa's hay mattress. Mr. MacLeod sat, and she trained her eyes on him. *Stop sitting close. Go away.*

Shifting in his seat, he cleared his throat. "Were the bruises between your legs from your pa, or the young sailor you kissed at lunch?"

"You mean Jack?"

"Ah. *Jack.* He bruised you? You're not in trouble."

"Jack loves me."

"Ah. It was him? Was it rape or did you want this?"

Mrs. Otis raised her voice, "Do those bruises look like she was having fun?"

A flute joined the drum, sounding like something soldiers played.

Mr. MacLeod's face stilled. "Annaliese, I need you to tell me the truth. Rape is a serious crime that leads to hanging."

Annaliese rolled her eyes and muttered, "Ain't matter none." *What a bufflehead. Who does MacLeod think he's gonna hang? Daniel Crowan is rich. His daddy is gonna be the next governor. Mr. Daniel ain't never gonna hang. Plus, Pa owned me—he could rent me out to whoever he wanted.*

Mrs. Otis said. "Are you sure you want to put the girl through a trial, Mr. MacLeod? She'll become even more of a pariah. Who'd ever marry her?"

The adults spoke in hushed tones as the sky shifted from pink to black. People danced and clapped downstairs as the music got rowdier, and the drums beat louder, louder, louder. Annaliese squeezed her eyes shut and covered her ears. "It's too loud."

"I'll leave you." Mrs. Otis picked up the wet towel from the floor on her way out.

MacLeod struck a gentle but firm tone. "This is important, Annaliese. I need you to look at me. Keep this secret. No one ever needs to ken your past. It'll only hold you back."

Annaliese cracked her eyelids open. *This man is so stupid.* "Why would I tell anyone?"

Now he blushed. "For what it's worth, I'm sorry this happened to you. I'm ... sorry."

Why's he apologizing? Polite clapping followed the song. *I should have run earlier. I'd be with Jack on the river by now.*

Mr. MacLeod caught a glance of his reflection in the mirror and scowled at the blood on his shirt from fighting Pa earlier. Loosening his jabot, he tugged off his shirt. As he washed his face and underarms, she stared at a small sachet tied around his neck.

"What's that?"

Drying himself off, he chuckled. "It's a protective charm from my wife."

"She a witch or something?"

"Dinna you ever say that again, aye?"

His angry voice scared her. She curled in a ball, covering her face.

MacLeod cleared his throat and spoke nicer. "Sorry, I didna mean to snap at you."

She peeked at him.

"Ack, it's nothing but silliness. See?" he said, taking off the sachet and opening it. "Some seaweed and mugwort leaves for a safe voyage. It's common for sailors to carry such things for luck."

Cinching the strings, he tied it on again and put on a new shirt. "I'm getting a drink. Get to bed. Sweet dreams." He blew out the candles and turned the key, trapping her in a room bright from too many windows.

Annaliese knew all the sounds in the cabin, but here, every time she nodded off, an unfamiliar noise scared her. A new tune started. Men's voices got louder and sloppier. Gossiping women stomped the creaky stairs to their rooms.

In the middle of the night, she left the bed and curled in the far corner on the floor and finally had a good, hard cry.

She must have blacked out because Mr. MacLeod carried her back to the bed. She kept her eyes closed. It would be easier if she pretended to be asleep. *Here it comes. He's gonna touch me now because he owns me.* Her mind got ready to drift.

But he tucked the blanket snug around her, pulling it under her chin, then smoothed her hair like Ma used to, gently. Mr. MacLeod pulled his sword and knelt with his head bowed.

"I'll take her to London, Eleanor. My oath, I will protect her."

Chapter Eighteen

LADY MARGARET

London

The trap had been set but everything had to come together flawlessly for it to work. Lady Margaret waited outside the boxing match at the Bartholomew Fair, knowing Viscount Percy's father would attend. Avoiding her signature red, she dressed in gray beneath a dark cloak to blend in. She spotted the old earl exiting the tent, stooped over a bronze dog-handled cane.

"Lord Monroe," she called.

A frown answered. "Lady Hallewell. You made a bad day worse, madam," he said, spinning on his heel.

Oh, he has no idea. Weaseling her arm through his, she knew he'd be too polite to decline in public. Enormous crowds brushed past them. A woman carrying a heavy basket sold pears to laborers drinking cider.

"How is your son?" She guided him toward the stage.

"Ask him."

"My husband's henchman, William MacLeod, treated your son despicably."

"From what I hear, Percy had it coming."

Rather cold response. They stopped below a raised platform serving as a stage, and the old earl stared silently as costumed knights spouted Shakespearian verses.

Thumbing his cane handle, he said, "Does your husband know you're here, madam?"

"No," she admitted.

Actors clashed swords, delighting the crowd.

"If Lord Hallewell wishes to apologize, tell him to call on me directly, otherwise, we have nothing to discuss, and I entreat you to remove your claws from my limb." Lightly shaking her free, he hobbled in the opposite direction.

Isn't he a challenge? He's headed the wrong way. Pursuing him past two little girls teetering on tiptoes, peeping into a wagon filled with exotic birds, she called, "Perhaps you should put your son on exhibit. People might pay two shillings to gawk at his amputation."

Facing her, his nostrils flared. "Why harass me over a son I detest and against your husband's wishes?"

"Percy seeks revenge against William MacLeod. I thought you'd like to join the fun."

"From what I hear, you caused my son's misfortunes. For all I know, you and your son hatched a scheme to justify stealing my boy's ship."

Shaking his cane at her, she stepped back and held her hands open for him to calm down.

Lowering his voice, he said, "As for my pathetic excuse for a son, I hear he aimed for MacLeod's head and missed. He's lucky to be alive. My son is a leech, your son is an idiot, and you, madam, are an odious parvenu. Follow me further and I shall strike you."

Lady Margaret scanned the crowd. No one seemed to be paying attention to them, thank God. *This isn't going as planned. How does he know such details? Percy swore they hadn't spoken since before the incident.*

Percy peered from behind the curtain of the player's tent, and she signaled him to approach, hoping none would recognize him.

Tailing the crotchety old earl, she passed a merchant selling hot pies and sausages. In ill-health and ailing, Lord Monroe stopped to catch his breath and watched a father purchase treats for his three children, lifting the youngest boy to see the display. Lord Monroe slumped his shoulders.

"Percy has been such a disappointment. He gambles away his inheritance, associates with the lowest people," he said, marking her, "and expects me to rescue him constantly. Well, I'm tired, Lady Hallewell. I'm tired. You'll need to find someone else for your fun."

"Am I wretched to you, Father?"

Viscount Percy emerged from the crowd dressed simply: brown breeches and a loose white shirt, exposing the knob of skin-covered bone where his hand used to be. Without his wig, his blond curls made him appear younger.

"My God," whispered the earl, covering his mouth as he gaped at his son's arm.

Lady Margaret had meticulously planned this moment. If the earl wanted a humbled son, that would be delivered. Giving the signal, a jester with a full lacy collar juggled rings in front of them as a man banged a drum behind. Throngs of people pushed the trio toward the stage.

"Come in here, where it's not so loud." Lady Margaret pulled back a tent curtain to an actors' dressing room. "We should talk."

Surrounded by stage props and costumes flung over chairs, the earl inspected his son with pained eyes. Lady Margaret hovered near the entrance.

"William MacLeod's taken everything from me, Father. My livelihood, my reputation, my very hand. I don't deserve your love, but I beg for your help with vengeance."

"I'm too old for a duel, and from what I hear, you weren't entirely without fault."

"Fault or not, I am your son," Percy said, exasperated as he squared his shoulders. "I want MacLeod dead."

The earl waved him off.

"Father, I'm begging. Give me enough money to hire a mercenary to kidnap his wife while he's in the colonies. When he returns to claim her, I'll be waiting with my pistol."

"Listen to yourself, son. Your passions run far too hot. Do you learn anything? Mr. MacLeod spared your life. You repay his mercy thus?"

"Percy, your father is beyond persuasion." *Hurry.*

"You trust rumors from drunken sailors in taverns? MacLeod has no honor, Father. He came to me with his weapon drawn while I was utterly defenseless."

"You mean, while you were fornicating with a courtesan?"

Viscount Percy blinked.

Forgot to mention that part, love. Peering out the curtain, she saw the show was ending. "Percy, the players are taking their bows."

"Mr. MacLeod visited me after the incident, explaining exactly what transpired."

Percy flushed red. "You believe him over your son?"

With a burdened sigh, the old gentleman put his hand on Percy's shoulder. "I'll get you another ship, an entire fleet if you like, but I'm not paying for an assassin. Go to the country and find an honorable wife. Stay away from vultures." Lord Monroe glared at Lady Margaret.

What unwise invective. "The players exit forthwith."

Percy froze like a panicked little boy.

"Your mother and I worry about your lacking character. She's brought to sobs, terrified you'll provoke the wrong man and end up dead. Maybe, strangely, this was for the best. It lets you choose a new path."

The earl's eyes burst open as Lady Margaret slit his throat from behind. His cane dropped from his withered hand as he collapsed with a shocked expression.

Percy's eyes flooded as he cradled his dying father and he raged, "Why didn't you just give me the money? This is your fault. I never wanted to …"

His father gurgled and choked on his own blood until he lay motionless.

Percy was a confused little boy. *He needs me now, more than ever. He'll never question my love again.* "Remove his wedding band. Take his money. Make it appear like a robbery."

"I had no choice," Percy muttered. "Why wouldn't you help me, Father?"

"Percy, focus. The actors are coming."

Wiping the tortoiseshell razor on the earl's coat, she returned it to the dressing table. *I knew Percy lacked the fortitude to get the job done.*

Percy pried the wedding ring off his father's dead finger and pocketed his cash.

Tossing Percy a fresh shirt and long coat from the costume rack, she said, "Hand me your soiled shirt. I'll burn them in the fire pit with the roasting kidney pies."

He passed her the blood-soaked garment in a daze. Stroking his cheek, she commanded, "Go to your mother. You need to establish an alibi."

Percy stared at his father lying in the dirt and picked up his cane. Blood spread from the earl's sagging neck, forming a dark pool. "Should we hide his body?"

Lady Margaret glanced out of the tent curtain. "He needs to be found. How else will you become the sixth Earl of Cheshire?"

Chapter Nineteen

WILLIAM MACLEOD

Would Lady Margaret really destroy my family for not murdering an innocent child?

William MacLeod dressed in his breeches and coat again. Time to return to order, even if it was hot. As the sun rose, he polished his claymore. Rust speckled the deep grooves of the inscription *Justice*, but it was beginning to shine again.

He'd have an entire ocean voyage to plot how to hide the girl from Lady Margaret. First, he'd pay Rob Birch a wee visit. What were Lord Hallewell's instructions again? *Rough*.

Annaliese woke, rubbed her eyes and looked around the room, confused.

MacLeod was determined to try to like the girl, at least for the next eight weeks, until he could dump her in a school. "We started on the wrong foot yesterday. Get dressed and we'll aim for a pleasant day."

"How?"

"Maybe we can watch a play if they have a theater or—"

"No. How do I wear all them things?"

They puzzled at the collection of shifts, stays, pockets, panniers, petticoats, stockings, garters, gowns and mop caps. He ken nothing about clothing for girls.

For a price, of course, Mrs. Otis taught her how to dress while MacLeod went to the bar. After paying for his drink, he pulled the runaway slave advertisement from his pocket pondering the tangled web between the Crowans and Rob Birch. If only he could go back in time and have found a different solution to get Eleanor out of the way. Annaliese's scrawny tortured body flashed in his mind. Knotted hair dripping wet, eyes full of shame. Whiskey burned down his throat.

"She's ready," Mrs. Otis called from the top of the winding staircase.

Pocketing the flier, he entered the room and the girl's transformation took his breath away. Annaliese looked adorable. Wee ginger ringlets framed her beautiful face. No one would guess the damage beneath her pale blue gown with white sash and matching shoes.

"Dinna you look bonny."

Clearly uncomfortable, the girl shrugged, until she caught her reflection in the ornately framed mirror. Annaliese was dumbstruck. Tears pricked her eyes as she touched her clean face and silken dress. "That's *me*?"

Mrs. Otis smiled and pressed the money back into his hand on the way out. "No charge."

MacLeod and Annaliese stood awkwardly.

"If we can teach you proper manners during the voyage, I might be able to arrange a brief meeting with Lord Hallewell. I think he'll be delighted by how much you resemble Eleanor."

Annaliese frowned, then took a deep breath. "Mr. MacLeod, I ain't goin' to London. I'm grateful you got Sam away from Pa, and it's nice you bought me clothes, but I ain't need another pa. I'm grown. I'm going to marry Jack."

"The lad who thinks he's a pirate?" MacLeod laughed out loud as he sorted through papers.

"Don't laugh at me. I'm his girl, and he done found me a job, too. I was gonna run away yesterday to Black Swan Tavern, but then you came."

"The brothel?"

She blinked. "Naw, he keeps a room there is all."

"Jesus, Joseph and Mary. So, tell me, lass, what job did he find you?"

"Workin'. And soon we'll have enough money to raft the river and build a cabin. He said pretty girls git hired easy and make good money, too."

He faced her. "Spreading their legs."

"Naw, that ain't ... I'm his girl," she said, biting her thumbnail.

MacLeod clenched her arm. "Did you fornicate with him? Were the bruises from him?"

"Ain't none your business."

"It is my business," he said, pointing in her face. "Have you prostituted yourself with Jack?"

Freeing her arm from his grip, she said, "No. He ain't even been with me yet. I ain't no whore. Jack loves me. He brings me food, and he's gonna take care of me and Sam—"

MacLeod shook his head. "Exactly like your mother."

"I ain't nuthin' like that bitch."

"Annaliese, Jack's not your friend."

"Oh, but you is?"

"No. I'm not your friend. I'm not your father. I'm here to take you safely from Point A to Point B. I'm the delivery man." Recognizing the gleam of a willful child about to do something stupid, he said, "To hell with your other clothes. We're going to Yorktown now."

"No, I ain't. You cain't make me leave."

"Watch me," he said, putting on his tricorn hat.

The girl moved quick. Racing past him, she jumped four stairs at a time and out the front door before he even realized she was leaving. Pursuing her through the narrow alleys, the lass pointed to him as she ran. "Scottish thief!"

A group held MacLeod back. "Brute like him chasing a young lady?"

"She's my ward, running away."

"Call the sheriff."

Sheriff Brown's familiar laugh echoed as he trotted over on his horse. "MacLeod's no thief," he told the crowd. "Regretting your decision to take custody yet?"

"Ack, you have no idea. Where can I find the lad, Jack? Where does he work? Would she have run to the brothel? She mentioned rowing to a cabin. I have to find her."

"Grab your horse, Mr. MacLeod, I'll help you."

Chapter Twenty

ANNALIESE

Annaliese ran to the busy warehouse, past a man filling out paperwork on a table, to the back wall where a group of men were stacking heavy barrels. "Jack."

Jack tilted his head. "Can I help you, miss?"

Annaliese threw her arms around him, hugging him tight, feeling his sweaty back. "It's me, Annaliese. Mr. MacLeod bought me new clothes. He wants to take me to my new pa in London, but I told him I'm your girl and you gonna marry me."

A Negro man with gray hair laughed. "Oh, Lord, now I heard everything."

Jack took a step back and inspected her. "You were pretty in rags, but *Jesus.*"

For the first time, she believed him. He kissed her and she noticed the dirt around his fingernails, the stink of his sweat. Leading her behind a shelf overflowing with stray hammers and rolled up twine, he said, "Where's the Scotsman?"

"He chased me, but I losted him."

"We need to hide you." Jack peered out the open door.

"I love you. I love you so much, Jack." Wrapping her arms around his neck, she couldn't stop smiling.

"I love you, too, but stop. We have to get there."

They dashed out back, down the uneven red brick alley, and snaked through the muddy streets, past two tailor shops and the silversmith, until they reached Black Swan Tavern.

"Jack, he's gonna know this is where you'd take me. He ain't dumb."

"Neither am I."

Annaliese tried to kiss him, but he seemed distracted. "What's the plan? How we gonna rob him? When can we git Sam and row down the river to the cabin you mentioned?"

Jack pounded on the back door until it opened. Music, laughter and the scent of stale beer hit her. A middle-aged woman with a fancy hairstyle spoke with the low voice of a smoker. "Well, ahoy, handsome."

Jack kissed the madam's hand. "Ahoy, beautiful."

Why is Jack calling that lady by my name? I'm Beautiful.

"Is he here?"

The madam went inside a room packed with ladies sitting on men's laps. Sailors, rich out-of-towners and locals laughed and drank as a bawdy woman wearing a gentleman's tricorn hat dealt cards.

Annaliese chewed on her bottom lip. *MacLeod ain't known what he was talking about.* "What job am I gonna do? You never said."

Jack didn't look at her and her stomach suddenly felt queasy.

"Well, good morning." Daniel Crowan appeared with a gap-toothed smile on the arm of the madam.

Her stomach churned. *This cain't be happening.*

"Here she is. Five pounds," Jack said.

Annaliese recoiled. "Jack, no. I'm your girl, you said—"

"This is business, honey."

Mr. Daniel handed him the cash. Jack shoved her into him and ran off. Inching toward the door, she said, "I-I have to get b-back to M-mr. MacLeod."

He laughed. "You sound like Sam." Mr. Daniel asked the madam, "Any rooms available?"

"You can use the cellar while you're waiting. I know how you are when you get a new little plaything."

Annaliese bolted, but he caught her arm and dragged her to a root cellar's hatched doors as she struggled, digging her nails into his hand.

Opening the hatch, he shoved her into the chilled darkness, where she landed with a thud among beer barrels and vegetable crates.

Two carpenters covered in sawdust headed toward the brothel. "Help!" she called.

Mr. Daniel tapped his tricorn hat at them. "Gentlemen."

They hesitated briefly, then kept walking, like it was normal to watch a girl forced into a cellar. Hinges squeaked as the doors banged shut.

I'm so damn stupid.

A splinter of light between the doors fell across his excited face. Exhaling mint julep, he lit a short candle on a shelf stuffed with pickle jars. "You look completely different. I might have to put you back in rags. It's more novel when you're filthy."

Only one exit. Backing against the cold, damp brick wall, she stumbled on a bushel of fermenting apples as candlelight flickered behind him. His soft hands stroked her cheeks.

Annaliese bit his hand till she tasted iron.

"Ow. Little brat," he said, shoving her into a sack of potatoes. His voice echoed in the small space.

Blowing out the candle, she crouched behind a barrel. *Think, Annaliese.*

Shaking the pain from his hand, he hunted her. "You do like your little games." A basket scraped as he knocked it over. Root vegetables thumped and rolled. "You want to play?" He grunted, throwing something heavy. A bottle cracked and the floor grew wet with the bitter stink of vinegar. "This cellar isn't big, and I won't be gentle when I find you."

Dozens of footfalls ran past the cellar doors. "What's going on?" asked a woman above.

"Raid. Get out before you're arrested."

Annaliese made a desperate dash, partially lifting a hatch door before Mr. Daniel jerked her back inside. Glass jars clinked as she stumbled against a wooden shelf. Both doors swung open, blinding her with sunlight. Mr. MacLeod jumped down and pinned Mr. Daniel against the wall.

"Are you hurt?" MacLeod asked over his shoulder.

"N-no," she stammered.

Squinting at Mr. Daniel's face, he asked, "Matthew Crowan's son?"

Sweat beads formed on Mr. Daniel's upper lip. "This isn't your concern, Scotsman. I just bought her. A young warehouse worker—Jack?—sold her to me for five pounds."

Annaliese trembled uncontrollably next to a wine cask in the corner. Eyeing the hatch doors, she knew she was in heaps of trouble no matter who she ended up with.

Mr. MacLeod glanced between them. "Is this the man who raped you?"

Her throat felt scratchy, and she avoided Mr. MacLeod's gaze as she hung her head. *Ain't no need for secrets now.* "Pa had debts."

The men's eyes narrowed on each other.

"Rape is such a strong word," Mr. Daniel said, grinning. "My daddy will need a lieutenant governor. I'm sure we could work something out." His head lifted high with certainty as Mr. MacLeod stepped away. "Everyone has a price, after all."

Mr. MacLeod's fingers flexed, and his legs planted wide. Sensing danger, she moved back. Mr. Daniel fumbled for his pistol, but before it left his sheath, MacLeod slashed off his head. Mr. Daniel's body dropped, and the blood glugged as it spilled over his jabot onto the hard-packed dirt floor.

Blinking rapidly, her jaw opened but no sound came out. Covering her mouth, she stumbled back from the gap-toothed head resting in a bloodbath.

"MacLeod, you down here?" Sheriff Brown came downstairs and fixed his eyes on the body. "Hell and damnation." Slamming the hatch closed, he rubbed his forehead. "That's Matthew Crowan's boy. How am I going to explain this?"

"Rape." Mr. MacLeod wiped the blood from his enormous sword on Mr. Daniel's fancy coat, returning his blade to its sheath.

Only a strip of sunlight shone through the gap in the cellar doors, but it was bright enough to see Mr. MacLeod face her with a fury to match Pa's. Backed against the brick wall, her legs felt weak as he shook her by her arms.

"What did I tell you about Jack? I told you he would bring you here. How many bruises between your legs do you want? Daniel Crowan could have killed you. What would have happened if I hadna come with the sheriff when we did? What would've happened if Jack hid you in some cabin and we couldna find you?"

Her lips quivered as she tried to twist from him. "I didn't think—"

"No, you didna think, Eleanor." He shook his head. "Annaliese."

Sheriff Brown's lips pressed together in a grimace. "This is a heaping pile of shit."

Mr. MacLeod let her go and faced him. "If you're going to arrest me, take the lass to Mrs. Otis at the tavern. She can testify to the girl's injuries. The bairn was raped by that swine."

Sheriff Brown shook his head and muttered, "How does arresting you help anyone?" Exhaling, the lawman thought things through. "The soon-to-be governor isn't going to want his deceased son smeared through every newspaper in the thirteen colonies. I'll take care of this." Scowling at Mr. Daniel's severed head, he said, "Daniel liked 'em young and poor. Worst-kept secret in town. You've probably saved a lot of children from suffering. I reckon when you're rich and your father's powerful, you can get away with anything."

"For a time," MacLeod said.

Annaliese raised her chin.

"Take your ward to London, Mr. MacLeod. The sooner the better."

Mr. MacLeod nodded, then led her by the scruff of her neck out the cellar. Walking past the retreating women, he stopped. "Look at the prostitutes, Annaliese. That's what you would have become, you damned fool."

Hard faces, cheap clothes. Annaliese locked eyes with a girl about the same age going back inside, and it sunk in. *Jack never thought I was beautiful.*

Chapter Twenty-One

WILLIAM MACLEOD

I killed my friend's son. Matthew Crowan is the richest man in Williamsburg; next in line for governor; my old friend from Oxford. MacLeod went into the main tavern to find Mrs. Otis. "I need to buy a wagon."

"I'll sell you mine. For a price," Mrs. Otis said. They sorted out the cash. "Wagon's in the barn. The horse is a gray gelding. I'm going to miss you, Mr. MacLeod."

"Could you help Annaliese pack? Dinna let her leave your sight."

Annaliese, still in shock, quietly disappeared up the stairs.

"God, I need a whiskey," he said, sitting at the bar.

The bartender poured him a dram. MacLeod lifted his glass to his lips with trembling hands.

Click-clack.

A cold metal rifle barrel pressed against his skull.

"You got something that's mine," came Rob's drunken slur. An assorted crew of poor farmers surrounded Rob Birch with guns. Jack hovered nearby with a blackened eye.

Ah, shite.

"I've had a gun pointed at my head before today, lads." MacLeod finished his whiskey. If he was going to be murdered, at least he'd die with alcohol-infused bravado. He reached for his claymore, but they pulled his arm behind his back.

"Take his sword, Uncle Hal."

"This fetch me a good price," Uncle Hal said, feeling the sword's weight in his old hands.

"I told you he had a room here," said Jack. "Can I please go now?"

Rob cast him a side eye. "You can leave, pretty boy." Cracking Jack's nose with his musket butt, the lad dropped to his knees. "Guess you ain't pretty no more."

Jack scrambled from the bar, blood spilling from his face.

"We don't want no trouble in here," the bartender said, removing glasses as customers fled. Some men fingered their own weapons.

"Ain't no one talkin' to you, boy," Rob said. His glassy eyes focused on MacLeod. "People say she left the brothel riding on a horse with you. Now git me my girl."

Birch's crew gripped their muskets tighter.

Five guns versus my wit.

"Annaliese said you'd come. I thought it might take you a wee bit longer to spend the fifty pounds I gave you."

Uncle Hal flinched. "That right?"

"Oh, didna he tell you? He sold his son to me. The girl was never his legally, but I paid him for both."

"You sold Sam? You ain't said nuthin' about money," Uncle Hal said, his posture stiffening.

"If money's what you want, I'll ensure everyone goes home happy," MacLeod said.

Sunburned and grimy, Rob's friends looked between themselves. "When we came on Thursday for our money, Rob told us you kidnapped them. He ain't said you bought them."

Rob said, "I was gonna tell you about the money. Look, he only paid for the girl, not Sam. He took my kin."

MacLeod said, "Your kin? How much money did you make prostituting her?"

"Now wait," Uncle Hal said. "He ain't never whore her out. Shoot, the girl ran wild like her mama."

"I saw the bruises. She's lucky to escape disease."

Uncle Hal closed his eyes, slowly shaking his head. "You whoring her? She ain't even ten. What the hell's wrong with you? No wonder she runs." Hal's lips pinched tight, and his forearms grew taut until he knocked his rifle against the back of Rob's head.

MacLeod stared at the old man as Rob moaned on the ground. Rob's friends backed away. A man with a red handkerchief around his neck lowered his rifle. "You lied, Rob."

Uncle Hal said, "You can have him for the six pounds he owes me."

"I'll give you ten if you give me back my sword."

"He owes us twelve," said the man with the red bandana.

MacLeod paid everyone to leave and returned *Justice* to her holster. Uncle Hal spit on his nephew. "Rot in hell, Rob."

༺༻

The Public Gaol was a red brick building with a thick wooden door. Mr. Smith, the gaoler—a burly, no-nonsense man in his fifties—said, "We have other Negroes for sale. Why him?"

"Does it matter?"

Mr. Smith chuckled. "The office is right through there. I'll bring him to you."

MacLeod peeked at the prison courtyard as the gaoler passed walls with weeds sprouted at the base and stained with black drips. Men crammed against the iron bars across the peepholes in the door to watch. Beyond the walls, tall maples blocked the blood red sun.

Inside the office, a small window facing the courthouse cast light on a dozen hooks on the wall, each holding a numbered key. MacLeod removed his tricorn hat to wipe his brow with a handkerchief from his overcoat. *Jesus, Joseph and Mary, English fashion is burdensome.*

Heavy chains scraped against the floor as the wretched soul entered, hunched over and scabbed. It looked like dogs had mauled his calves, and some scars from the whip showed through his soiled shirt hanging off his shoulder. Was anyone unscathed after an encounter with Rob Birch?

"Matthew Crowan wanted him sold to the Deep South, but money is money." Mr. Smith opened a thick prison roll book. "Besides, he's too busy grieving to worry about a runaway."

MacLeod raised his brows. "Grieving?"

"A farmer found Crowan's son, Daniel, dead on the road. Sheriff says they're hunting for highwaymen who robbed and murdered him. They decapitated the poor sot."

Mr. Smith noted the runaway biting his smile at the mention of Daniel's murder. "Happy to hear about the murder of your master's son, boy? You think that's funny?"

"My *former* master murdered his own Black daughter and didn't shed a tear. Why should I be upset with the murder of his white son?"

Peering at MacLeod, the gaoler said, "You sure you still want this blackbird?"

"Aye."

Mr. Smith sighed and wrote the sale price in the ledger. "Moses, this is your new master, Mr. William MacLeod."

Unlocked from his irons, the slave rolled his ankles then followed MacLeod outside.

Sunlight warmed MacLeod's face as he left the prison. Returning the tricorn hat to his head, he indicated for the runaway to sit next to him.

Staring at the lumpy blanket wiggling in the back of the wagon, the slave pinched his nose at the rancid stench.

"Raise the blanket," MacLeod said.

Tentatively peeling back a corner, the slave jumped. Rob Birch lay bound and gagged. When Birch recognized the runaway, he screamed as loud as he could with a handkerchief shoved in his mouth.

"I understand you ken each other. I want to teach Birch a lesson, but I think it will be more memorable coming from you, Moses. Cover him."

Laughing at his luck, the slave said, "Moses is a slave name. My real name is Chibuzo. I promise Rob Birch will remember a lesson from me."

Into the wee hours, they beat Birch in his own cabin. Rob's arms stretched high above his head, with his hands tied to a sturdy peg in the cabin wall.

"Wake up, Birch." Chibuzo doused him with a bucket of cold well water, shocking him conscious, then delighted in using Rob's own whip against him for one final lash. It whistled through the air before landing with a loud crack.

MacLeod said, "Put him in the chair."

Chibuzo cut the ropes and Birch's bruised and bloodied figure fell like a sack of potatoes. Spying a jar of salt, Chibuzo rubbed a fistful of it into Rob's back, clearly savoring how Rob twisted from the burn, then tied him to the chair.

MacLeod leaned against the lopsided table. "Mr. Birch, look at me. That wife you loved to beat was my lord's mistress. And I am his retribution. Chibuzo, get the fire poker."

"No," Rob panted. "Eleanor lied. I never beat her bad. You ain't known her."

Chibuzo grabbed the fire poker, roasting it over the flames.

"She'd throw things. Got mouthy." A sweat drip rolled past Birch's ripped ear. "Only slapped her when she was asking for it, same as any husband." Staring at the metal tip glow red, he began to tear up. "I loved Eleanor. She's the only person ever loved me," Rob gasped.

"Chibuzo, he's not showing accountableness, is he? Give him the fire poker."

"No. No. Wait," Rob said.

Chibuzo pressed it into Birch's shoulder. Rob shrieked in agony. Chibuzo pulled away the poker then shifted his own shirt to the side, exposing the Sweetwater Plantation symbol. "How does it feel to be branded?"

"Fuck you," Rob muttered, head hanging. "Crowan paid me to do it. You slaves have a place to live. Food. No one gave me shit." Rob blew the shiny red mark on his blistering shoulder.

"It was your duty to provide." MacLeod lowered his voice. "But let's move on to Lord Hallewell's daughter in your care ... I saw the girl's body."

Rob huffed. "Maybe, maybe I was a little rough, but you ain't known what it's like to raise your wife's bastard." He gasped. "Always looking at some other man's face."

MacLeod stared into the distance. *His belt rained down on Broderick's back as the boy cried. "Da, stop, please."* MacLeod shook off his memories.

Rob spit. "Yeah, I beat her, but she had it comin'. That girl ain't nuthin' but trouble."

"Give Rob the fire poker again."

Rob twisted to avoid the scorching metal tip, but soon his skin sizzled on his side, filling the room with the smell of human meat. Rob screamed into the night. A layer of skin peeled away and stuck to the poker.

"Shut your gob, you wee shite." Scanning the grimy room, he told Chibuzo, "Get the broom, please."

Chibuzo dropped the poker. Tripping over rubbish, he grabbed a splintered broom and plucked off the webs.

"I love the girl," Rob's breath hitched, "in my own way." Tears and a long line of snot dripped off his nose. "I'm a good pa."

MacLeod delivered a jaw-crunching punch, splattering blood against the wall. "You sold your children for a card game. One more lesson, and my lord requires that it be rough." MacLeod slammed Rob over the table. "You raped the wrong wee lass."

Birch eyed the broomstick, crinkling his brows until horrified understanding fell across his face. "No. No. Please. *I* never raped her." He panted hard. "Daniel Crowan was gonna take my land," he wheezed. "Only let him have two minutes of fun," Rob gasped.

MacLeod pulled Rob's breeches to his ankles and nodded at the runaway. "Let's see how fun it is on the other end."

Rob tried to escape, but MacLeod easily overpowered him.

Chibuzo froze, glancing between the broomstick in his hands and his former oppressor, now defenseless and pleading. Placing his left hand on the small of Birch's sweaty back, the slave readied himself.

"Mercy," Rob sobbed. His left eye had swollen shut.

MacLeod stared at the runaway. "What are you waiting for?"

Chibuzo dropped the broom and retreated a step. "If you want me to kill him, I will kill him. But I won't become him. I won't let him—or you—take away my soul."

MacLeod's head lifted; his plan disrupted.

Tears rolled down Rob's bloodied face. "Let me go."

"I know you," said Chibuzo. "You don't remember me, but I met you in London when you threw the slaver overboard. You made the soldiers feed us. You showed us mercy."

MacLeod's mouth dropped open. Studying the scar over Chibuzo's eye, he said, "You held a dying child in the cage, aye?"

Chibuzo nodded. Fire crackled as Rob sobbed, broken. "Do not become a man you hate."

Fiona glared at him. *"The man I married despised brutes, yet it's what you've become."* MacLeod's breath quickened with the realization his savagery was as abhorrent as Rob's. Birch was reduced to a victim sniveling on the table. After a long minute, MacLeod cut the ropes. "You're lucky the African has more compassion than I. Pull up your breeches, Mr. Birch."

Rob's hands shook as he covered his nudity, avoiding their eyes. He wiped his face on his dirty shirt, sobbing.

"Quit crying like a wee lass. Live with your sins, and the memory of this reckoning, for the rest of your pathetic life." MacLeod grabbed Rob's gun from the pegs and opened the door as dawn's gray light overtook the sky. Chibuzo followed him to the wagon, his feet crunching the dried leaves. MacLeod shook out his bloody fist, stretching his fingers.

Rob stumbled out, pulling an ax from the woodpile, ready to throw. "You think you're better than me?"

Bang.

MacLeod killed him with one shot to the brain.

Chibuzo and MacLeod carried Rob to the York River where they found an abandoned boat and rowed out. In the quiet of sunrise they cuffed the heavy metal ball to Birch's ankle and dumped him overboard with a loud splash. Watching his body submerge in the murky water, Chibuzo said, "He could have lived, but for his hatred."

"I suppose my lord will be happier with these results." MacLeod threw Rob's musket overboard. They rowed back, leaving the canoe on the shore and returned to the wagon in silence. Deer crossed the road, finishing their feeding.

Chibuzo said, "What becomes of me now?"

"I hadna considered it." MacLeod hit the reins, staring at the road ahead. "Well, you're paid for. I suppose you'll come to England with us. I ken Lady Margaret wanted a slave, but honestly, she dinna deserve a prize."

Chibuzo sighed.

"I suppose you dinna like London."

"I do not like slavery. I have no opinion of London."

"Strange our paths crossed again." A red leaf fell on MacLeod's shoulder, and he brushed it off. "I dinna like slavery, either, but—"

Chibuzo smiled bitterly. "Yes. I have heard this. I do not like slavery, but it's a necessary evil. I do not like slavery, but it's for their own good. I do not like slavery, except I do."

Silence hung as they rode to town. MacLeod stared at the dusty road, deep in thought. The strong scent of pine needles and brackish water made him miss his own home. For the first time, he wondered what Chibuzo's home might be like, what smells he missed, what family he had lost. "Chibuzo, I want to free you—"

Breath caught in the runaway's throat as a smile formed.

"But there are laws about filing manumission paperwork. I'd have to petition the governor and prove you performed meritorious services. Matthew Crowan will probably be the next governor. I'm a good barrister, but I dinna see that miracle happening in my lifetime."

Chibuzo's face fell, and his body stilled. "I understand." He unearthed Rob's hunting knife from his breeches and held the blade against MacLeod's neck, pulling the reins with his other hand. "Exit the wagon. I do not want to kill you, my friend, but I will."

MacLeod's hand rested on *Justice*'s hilt. They locked their eyes, knowing either, or both, might not survive.

Is this who I've become? Forcing an honorable man to become Lady Margaret's slave?

MacLeod hopped off the wagon onto the country road and removed his tricorn hat and overcoat. "This should disguise you a wee bit. Safe travels," he said, handing them over to a very startled Chibuzo. MacLeod grinned. "You're not the only one with a soul worth saving."

Chapter Twenty-Two

Annaliese

Stretching with a yawn, Annaliese said, "Where was you?" Noting MacLeod only wore breeches and his shirt, her eyes rested on his scabbed knuckles. "Looks like you punched someone hard."

"We're leaving," Mr. MacLeod said, pulling out another coat and a burlap package from his trunk. "Damn. No time to buy another hat. Get dressed before the coachman arrives."

Dropping the package on her new trunk, he stared out the window with perfect posture, one hand resting in the other behind his back while she dressed. When he unexpectedly came to help tie her bodice strings, she shuddered, holding her breath till he finished.

Soon a coachman in a blue coat and brown bob wig knocked on the door. "Ready, sir?"

Following the men past the dining room scented with bacon and coffee, she watched MacLeod grab a biscuit and the *Virginia Gazette* on the way out.

"My lady," said the coachman, offering his hand to Annaliese as the crisp morning air hit her face.

It took a minute before realizing the coachman meant her. *Me. A lady.* She snorted then sat in the carriage inspecting everything. It smelled like horses and leather. Stroking the soft cushions, she couldn't help but let slip a smile because she always wondered what it would be like to ride in a carriage.

MacLeod sat next to her and handed her the package.

Annaliese cocked her head. "Huh?"

"Your real father thought you would like it."

Biting her lip, she stared at the burlap sack. *Must be something good—MacLeod's acting pretty pleased with hisself.* Her fingers fumbled untying the string. "Ain't never got a gift before," she said a bit too excitedly. Then she saw it. "What you give me a stupid poppet for? I ain't no baby."

MacLeod cleared his throat before speaking. "You kept staring at it in Mrs. Woollery's store, and it certainly wasna cheap. I thought—"

"You thought wrong," she said, tossing the doll back.

He scowled. "You're determined to be unlikeable. You dinna want nice things? Fine. I'll give it to a girl who appreciates it." MacLeod snapped open the newspaper. Daniel Crowan's portrait made the front-page news.

The coachman hit the reins, and they left Williamsburg with a lurch forward. Soon the church steeple disappeared with the road curve. Crossing her arms, she said, "Knew it. You just like everybody else."

MacLeod lowered his paper. "Excuse me?"

"Pretend to act nice. Give me a poppet, then give it away. You just like Jack, all lies."

"You want to talk about Jack? Remember when I told you Jack wasna your friend, and you should stay away? But no, you deliberately disobeyed me, and look what happened."

"Hate you," she said under her breath, showing her back to him.

"For what? Rescuing you, and buying you new clothes? Look at me, you unlicked cub. For the next forty-four days, you're going to act civilized, so fix your countenance and eliminate those hostile eyes." Returning to his paper, he muttered, "I told you Jack didna love you."

His words landed like a punch, making her slump lower in the carriage. They bumped over logs laid at six-foot intervals across the muddy road, making her teeth clack with each thud. MacLeod ignored her, flipping pages.

She kept replaying the moment Jack sold her and her throat squeezed shut. "What you want me to say? You was right?" Her voice cracked. "Fine, you was right. Jack never loved me. I'm stupid, all right? You happy?"

Lowering his paper, he softened his tone. "You're not stupid, but you do dangerously impulsive things. Annaliese, you're a child. Being exposed to adult situations dinna make you an adult."

Furiously knuckling away her tears, she wanted to punch something. MacLeod offered her a handkerchief which she took, but only because her nose was running something fierce. Splitting his biscuit, he gave her half, which she shoved in her mouth without thanks. Shaking his head, he returned to reading.

They passed a zigzag fence covered with green moss spots that encircled a farmstead. Annaliese stared at a little girl tending chickens, holding a rag doll in one hand. Annaliese felt a little bad. MacLeod was trying to be nice, after all.

"Thank you ... The toy."

He peered over the paper, surprised. "You're welcome."

Annaliese examined the wooden doll. *Ma always said my real father would give me one.* It had painted brown eyes, pink cheeks and a little pink mouth. Annaliese rubbed its curled brown hair between her fingers. "I had a poppet once."

"Yorktown," called the coachman.

Tasting salty Atlantic air on her tongue, she watched cawing seagulls fly over the port town. Bustling with passengers, merchants and huge European ships jostling to berth at the harbor, she wondered if London looked the same. They stopped beside a rickety warehouse.

A short, stout man barked orders to two sailors, directing them to load passengers' trunks on board. "Blimey," he said, blinking at Annaliese as she stepped out of the carriage.

MacLeod said, "Annaliese, this is the ship's master, Mr. Grubb. He navigates."

When she stood still, MacLeod cleared his throat, and she offered a sloppy curtsey.

Mr. Grubb stared at her with a distinctive frown. "I wasn't aware you'd have a girl with you, sir." He was speaking in that careful tone Pa used when he tried to hide how drunk he was.

"Now you are," MacLeod said with a hard smile. "See to the trunks."

Putting two fat fingers in his mouth, Mr. Grubb whistled, and some sailors took their luggage. Another sailor's eyes bulged. "Don't whistle, Grubb. You want to bring wind on us?"

Mr. Grubb muttered to the sailor, "Forget the whistle, look around. Too many womenfolk, too many redheads, plus the cloudy weather? I dursen't but it's a bad omen to sail."

MacLeod rolled his eyes and handed Annaliese the doll. *He's letting me keep it, after all?* Grabbing her hand, they strode to the warehouse. Teams of oxen pulled hogshead barrels of tobacco to the wharf. Other merchants carried wagons loaded with lumber or crates full of greens.

"You ain't have to hold my hand like a baby." Annaliese pulled away but MacLeod gripped tighter.

"Dinna I? For all I ken, you'll get an itch to swim."

They went inside the weatherworn building decorated with rusty anchors and paintings of sea monsters. Gaping at their open jaws, Annaliese swallowed hard.

"Those are sharks," MacLeod said with a smirk. "Stay on the ship and you'll be fine."

Peeking around the noisy room, she gripped her doll to her chest. Most passengers lined up were wealthy gentlemen in expensive coats who smelled like rum and pipe smoke. Some had wives dressed in flowered bodices and fancy straw hats to shield the sun. A few children chased each other holding carved animals and tin soldiers. MacLeod cut to the front of the line.

"Captain Adams, this is my ward, Miss Annaliese Cameron."

Without a reminder, she curtsied. Captain Adams stood, opened his mouth to comment, but thought better. Bowing courteously, he returned to writing people's names in a large book.

MacLeod called to a boy in Gaelic, who nodded and grabbed a mason jar from a shelf full of ropes and folded sheets of canvas. MacLeod said to Annaliese, "Seamus is our steward."

Annaliese scratched the back of her neck. "What's a steward?"

"A servant."

Bouncing on her toes, she asked, "I got a servant?"

"No, I do."

Seamus handed her the jar. Her head flinched back slightly, not sure what game this was.

MacLeod said, "Scoop some sand and shells to keep as a memento. It's good to have a wee bit of home with you. Seamus, please chaperone her."

The Gaelic boy guided her to the small patch of beach.

"I ain't known one face could hold that many freckles."

Saying nothing, the boy frowned and blushed.

Ships of all different sizes filled the harbor and she sighed. *Sam would have loved it.* She distracted herself from crying by picking the prettiest shells she could find in the gritty sand as small, choppy waves splashed ashore.

Mr. MacLeod called, "Annaliese."

She followed Seamus to the long pier, where people wabbled on gangplanks to board the ship. A breath caught in her throat. *This is really happening.*

Raindrops fell, then stopped, and the sun reappeared burning her face, acting as topsy-turvy as she felt. Taking a few steps back, she checked over her shoulder, saying to MacLeod, "You think Pa will come?"

"No." Placing his hands on her shoulders, he steered her aboard as Seamus followed.

They stopped near a brass bell engraved with letters. "What's the bell for?"

MacLeod said, "It signifies shift changes and mealtimes. That engraving says *Icarus*. An utterly ridiculous name for a ship, but I'd expect nothing less from the former owner."

Annaliese hammered her knuckles on it, making it gong loudly to her delighted laughter. MacLeod nudged her forward, quieting the noise, while Seamus bit back a chuckle. Triangular and square sails were being raised by the dozen up the tall masts. Gawking above, she bounced on her toes. "I cain't wait to climb it."

"No," said Mr. MacLeod flatly.

Elbowing Seamus, she whispered, "I'll do it, anyway. Every spring my brother and me climb trees tall as the mast to collect them baby squirrels from their nests. My pa sells them to all the rich gentlemen for their little brats."

Mr. MacLeod arched an eyebrow. "You try anything as dangerous as climbing the mast, and I'll skelp your wee behind."

I hate him, she thought, inching away from his reach.

Seamus gazed at her with a tilted head. "Beggin' your pardon, miss, but I didn't think young ladies climbed trees."

A bosun called, "Yeo-a-hoi." The crew sang "Yeo-a-hoi" until the anchor raised.

Women hollered goodbyes to family on the pier, wiping tears as the ship separated from the dock and navigated the crowded harbor. Annaliese kept searching the crowd, tapping her fingers against the rail as raindrops wet her new gloves, but Pa wasn't there.

Passengers climbed below with their sacks and chests. Mr. MacLeod led her to the quarterdeck, which was raised above the stern and enclosed by a rail. The sun reappeared and she squinted before a dark cloud hid it again. Tucked in a corner of the foredeck was a small pen holding goats. Chicken coops sat behind an enormous wheel minded by two men.

Wind filled the sails, and she covered her ears at the deafening flap. Barefoot sailors in loose, ankle-length trousers and checkered linen shirts ran from end to end, cracking ropes and obeying yelled orders.

Mr. MacLeod rubbed his thumb across his lips and muttered to himself, "Well, you're committed now, MacLeod, Lady Margaret's wishes be damned."

Warehouses and their fish stench faded away. Annaliese moved in one direction and then interrupted herself. When there was nothing to see but the gray ocean, her restless pacing stilled. She eyed MacLeod's knuckles again. "I thought for sure Pa might come."

"Say goodbye to the wilderness, Annaliese. This is what your mother wanted."

"Ma only cared what was good for her, not me." Annaliese tugged on her cloak hood to block the dreary drizzle. "That wilderness is my home. My brother's there," she said, feeling her throat get scratchy. *MacLeod ain't gonna see me cry. To hell with him.* Squaring her shoulders, she forced a fake smile. "Ain't matter none. You got me a fancy poppet and a jar of dirty shells, so that's nice. We goin' below deck?"

Mr. MacLeod's face was unreadable, so she broke her stare. A bell rang three times. Sailors climbed off the rigging while new crew mates took over.

Waiting a moment, he finally said, "It's not fair, is it? You're traveling to another world with a man you barely ken. It's understandable you're scared and angry. I see the tempest in your eyes, vulnerable and brave."

Her tight grip on the doll made her knuckles white. She felt naked, like he could see everything she didn't wanted him to see.

"Annaliese Cameron, you have an opportunity to create a new life, as I once did. Dinna squander it."

Chapter Twenty-Three

LADY MARGARET

London

 Madame LaCroix's assistants sewed Lady Margaret into her new robe à la française sack dress—in red, obviously. Viscount Percy Monroe, now *Lord* Percy Monroe, sixth Earl of Cheshire, swanked into the mantua shop with the aura of power sporting his father's dog-head cane. Apprentices silently left as he paid them.

 "My lord." Lady Margaret gracefully curtsied. "How does it feel to be an earl?"

 "Overdue." Swiping aside her white lace fichu with the bronze dog handle, he nuzzled the tops of her breasts. "Stunning as ever, Margaret."

 "My love, let's not get distracted," she said, pushing his new toy away. "We decided we must focus on Lord Hallewell."

 "Did we?" he said, nonchalantly sliding onto a rose-colored armoire, stretching out his legs. "I'm a schoolboy, mistress, learning the art of war from you. But I've decided my first act of vengeance must be against MacLeod, as he stole my honor."

 Perhaps that would be best. It would be delightful to let MacLeod murder Eleanor and the little bastard, and then let Percy kill him and my husband.

Percy stared at his new mechanical hand, a combination of metal catches and springs held onto his forearm with leather straps. "Sometimes my hand still hurts even though it's gone."

Lady Margaret frowned. "How awful for you."

"Father was right. This is my new start. Did you know a Roman general who lost his hand in the Second Punic War won battles with an iron hand? The armorer who made my prosthetic told me. I've spared no expense. See how the thumb and fingers are jointed at each knuckle? Once locked in place, like a handcuff, I can hold reins to my horse, a sword, a quill, anything. MacLeod supposes he weakened me. He awakened me. I'll annihilate him."

"Can you fire a pistol?" she asked, sitting next to him, holding his iron fist in her own hand, noticing the aesthetic details of etched fingernails and sculpted palms.

"Unfortunately, it lacks the dexterity to pull a trigger, but I've been training to fire with my left hand. Thank you again for the gift."

"You mean the loan? Quite the warrior, aren't you?"

Percy truly seemed a serious man, one with power, drive and a fortune. *United, we'd conquer the world*, she mused, standing to admire her own reflection. *Be patient with his whims. Soon you'll wear a widow's black—and your third bridal gown.*

Lord Percy touched his thumb to each mechanical finger, fixated on the movement. "I don't want to just kill MacLeod. Teach me how to hurt him."

Tucking a hair behind her delicate ear, she said, "Percy, my apt pupil, perform due diligence. He's a barrister. They keep records on everyone. Convert his allies into enemies."

A chime rang, and a merry voice called, "This room?" The gloved hand of a plump young woman with rosy cheeks pulled back the curtain. "Goodness, forgive me. I thought—Viscount Percy Monroe? Or, shall I say, *Lord* Percy Monroe?"

"My lady." Percy playfully made the dog handle kiss her cheek as she giggled stupidly.

Lady Catherine positively gushed over Percy before noticing Lady Margaret. "You're Alexander's mother, aren't you? Is he here?"

"No," Lady Margaret said, coldly. *Bugger—My reputation.* "Alexander and Lord Percy escorted me here. Alexander went in search of a privy." She nodded at Percy to play along.

"Hopefully he won't get lost," he said with a smirk.

"What a splendid color on you, Lady Hallewell. Mama says women past a certain age stop wearing red, but here you are proving her wrong. Brava."

Dowager Lady Granger, the debutant's mother, came into the dressing room. "What a consort back here. Lord Monroe, my deepest sympathies for your father." Sandwiching his good hand between her aged ones, she said, "What is this world coming to?"

Outside the room, the seamstress tentatively knocked.

"Yes?" Lady Margaret called testily.

Madame LaCroix came in, curtseying to Lady Granger. "Excusez-moi, your grace. My assistant should have shown you to another room while this one is in use." She glared at the shamefaced apprentice. "Lady Hallewell will soon leave."

Weaving her arm through Lord Percy's, the Dowager conducted him out of the fitting room. "Catherine just finished her first season. You must come to our harvest ball. The men all go hunting the following day. You know, my cousin, King George II, is supremely fond of Catherine. Shall I seat you near him?"

Lord Percy pretended to pay attention to the old bat while he mocked the Dowager behind her back. Lady Catherine struggled against fits of giggles as she trailed them.

Lady Margaret fumed at the haughty old boot's bald ambition, and Percy's blatant flirtation, then pivoted to the seamstress. "How dare you let them in while I was dressing? It's astounding you—"

"My lady, your husband sent word your allowance has been cut off indefinitely and if I continue to indulge you on credit, not a court in the land will force him to pay."

Lady Margaret's lips grew tight. "Clearly there's a mistake. I've spent thousands at your shop, and you dare deny me anything?"

"My lady, I'm in the middle. Between the silk damask and the hours of detail work for the embroidery, I would be out a fortune if I let you leave with the gown."

"I am leaving with this dress, and then I'm telling all my friends to boycott your shop. You'll be ruined by month's end."

Madame LaCroix put her hands on her hips. "Your threats do not frighten me. I did not rise to the top of the London fashion market by kowtowing to aristocrats in weakening circumstances. The constable stands in the lobby ready to arrest you if you attempt to steal."

"Surely Lord Percy will pay. I loaned him the money for his prosthetic hand, you know. Ask him."

An apprentice left to convey the message while the women faced off. A few moments later, the nervous girl returned and delivered the message. "Lord Percy said he's positive Alexander will pay when he returns from the privy. He's left with Lady Granger."

Lady Margaret produced a stunned squeak.

Madame LaCroix snapped her fingers and five apprentices appeared. They unpinned Lady Margaret's ruffles, ripped off her gown, untied her pannier, pulled the stays over her head—wrecking her elaborate hairstyle—and stripped her to her mere shift and garters.

Lady Margaret let loose such a ferocious scream that the constable ran in. He found her sufferings delicious, no doubt.

Chapter Twenty-Four

ANNALIESE

"Watch out," MacLeod said, helping Annaliese down the narrow ladder to the 'tween deck.

Each timber on the floor seemed to move in a different direction as her wobbly legs tried to find solid footing. MacLeod had to crouch under the low ceiling as they passed passengers setting their trunks beneath sleep shelves. Without windows, the main light came from the open hatches and grates above. A few lanterns hung on hooks. Another ladder led to an even lower deck.

"What's down there?" Annaliese peered into the darkness and plugged her nose at the stench that hit her like a wave of escaping misery.

"The orlop. It's a labyrinth of tobacco barrels, supplies and trunks. Brig's there, too."

"What's a brig?"

"A gaol. Try not to end up there, aye? Your mother would have traveled there as an indentured convict."

Thinking of Ma locked in irons in the darkness made her shudder. "I would have been in her belly, huh? Is peoples there now?"

"Poor people go from London to Virginia, not in the opposite direction."

A sailor in a blue coat climbed from the orlop ladder with a quarter cask and called, "Ahanu, grab this."

A tall, lean Shawnee man dressed in typical sailor fashion except for two long braids and a beaded necklace took the handles.

Annaliese said, "He Laughs. Ain't that what Ahanu means in Algonquin?"

The man laughed in response, which made MacLeod's eyebrows raise.

"You ain't the only one who knows another language. Well, a few words at least. My Uncle Hal taught me."

Ahanu gave a nod and strode in the opposite direction, flexing his knee as the ship heaved. MacLeod grabbed a handhold on the wall as Annaliese crashed into him. An older man threw up in a bucket, his powdered wig on the ground beside him.

"Where do I sleep?" Scanning the floor, she searched for the safest corner, away from others but close to a ladder in case she needed to escape.

"The officers sleep in forecastle cabins and sailors hang their hammocks there. We're in the windward quarter of the quarterdeck. Captain Adams is jealous, but it's the only spot not stinking from ballast fumes. Mind the ladder, it's steep."

Blinking at the news, she followed him into a private room almost as big as Pa's cabin. Seamus had already placed their trunks beneath seven inward-sloping windows. A bed was framed in the left wall and a hammock hung on the right. Next to the door was a desk with a small shelf above it.

Dropping her poppet and shells on the desk, she asked, "How come we sleep here?"

"Your father owns the ship."

Her jaw fell. "Thought only kings owned ships. Ain't known regular peoples did."

"Regular wealthy people, if there is such a thing. And the plural is *people*, not peoples. There's your bed."

"My own bed?" Crawling on it, she checked the mattress's firmness, inhaled the soap scent from the clean sheets and stroked the heavy woolen blanket. *My own blanket.* Bouncing off the bed, she said, "Where's the chamber pot?"

"You use the head on a ship. It's like a privy. The waves clean everything. Works splendidly."

"What's this?"

"My hammock. Have a try."

Climbing in, she swung until it dumped her to the floor with the blankets piling on top.

"Saw that coming," he muttered.

Laughing hard, she said, "Sam would love this here hammock." Leaving the bedding on the floor, she staggered to the elegant windows that angled into the room and knocked on them. "That there's real glass, Mr. MacLeod." Her knee buckled with a dip of the hull.

"Careful. You dinna have your sea legs yet," he said, unpacking his papers and candles.

Cocking her head, she said, "Sea legs?"

He smirked. Annaliese had never noticed his dimple before. Maybe he never smiled before.

"It's an expression, lass. It takes a few days to balance walking along the shifting ship. Hopefully, you winnae get seasick. Put your shells away before you break the jar."

Opening her trunk, she shifted through her dresses with increasing urgency. "Where's Ma's book?" Flinging the dresses on the floor, she said, "Did Pa take it? I known I packed it." Marching to MacLeod's desk, she yanked his arm. "Ma's book ain't here. We have to go back."

"We've left the harbor," he said calmly.

Pulling harder, she spoke louder. "No, we have to git it. It's Ma's."

The ship lurched. MacLeod's papers slid to the floor as she bumped into the desk.

"Calm down. Mrs. Otis will send it if it's at the tavern," he said, gathering his things.

Her wheezing came quick and shallow. "How's the tavern keeper gonna known where I live? I ain't even known where I live. Pa token it, I known he did. We have to git it from him."

MacLeod placed his hands on her shoulders to steady her. "You'll live just fine without your mother's diary. Trust me on this. Deep breath."

He held her eyes until she exhaled, but she still felt a painful lump in her throat. *MacLeod ain't understand nuthin'. Sam's gone. Now the last of Ma is gone, too.* Hiding her face, she blinked back a tear. *I hate Pa.*

"Put my blankets back, and your dresses, too. Neatly. Your pa may have liked to live in filth, but I dinna."

Tossing the bedding on the hammock, she folded her clothes in a huff. *Pa wants to hurt me, mean bastard. He's jealous I'm creating a new life while he's stuck in a shitty cabin with one grease-paper window.*

A girl with light brown curls and a shiny blue dress covered in bows peeked around the open door. "Bonjour, Monsieur. I'm Jacqueline Gauthier." She curtsied, then smiled at Annaliese. "Want to play?"

Annaliese whiffed the rich girl's lilac perfume, then hugged a folded petticoat close to her chin. "Uh, I ain't allowed."

MacLeod said, "You may play. Dinna bother the crew and come when I call."

Annaliese put the petticoat in her trunk and felt heat in her brand beneath her glove. Glancing between MacLeod—already engrossed in a ledger—and the smiling rich girl, she felt torn. *Jacqueline seems nicer than the people in Williamsburg, but what if it's a trick?* Annaliese swallowed hard. *You making a new life now, Annaliese Cameron. She ain't never gonna see the branding under your glove.* Annaliese straightened her shoulders and followed Jacqueline into the 'tween deck, noisy with people unpacking.

"The girls in Williamsburg ain't like me much," Annaliese said, almost like a challenge.

"Girls can be mean." Jacqueline's petticoats were so wide at her hips, she had to twist to climb the ladder. "But I'm not. Except to my brothers, but they live in France and deserve to be slapped."

I like her already. "How old is you?" Gripping the ladder sides, she tried to time her climb with the heave of the deck to not get knocked off. Above the deck, blue-green ocean and sunlight stretched into a hazy horizon.

"Eleven. I'm from Paris, but we've been living in Maryland while my father served as chef for the governor. My maman and I are traveling ahead, and he'll meet us in London where he has a new position with the ambassador." Jacqueline waved at another girl beside solemn parents. "Bonjour. Who might you be?"

"Rebecca Mercer."

The girl looked like a ghost. Dead-white skin, pale hair, gray eyes. Her charcoal petticoat and bodice next to her starched white apron and mop cap looked dull as a tombstone, which made the golden cross sparkling around her neck more striking. Rebecca regarded her father, who waved her off with a wrist flick.

They moved aft, holding whatever they could to stay upright as the ship pitched. Sailors kept busy splicing ropes and mending nets.

"How old is you? You a Quaker or somethin'?" Annaliese asked.

"Quaker?" Rebecca held her hand against her heart. "Heavens, no, we're Calvinists. I'm ten. My father is getting his own church in England."

"So? I'm nine and a half and my pa owns this ship. I can do whatever I want." Annaliese jumped into a puddle, splashing Rebecca's white apron. Ghost girl stood with her mouth open, too stunned to scream.

Jacqueline said, "Look. Dolphins."

Annaliese and Jacqueline ran past a crew mate fixing his neckcloth, with Rebecca trailing behind, shaking her dripping apron. Two dolphins jumped in semicircles, making *click-click-click* noises. Annaliese climbed the rail for a better look.

"No, Miss Cameron," called Seamus, running up. "You might fall overboard, and the Lord in heaven only knows what Mr. MacLeod would do to me for letting it happen."

"Ain't you gotta work?"

"Aye. Mr. MacLeod sent me to chaperone you."

"I ain't need no one to mind me. I raised my brother since I was five," she said, poking his patched jacket. "Hell, I was practically married. I'm grown."

The ship titled. Both she and Jacqueline stumbled into Seamus, who gave a smug little grin. Annaliese's head hurt from the motion.

Rebecca held onto a barrel. "Married at nine?"

Annaliese covered her mouth. *Ain't Mrs. Otis say people would treat me like a pariah if they knew I'd laid with men?* "Just jokin'. Never mind. This here's Seamus. He's ten, too. He's Scottish."

"I'm twelve, not ten, and I'm Irish, Miss Cameron."

A woman in a green shawl raced to the deck, retching loudly overboard.

"I used to be Irish," Annaliese said. Two nearby sailors overheard and laughed. *Stop laughing.*

Rebecca snorted. "Used to be? You're Irish or you're not."

Annaliese felt her face burn. "Well, I thought my ma was Irish, but Mr. MacLeod say she were Scottish like him."

Rebecca whispered to Jacqueline, "She's so stupid. Her grammar's atrocious."

"I ain't known what grammar or atrocious means, but I known I ain't like you." Annaliese aimed to throw a punch, but Seamus caught her fist.

"Whoa. No tussles on my watch. Mind me, lass, or I'll tell Mr. MacLeod."

Twisting away, she squared against Seamus now. "Ain't afraid of MacLeod none. He already beat me once and it ain't hurt too bad."

Jacqueline said, "Stop fighting with everyone, ma chère. Let's play tag."

Annaliese shoved Rebecca into a rope cord. "Tag."

Rebecca ran after her faster than a hound chasing a squirrel. As the ship moved further out to sea, more gentlemen came on deck, vomiting into the salt water, their tricorn hats blowing across the deck. Some didn't make it to the rail in time, falling to their hands and knees, shitting their bacon and eggs through their teeth.

Waves grew larger on either side, sending spray onto the already slippery deck. Annaliese darted through the crowd, shoving aside sailors mending a canvas and passengers with cold, sweaty faces. Not used to a shifting ship or heeled shoes, Annaliese tripped face-first in a vomit puddle. Rebecca howled.

"Goddamn it." Annaliese rose, shaking wet bits from her gloves.

"Blasphemy," Rebecca said, pointing.

Jacqueline covered her mouth as Seamus made the sign of the cross. Mr. Grubb, who watched the entire exchange, strode over and gave Annaliese a good walloping with a rope end as MacLeod came on deck. Rebecca's grin spread.

"What's going on?!" MacLeod bellowed.

Rebecca tattled, "Annaliese said you own the ship, and she can do whatever she wants, and she's not afraid of you."

Annaliese's jaw dropped. *Damned bitch.*

Mr. Grubb kept a tight grip on her arm, not letting her escape. Wiping the slimy filth from her face with her other arm, she felt nauseous from the stench of vomit mingling with the scent of rum on Grubb's breath.

Is the ship spinning?

"Thank you, Mr. Grubb. I'll handle it from here." MacLeod looked thoroughly unhappy with Annaliese. "Come, Annaliese, you need fresh clothes."

Rebecca continued, "She also took the Lord's name in vain, even though I told her it was a sin. She deserved the whipping."

Ah, hell. Annaliese raised her arm to protect her face, waiting for a beating from MacLeod. It ain't come. "Thought you said you was gonna beat me for cussin'."

"I said you'd be whipped. I didna say I'd be doing it every time."

"Spare the rod and spoil the child," the old salt muttered as he coiled his rope.

"If I want your advice, I'll be sure to ask."

The ship hit a swell and her stomach felt like it flipped three times. Annaliese tripped into MacLeod, dampening his shirt with puke. "I'm gonna be sick."

Letting loose a loud belch that promised worse to come, she stumbled to the rail and spilled her stomach into the sea. Rebecca said to Jacqueline, "Serves her right. I'm telling my father."

Mr. MacLeod said in an angry hush, "Why are you telling people I own the ship?"

Wiping her arm across her mouth, she said, "Naw, I said my father did. You told me."

"Even worse. Now people know who sired you."

"You ain't never told me to keep *that* secret." Annaliese retched into choppy waters.

"Jesus, Joseph and Mary," he muttered. "It's your own fault, MacLeod."

Her head throbbed. *Some new life. I'm gonna hurt that little witch Rebecca for tattling.*

Chapter Twenty-Five

FIONA

Scotland

Rain drummed against Fiona's bedchamber window as she repetitively rubbed her hands down her thighs, trying to forget her stormy visions. It had been four months and still no word from William. Only magic could help. The house was quiet.

No one will find out.

Fiona extracted her wooden box hidden under the floorboard beneath the bed. Gently blowing away fifteen years of dust on the lid, she gingerly unearthed her leather-bound grimoire. True, she told William ages ago she had burned it, but how could she? It was the first thing she created once William taught her to read and write. Her fingers caressed the recipes for spells, and she sighed at her detailed herb diagrams with their uses. Rosemary to ward off evil spirits. Sage for treating fevers. Pennyroyal to provoke the menses.

Fiona stroked her belly. *How different would my life have been if Reverend MacDonald never spied my salt circle?*

Turning from her notes on seership, she peered inside the box and smiled at her tools like lost friends. Brushing aside the flint, crystals and bone, she extracted the white-handled knife. Previously consecrated and sained, it was ready for divination. Taking an apple from her pocket, she sliced it in half, showing the pentagram on each side.

The left half shone one damaged seed. Someone from the past was coming to haunt her.

Colonel Wilkes said, "Why, Mrs. MacLeod, you are a mysterious creature, aren't you? What's your specialty then—palmistry? Dreams?" He leaned in and she stared into his dangerously handsome face. "Shh. I won't tell your husband if you don't."

Fiona twisted her wedding band and studied the right half of the apple, full of rotting seeds signifying family quarrels and problems with land and finances. Tossing both halves into the fire, a draft blew through the chimney, flipping the pages open to the Black Arts section.

Auntie Matilda only did natural magic but taught her everything. Wormwood for revenge. Hellebore can only be picked on a moonless night. Screaming Mandrake roots held power to soothe or kill. Her chest flushed. *How far must I go to protect my family?*

"Mam?"

Fiona snapped the book shut, but not before James entered. "Dinna you wait to be called in? What do you want?"

James held up his hands. "Ack, dinna bite my head off. I need to return to Glasgow in the morning. My wife misses me, and I need to prepare for court."

Crinkling her brows, she asked, "Who's going to oversee the harvest?"

"I'm sure Da will come before your birthday."

Violent waves from her vision flashed before her as the wind outside rattled her windows. "Are you? Because I'm not. I have a bad feeling," she said, tracing a finger over her diamond and emerald bracelet.

James jutted his chin. "What're you reading?"

Dropping her shawl over it and the box, she sat on the bed and patted, so he'd join her. Nodding at their first family portrait hanging above the fireplace, they both grinned.

Wee James snuggled in her arms wrapped in Auntie Matilda's quilt. William stood behind, proud and strong in his dark green kilt and waistcoat, a thrum bonnet over his wild hair.

"Your father wanted to wear breeches and a coat, but I told him I wouldna sit for a portrait unless he donned a proper plaid. He made me move the painting here so no one would see it but us."

She chuckled but then felt her smile fade. How very ashamed William seemed of their past. Clearing her throat, she said, "You should move here with Nelly until harvest is done. It's a grand manor. This is your inheritance."

"Inheritance? Mam, he's not dead, he's on a trip for Lord Hallewell. You ken I cannae stay forever. My life's in Glasgow. The boys will help with harvest before they leave for school."

Fiona crossed her arms over her stomach. *How can I pay for tuition with my life savings gone and no new money coming in?* "Tenants keep stopping by, telling me of their poor harvests and woes. You're the man of the house now. When are you going to fill the void?"

James strolled to the portrait. "I have my own family to think about." A smile spread across his face. "Nelly's expecting."

"The tincture worked." Fiona grinned.

"What?" His smile dropped.

Fiona traced the thistle pattern on the quilt. "Auntie Matilda sewed me this. She taught me which herbs soothe, which prayers to keep fairies from transforming bairns into changelings, how to interpret dreams. Dinna fash about potions from a wise woman."

James scowled at the book peeking beneath the shawl. "I'll say an extra prayer at church for Da's speedy return." He rocked on his feet, then kissed her cheek and left.

Rain pounded the roof. Fiona locked the door and stared into the fire where the apple had charred to ashes. *Bills coming due, snakes closing in and no letter from William in months. I cannae do it alone.* Hugging the grimoire to her heart, she cast the spell. *Eisd rium a Dhia. Make James stay. With harm to none, so it be done.*

Chapter Twenty-Six

ANNALIESE

Curled in a ball, still shaking from a nightmare, Annaliese overheard MacLeod and the officers talking in the hall.

Surgeon Johnsson, a friendly Swede, said, "Quite a storm last night, ja?"

"Aye," said the captain. "We're blown off course. My men have been grumbling all morning about the delay."

"Maybe if MacLeod kept his little ward quiet, people wouldn't get angry, and we'd have good weather again," Mr. Grubb said, not entirely joking.

MacLeod said slowly, "I dinna understand your meaning, sir."

Annaliese cracked open her eyelids and peeked into the hall. MacLeod's chest seemed to expand into Grubb's space, and the old salt shuffled back a step.

"Upon my word and honor, sir, it's not me saying it, mind you, I'm telling what some others be saying. Her nightly screams worry the men. Storms follow, aye?" Mr. Grubb's eye contact fleeted away to the buttons on his coat, which suddenly needed a good tidying up.

Captain Adams asked the surgeon, "Can you give her something to sleep peacefully? Just until we arrive in London?"

Surgeon Johnsson said, "We've already tried warm goat's milk and lavender tea. I only wish I had the ingredients to make a tincture of laudanum."

"Cheese," Mr. Grubb said, tugging at his falling hose. "She needs to stop eating cheese entirely. My mother told me that as a boy."

"Or a stronger dose of grog before bed," the surgeon suggested.

"Gag her," Mr. Grubb said.

"I'm not gagging and intoxicating the wee lass because some crew members believe in old wives' tales. Childish nightmares dinna cause storms."

Captain Adams said, carefully, "Sailors—they're a nervous lot. Superstitious. We can explain away one nightmare. But every night since we left port? Sometimes seamen will make connections where learned men, such as us, would not."

"Meaning?"

"Pray she gets a good night's sleep."

The men walked away, but Grubb held back a moment to drink his flask of rum in secret. When he left, she made sure the door was closed and she rocked with her doll. Her head hurt something awful. *Will these dreams stop already? Even on a ship across the world Pa manages to ruin everything for me.*

A few hours later, MacLeod returned. "I think it's best you join the rest of society. Grab your hornbook. You'll be starting dame school today with Mrs. Mercer. She's teaching all the children aboard."

"You ain't gonna teach me?" Weeding out her mason jar from beneath her pillow, she sat on the floor and poured the sand and shells through her gloved fingers.

"Jesus, Joseph and Mary, how hard is it for you to stay clean? I just said you were starting school." MacLeod snapped his fingers and opened his palm. "Give me your shells."

Pouting, she swept the contents back into the jar and handed it over.

"All of them," he said, staring at her pocket. Exhaling in defeat, she handed over a conical auger. Tucking the jar in the shelf above his desk, he then dusted off her dress. "Dinna fash. You can earn them back with good behavior."

Annaliese followed him onto the 'tween deck holding her hornbook like a shield. Tables hung from hooks in the ceiling with benches beneath where people were eating burgoo with molasses and dipping hard tack biscuits into their coffee.

Even seated, Reverend Mercer seemed tall, and his wife looked like a bitter shrew. They were perfectly paired—both allergic to joy. Rebecca sat with straight-laced posture. Annaliese stared at the thin golden cross dangling from her neck, noticing how she stroked it. Annaliese stabbed Rebecca with her eyes.

Reverend Mercer wiped his mouth with a napkin and said to Rebecca, "Help Mother set up for school." His bottom teeth were crooked and overlapping. To Annaliese, "Your guardian tells me you are new to God."

"I'm practically thirteen. I ain't that new to Him."

"She's nine," MacLeod said.

Scowling, the reverend said, "He knows you, certainly, but you don't know Him yet, which must explain why you broke the Third Commandment."

Holding up both hands, she said, "I ain't break nuthin', Mr. MacLeod."

Reverend Mercer gave a knowing nod. "Ah. You truly don't know the Ten Commandments. Because if you knew your actions' ramifications, surely you would not curse the Lord, our savior."

Blast it. I known Rebecca would squeal. "You gonna whip me?" she asked, inching away.

"A whipping is naught compared to damnation. Hell is real, Annaliese."

A sailor rolled dice on a triangle carved into a barrel top. His friend cussed after losing the bet. Grinning, the first sailor counted his coins, and she remembered Pa smiling at his money after selling her and Sam. "How's hell worse than living with my pa?" she mumbled.

Reverend Mercer raised his voice. "If you don't want your soul to burn with the witches, receive Christ and stop treating sin as inconsequential. Do you want to be burned?"

What? Her eyes darted for an escape, but where could she hide on a ship? The mast?

MacLeod patted Annaliese's shoulder, like he read her mind. "No one is going to burn you. We're no' trying to frighten you. We want you to understand how to behave. Your mother would have wanted you to be raised properly. Your father does, too."

As the reverend droned on about Jesus, she slyly pocketed half-eaten biscuits from the table. Her eyes wandered to Rebecca reading a Bible. *I'll corner her when she's alone and punch her gut a few dozen times. That'll learn her.*

MacLeod said, "Best behavior, aye? You'll learn how to be a polite young lady, like Rebecca. If you want to meet your father, you'll need to demonstrate proper manners."

Her stomach hurt as she trudged with Reverend Mercer to the class area. *What if I cain't never learn to be good? I won't meet my father?*

Jacqueline smiled and waved her over near the back, far from Rebecca sitting primly in the front row. Little boys filled in the middle.

"Mother will teach the lessons," Reverend Mercer said to the children, placing a gaunt hand on his wife's narrow shoulder. "Put in diligent effort. The Lord helps those who help themselves." To his wife, "I'll be aft if you need me, Mother."

Annaliese whispered to Jacqueline, "It's weird they call each other Mother and Father. Imagine them humping with his cock going in and out. 'Oh, Mother.' 'Oh, Father.' 'Ohhhh.'"

Jacqueline bit her lip hard to stop laughing, growing bright red.

"Annaliese Cameron, come here."

Blast it. That ain't take long. Everyone stared as she tiptoed to Mrs. Mercer, whose face looked as pleasant as her gray linen dress. *How much did she hear?*

A sailor above called, "Tighten the jib."

"Since you're talkative, speak to the class. Say your letters."

Her face got hot, and she gripped her new hornbook handle, afraid Mother might use it as a paddle on her. "I ain't known them," she muttered.

"You *don't know* them. Since you know nothing, stop speaking when I do. Sit."

"Yes, ma'am," she said, and slunk back to Jacqueline as a grin crawled up Rebecca's face.

As lessons progressed, Annaliese had to stand with little boys younger than Sam who could already read. Mrs. Mercer had her repeat 'ab, be, ib, ob, ub' for nine hundred hours. *How is this going to learn me reading?*

Finally, Annaliese got to return to Jacqueline while the flighty younger boys kept Mrs. Mercer's focus diverted. Annaliese glared at Perfect Rebecca up front, not a hair out of place, her delicate cross sparkling around her delicate neck.

"How come adults love her so much?" Annaliese whispered.

"She obeys," whispered Jacqueline. "Stop ruminating."

Annaliese bit off a thumbnail chunk. She chewed all her nails to the quick, even though MacLeod constantly pulled them from her mouth. "MacLeod cain't shut up about her." She imitated his brogue. "Rebecca's such a polite lass. Rebecca's so smart. Rebecca's so ..." she dropped the accent, "damned annoying."

Jacqueline coughed in her hand to camouflage her laughter.

"Annaliese Cameron, come here. I've warned you once about talking." Mrs. Mercer grabbed a switch of birch twigs.

Ah, hell. Annaliese dragged her feet along the swaying floorboards with all eyes upon her. It became difficult to breathe as the musty room grew hot. Now MacLeod is gonna be mad at me. *I hate the Mercers. I hate school.*

"Take off your glove."

While her cheeks scorched hot, her whole body froze. *Everyone will see my brand.*

Mrs. Mercer was angry with the delay and peeled off her glove, then gasped as she twisted Annaliese's hand back and forth. All the children in class leaned forward for a good peek.

Mrs. Mercer's eyebrows knitted. "How did you get those marks?"

Her eyes burned a hole in the floor. "I fell."

"Stop lying." Mrs. Mercer swatted Annaliese's palm, but the prickling sensation tickled compared to what Pa used to give. Heat rushed to her hand, now sticky with sap. Boys pretended to study their hornbooks, but they watched. "Tell me how you got those marks."

Hell with you. Annaliese thrust out her chin in defiant silence. Birch sticks whizzed through the air, biting her skin until the welts bled. Rebecca wet her lips as an unkind smile spread across her smug little face. *Stop laughing*. Annaliese wiped her bloody hand on her hip as she returned to her seat.

The day rolled on. Bells kept ringing, crews kept shifting and lessons continued. Everyone was allowed to leave once to use the privy, and that was all the time she needed. Annaliese snuck back into her cabin and exhaled; happy MacLeod was elsewhere.

When Annaliese returned, Mrs. Mercer said, "Rebecca, read to Annaliese while I work with Jacqueline on her Latin."

Annaliese groaned and sat next to Rebecca, who lifted two books from her pile.

Rebecca said, "*Book of Common Prayer* or *Compendium Maleficarum*? You probably want the second. It's about witches and has pictures."

Whoa. One picture showed the Devil—a muscled man with goat horns and wings—stealing a dead baby from a lady with a huge ruffle around her neck. Another picture showed people signing a thick black book, like Ma's book. But the third picture forced Annaliese into fits of giggles. A crowd holding whips surrounded a woman on her knees ...

Mrs. Mercer glanced up from Jacqueline's lessons. "Annaliese Cameron, what in heavens are you laughing at?"

Annaliese wiped her tears. She scarcely got the words out, gasping, "The lady in the picture be kissing the Devil's ass."

"My necklace," blurted Rebecca, kneeling to search the ground. Her death-pale skin grew sweaty and flushed.

"Your grandmother's cross?" Mrs. Mercer joined her daughter on hands and knees, digging into cracks in the timber.

Rage tears spilled as Rebecca pointed. "Annaliese took it. I know she did, she's smiling."

"I ain't tooken nuthin'. We was readin'."

"Mother, she did. I had it earlier, but now it's gone."

Jacqueline joined in the search. "Maybe the chain broke?"

Annaliese felt embarrassed and confused. *Why would anyone defend me?*

"I'm not stupid." Rebecca called, "Father, Annaliese stole my cross. She's coveted it since we met."

"Maybe a witch took it," Annaliese hissed.

Reverend Mercer approached, with furious eyes. God only knew what he'd do. Annaliese shoved past him and scampered above, past sailors on all fours scrubbing the deck with vinegar and sea water.

"What the devil is going on?" MacLeod asked, leaving Captain Adams' side. Annaliese hid behind him.

Reverend Mercer said, "Your ward is disruptive, disobedient and a thief. I've preached to savages with better children." Veins raised on his neck.

"Ain't want to be at your stupid school, anyway."

"Wheest," MacLeod said, holding her arm. To the reverend, "What did she do, exactly?"

Sailors kept their eyes focused on their tasks, but blatantly strained to listen.

"She stole Rebecca's cross in retaliation for some perceived slight and tried to blame it on witches. Wicked girl."

MacLeod slowly straightened, and Annaliese curled in her shoulders as she shrunk. Speaking in a low, firm voice, he said, "She kens not to steal. I made that very plain. I'm asking once. Did you take Rebecca's cross?"

Annaliese drew to her full height and shook no.

"Empty your pockets."

Pulling them inside out, she refused to break eye contact as she smiled smugly.

"Take off your shoes."

The deck tilted. Taking a step back, she swallowed. The men exchanged knowing nods. Slowly she removed her pink heeled shoes, rolling her hosed toes on the timber.

MacLeod shook one. Empty. Then the other. *Clink.* A copper coin fell and rolled in a circle until it dropped.

"I found it on the deck. I ain't tooken it from no one." Her back was against the mast. "Please don't whip me."

"A penny," MacLeod said to Reverend Mercer, pinching the coin between his finger and thumb, "but not a cross," he said to Annaliese with a slight smile.

He believes me?

"Inspect her room. My Rebecca is very careful, and your Annaliese runs wild."

Her chest tightened and fingers tingled. "You always believe Rebecca."

They moved to their cabin. MacLeod said, "Stand in the corner while I search."

Reverend Mercer had her say "Idle hands are the Devil's workshop" while MacLeod rifled through her trunk and flipped her mattress, finding only two partially eaten biscuits.

"No cross. Perhaps Rebecca did lose it."

Shaking his head, the preacher said, "You're too lenient. This girl dances with the Devil."

"Excuse me?" MacLeod towered over the reverend.

"It's merely an expression." To Annaliese, "The cross belonged to my mother, and this is all Rebecca has left to remember her."

A warm rush coursed through her veins. Annaliese felt a buzzing sensation in her fingers, like watching Pa getting his ear nailed, and she bit her lip to keep from smiling.

Reverend's eyes narrowed. "Perhaps we should take away something important to you?"

Her stomach sank. They both spied her poppet on the bed at the same time and the reverend snatched it.

"Please don't burn Charlotte. Please, I ain't steal nuthin'. How come no one believes me?" she pleaded with MacLeod. "You promised I could keep my baby." She stomped her foot. "You ain't fair. You stoled this ship and nuthin' bad happened to you."

Both men froze. MacLeod blinked about a dozen times before saying, "Says whom?"

"Mr. Grubb calls you Laird Pirate behind your back because you cut off the real owner's hand and stole the ship for yourself."

MacLeod's jaw went tight. "Mr. Grubb and I will have a wee conversation about slander." To the reverend, he quietly said, "It appears she's innocent. Perhaps you owe her an apology?"

Reverend Mercer tossed her poppet to MacLeod and left.

Chapter Twenty-Seven

LADY MARGARET

Wentworth Palace, Yorkshire

Lady Margaret sipped her champagne at Lady Granger's ball. The grand staircase, an elaborate gilded display of craftsmanship, overflowed with ladies waving fans, military officers in red coats, and noblemen in powdered perukes.

Lady Granger said, "Madam LaCroix delivered your gown after all? I hear she's in hospital now. But, oh, what a hubbub at her shop over payment. How terribly embarrassing for you to be cut off." The old bat loved being the town crier of Lady Margaret's misfortunes.

Lady Margaret stroked the rubies adorning her neck, an heirloom from her first husband, the one generous enough to die quickly. "I'm wearing the dress, aren't I? I know a thing or two about outwitting husbands."

"Do you?" Lord Hallewell said, unsmiling.

Ladies averted their eyes, stifling their smirks behind their flapping fans. Lady Margaret hadn't even noticed his approach. Sipping champagne again, she said, "I didn't realize you were interested in women's gossip, my lord."

Lord Hallewell stunk of port. "Your silence is more concerning than your chatter, wife."

God only knew what would fly from his mouth in his current condition. "Darling, shall we stroll the garden?"

Barely three yards into the courtyard, Lord Hallewell retched into a red poppy bed.

"It's rude to christen their vegetation."

"I can't help but fear this may be my last meal." Lord Hallewell wiped the saliva string from his lips.

"What are you carrying on about?"

"I fear Lord Percy wants to challenge me to a duel. Had I known Lady Granger invited him, I should have made a polite excuse."

"Leave then."

"I'm fine," he said, standing. "I accepted the invitation because Lady Catherine would make a suitable match for Alexander. She's a pleasant girl and brings a substantial dowery."

"Is it stored in her enormous double chin?"

"How petty you are. Think what's best for Alexander. We'll leave after dinner. I hope Lady Granger hasn't seated me near Lord Percy."

"Darling, Lord Percy's missing his right hand. If you must duel, the probability for success is clearly in your favor. I wouldn't worry."

Lord Hallewell grabbed the flask from his pocket and drank.

Snatching it from his hand, she hissed, "My lord, do you really deem it prudent to wash your fears with spirits? You are embarrassing me. I forbid you to take another drink."

Alexander stood a few yards in the distance, flirting with a half-dozen girls on a quest for a wealthy husband. An expansive four-story mansion stretched beyond, lit with candlelight. Gossip filtered through the air from the rounded portico packed with debutants and their suitors.

"You forbid it? To hell with you, Margaret. I'm playing cards." Lord Hallewell stumbled toward the party. Guests strolling the grounds noted his outburst, casually whispering.

Waving her son over, she said in a low voice, "Follow him to make sure he doesn't gamble away your inheritance." Alexander departed immediately.

Moving inside the estate, she climbed the winding marble staircase to the balcony above the ballroom for a better view. Stuffy nobles and tawdry merchants flush with new coin crowded the black-and-white-patterned marble floor. Revelers spun past life-sized Greek statues adorning the wall inlays between pink marbled columns supporting the balcony. At the center of it all, Lord Percy danced with Plump Catherine.

Lady Margaret's grip on the wooden railing matched the tightness in her chest at spying him flirt with a younger, more powerful woman. The crowd clapped politely. Lady Margaret noticed Percy watching her and grinned. They always sensed each other.

Within moments, he joined her, sporting his father's cane.

"Dancing with Her Graceless?" Lady Margaret asked. "Plump Catherine has grown even fatter since last I saw her, but she wears it well."

"I thought your favorite color was red, not green," he smirked.

More guests came onto the balcony, chatting by the prominent windows overlooking the courtyard. A servant gave each a champagne flute.

Percy said, "Lady Catherine's financial assets are as plump as her sweet arse. Beautiful women always threw themselves at me, but now mothers are parading their daughters before me, too." He laughed, sipping his drink. "As though I'd gander a merchant's horse-faced daughter now that I'm an earl."

Pompous ass. She hated feeling jealous—there was no power in it.

Percy noticed her grimace. "None are as seductive as you in that gown," he said, ogling her ample cleavage. "I'm surprised your husband let you wear it."

Swiping him aside, she asked, "You suddenly care?"

"You're in a testy mood. I bought it for you, didn't I?"

"After the fact. I would have paid for it myself if I hadn't given you my money. You used me to deal with your father, then abandoned me at the mantua shop. Madam LaCroix humiliated me, stripped me like a common peasant." Lady Margaret had an inkling to slap him, but too many people were near. "I don't want to be here—my husband demanded we come. Bride shopping for Alexander, you know. As for my husband—he doesn't care what I wear nor who paid for it, provided it isn't him."

Percy's sandalwood-scented perfume grew prominent the more he leaned in. "He must notice you in that dress."

She longed to kiss him, claiming him as her own.

"Where's your husband?"

"Avoiding you, I assume. It's ludicrous. You'll never challenge him to a duel."

"You think not?" he said nonchalantly, hovering close enough for a kiss, but she batted him away with her fan. People watched everywhere, all the time.

Lord Percy drank, irritated, then whispered, "Honestly, having *me* murder your husband isn't strategic. People already gossip about my father's untimely death. I need to keep distance between such plots. Didn't you say your husband had someone named Wilkes killed?"

"Colonel Wilkes, yes. On my wedding night, no less. MacLeod and his witch wife were involved somehow."

"Is she really a witch? The last thing I need is another curse on my head."

"No, fool. She's a simple farm girl from the Highlands who believes in fairies and such, but I know the rumors embarrass MacLeod. I told him if he brings my husband's mistress to London, I'd ruin Fiona's reputation, and I'd let Wilkes' son know my suspicions about their involvement in his father's murder. He's a lieutenant now, apparently."

"Margaret, the solution is right there. MacLeod will be gone for months, which means your husband is vulnerable. Tell Wilkes' son about the murder. He'll probably duel your husband and kill MacLeod when he returns so I won't have to. Let Lieutenant Wilkes eliminate both our problems."

Lady Margaret considered it. "Percy, your idea might prove terminal." She raised her glass to him, then let the champagne fizz down her throat. "Timing needs to be flawless. If I invite Lieutenant Wilkes for tea, my husband will be apprehensive. It has to be my husband's idea to tell Wilkes that MacLeod was the murderer. Revenge requires such tedious planning."

"Patience is a virtue I never acquired." Percy gave a slight nod, slipping into a room.

After a few moments, when no one was watching, she crept inside the drawing room decorated with green silk. They stood beneath a smiling portrait of the Dowager and Plump Catherine. Closing the door, he filled her mouth with his tongue.

Twisting away from him, she said, "Percy, it's too dangerous. My husband is playing cards in the other room."

"I know. That's what makes it exciting."

Applause rippled through the crowd at the end of the song. Lady Margaret said, "You should return to your fawning debutants, lest they miss you."

"I don't care a whit about them."

"Really? A glove masks your iron hand. Why? So girls won't be repulsed?"

"You are wily tonight, aren't you? I wanted to give you a gift, but you don't deserve it."

Dignity might have tempted her to leave, but his intoxicating nature held her in place. Percy kissed her neck, gloating in his supremacy over her. "I've brought you a small token of my dedication." Reaching into his waistcoat pocket, he pulled out a small, wrapped box and slid it into her palm.

Untying the ribbon, she lifted the lid. "Jesus Christ," she gasped.

A brown eyeball rolled inside, staring up at her.

Lord Percy laughed. "Did you hear highwaymen attacked Madam LaCroix? Such a shame. But I suppose a woman who owns the most fashionable mantua shop in town shouldn't disrespect the sixth Earl of Cheshire's lover."

She took a juncture to process all he said. "What a sight for sore eyes." They both snickered. "I shall cherish the sentiment but must retire it to you for safekeeping. Gifts are too risky for a married woman. A widow, however—"

He buried it in her pocket. Lord Percy was a tidal force, drawing her closer. "I trust you know how to hide things. That was my first gift. The second is information. Ever since you told me your husband's mistress was in the colonies, it made me curious how she got there."

"And?"

Unveiling his cock, he said, "You're going to have to earn that information."

Spinning her to face the door, he raised her petticoat to take her from behind and she moaned. Clapping his left hand over her mouth, he said, "Shh. You never know who's listening outside the door."

Chapter Twenty-Eight

WILLIAM MACLEOD

MacLeod pushed the door open a sliver. *Who is Annaliese talking to?*

Standing barefoot in her shift, Annaliese roasted her poppet's hand over a candle flame. "Stupid bastard. I wish you was never born," she growled. "You think I like burning you?"

Barging in, he snatched the toy. "What the devil are you doing?"

Fleeing to crouch in the corner, she covered her face with her battered hands. Her chest visibly pounded. Whenever he forgot about Rob Birch, an unwelcome reminder came. Approaching her slowly, he spoke in a gentle tone he'd use with a wild filly. "I winnae hurt you. Look at me. I'll never burn you."

Lowering her fingers only as far as her nose, she kept her shoulders raised as the *Icarus* creaked.

"You're supposed to be in bed."

Annaliese tore under the covers and raked her scattered little treasures—pebbles, hair ribbons, a half-eaten lump of cheese—against her chest. "You gonna give away my poppet to a good girl?" Swallowing hard, she squeaked, "You gonna whip me?"

Burned wood scent lingered in the air. MacLeod closed his eyes and rubbed his temples. *Rob Birch beat her enough to last three lifetimes.* "No," he said, handing back her doll.

Exhaling in obvious relief, she hugged it tightly, flushing beet red. After a pause, she chewed on her lip. "Pa would whip me something terrible for being bad."

"There's a difference between discipline and cruelty, aye? The former is to guide, and the latter is to humiliate. Tomorrow, I want you to apologize to Mrs. Mercer and tell Rebecca you'll help her look for her cross necklace. Get back in their good graces."

Currents slapped against the waterline below the windows. Her little brows crinkled. "I hate the Mercers."

"You dinna have to like them. You need to mind them. I've spent the last hour trying to smooth things over. Look at me, I'm being very serious now. No more laughing at witchcraft books. Conjuring is a crime, not a joke. I ken someone's aunt who was convicted and burned at the stake."

Annaliese sat up, eyes now wide open. "Could she fly?"

"Of course not. She wasn't really a witch, but because she was eccentric, people viewed her suspiciously. That's why you need to fit in. Watch Rebecca. Behave as she does. Be polite, obedient and quiet."

"Did she turn herself into a frog?"

"What? No, and that's not the point—"

"I bet she could change into a black cat, like it said in the book. She shoulda transfigured when they come to burn her. That's what I woulda done."

He stared at her a beat. "Go to sleep, lass."

After updating his ledger for an hour, he put down his quill and watched her sleep. Her whipped, burned hand rested over her singed doll. *God forbid she ever become a mother.*

Of course, I'm not winning any awards for being a good father, either. MacLeod undressed to his nightshirt. *Did I ever tell Broderick, "I wish you were never born?"* No. But *"You dinna deserve my surname"* came damn close.

Blowing out the candle, he crammed into the hammock, curling into a ball to fit in the drat thing. Staring at the pitched-covered timbers in the ceiling, he listened to the wind gradually gain strength. Annaliese snored softly, unaware of the storm rising around her.

If only the lad had resembled Fiona—it might have been easier then. But wasna that the same logic Rob Birch used to brutalize Annaliese? Am I different from Rob Birch? Not as violent, but I taught Broderick to cower.

Heavy rain thumped against the portholes, waves crashed against the ship and men called orders to lower the sails. The girl thrashed in her bed.

"Annaliese?"

Motionless now, she resumed a quiet slumber. *If only I could silence my own mind*, he thought, raking his fingers through his hair.

"Run," she shouted, springing from bed. Dashing to the darkest corner, she cowered behind her trembling hands.

MacLeod rolled off his hammock, crossing the ray of moonlight to shake her awake.

"No!" she yelled, biting his hand.

With a yelp, he let go and she crawled in the opposite direction, beneath his swinging hammock. He grabbed her bare foot, but she kicked his chin with all her might.

"Damn it, Annaliese, wake up. It's a dream," he said, clawing her back over the oak floorboards, keeping her from the door. "Wake up, lass," he said, shaking her shoulders.

Annaliese thrashed in a disoriented manner, like a threatened beast, then screeched loud enough to wake the dead.

"What's wrong?" Seamus ran into the room, rubbing his eyes. Other people stirred in the 'tween deck, with similar questions. The hull rose, then crashed down with a loud crack.

Now fully awake, Annaliese scanned the room. Her nightshirt stuck to her trembling, sweat-soaked body. MacLeod said, "'Tis only a bad dream." He called to the grumbling passengers through the open door. "Apologies."

"Again?" someone muttered. "What's wrong with that girl?"

"Sounded like a banshee crying for the murdered," said Seamus. Lightning flashed. "Your hand's bleeding, sir."

Wiping it on his nightshirt, MacLeod tried to make light of the situation. "Annaliese, your bite is as bad as your bark."

Her eyes grew wet. "I ain't mean to be bad. I'm even bad in my sleep."

"Oh, no, no, sweetheart. I'm trying to joke."

Seamus stared between Annaliese's mouth, wet with blood, and MacLeod's bitten hand and made the sign of the cross as he left.

That wasna a good sign.

Lightning flashed through the windows. MacLeod stood and gripped the doorframe for balance, watching rain drip through the open hatch in the hall before a sailor shut them in the dark. Annaliese hid in the shadows between her trunk and the bed, knees drawn in.

"You're safe. What were you dreaming?" MacLeod knelt beside her, but she recoiled.

Her breath wafted like smoke. Rocking on her heels, the rain grew louder.

"You're soaked. Dinna catch a chill."

Gently tugging off her damp nightgown, he toweled her dry, noting her bruises had faded to a sickly yellowish green. *If only her memories could fade.* The floor shifted as he chose a fresh nightgown from her trunk and tried to help her dress. She skitted away trembling like a rabbit.

"I'm not good at this. My wife handles all the nightmares. I wish I had one of her hag stones. Dinna fash. You're safe."

Rain dripped through cracks in the ceiling.

"No one's safe," she said.

∞

Sunlight spilled into the room, casting a warm glow as they readied. Annaliese dressed quietly as MacLeod splashed his face with washing water from a jug. He hummed as he took a short, bristled brush and mixed lather in a small bowl. Staring into the circular mirror hanging on the wall, he raised his chin to brush the foam on his whiskers.

Ambling over, she said, "Pa *never* used soap, just his knife."

"Sounds unpleasant," he said, dabbing foam on her nose.

Wiping it off with a chuckle, she grew quiet and gnawed on her thumbnail. "I'm real sorry for biting you."

"Ack, people get nightmares." MacLeod shaved meticulously with his straight razor, wiping the dark red hairs on a small towel.

Annaliese wandered to the window, staring into the blue. "Pa let Sam climb into bed if he had a nightmare, but if I did, he'd whip me something fierce for waking him. I guess no man's gonna love his wife's bastard."

MacLeod paused with the blade over his neck, staring into the mirror.

"You taught Ma to read, right? What was she like?"

Eleanor took a feather quill and stroked her cleavage, never taking her eyes off me. He cleared his throat. "More interested in fun than learning letters." He splashed his face clean, patting it dry.

"Not lessons. What was she *like*?"

"Bonny, witty and impulsive, which is why your father loved her. All traits you inherited. Make your bed."

Annaliese smiled, then straightened her blanket. "Did you like her?"

Slowly, he cleaned his razor. "Eleanor was my lord's mistress."

MacLeod checked his image in the mirror once more, then powdered his hair. He didna like all the fuss, but it was imperative he looked proper when representing the interests of Lord Hallewell. Sliding *Justice* in her sheath, he took a deep breath. He wouldna enjoy the upcoming task, but it was necessary.

"Flogging on board," called the bosun, as they stood on the quarterdeck to watch.

Gentlemen donned their grizzled wigs, and mothers pushed their children forward to witness justice and learn from it. Annaliese stood quietly between MacLeod and Seamus, watching Mr. Grubb strip off his fine navy coat and linen shirt to expose a back covered in moles and roles of fat.

Mr. Grubb's wrists were fastened to the mast shrouds to keep him from flying forward. Ordinary sailors weren't often treated to an officer's flogging. Crew mates elbowed and nudged for a better view, creating a wave of worn gray and blue coats moving on the deck.

Captain Adams rolled up his sleeves, standing a yard behind Grubb with his black leather cat-o'-nine-tails. "Cornelius Grubb, you confessed to having committed slander against William MacLeod and thereby Lord George Hallewell, this vessel's lawful owner. You will receive thirty-nine lashes."

A murmur went through the crowd, splitting their gaze between Grubb, strung up like a beast, and MacLeod, stone-faced and still. Annaliese smirked until MacLeod's rough pinch on the area between her shoulder and neck wiped her grin away.

Captain Adams, a good foot taller than Grubb, struck the first lash. Each leather strand had little knots on the end that dug deep, leaving pink welts.

MacLeod subtly darted glances at the others' reactions. Seamus watched with rapt attention, his fingers steepled by his lips. A few sailors who had had run-ins with Grubb savored the role reversal, but most sailors huddled in a group and scowled at the girl.

Captain Adams waited fifteen seconds between each blow for the full pain to register. Clouds swept overhead, casting dark and light shadows across the deck as Mr. Grubb moaned at the lash. Women winced at the whoosh of each swing, then cast dark looks toward Annaliese, who was shrewd enough to notice.

"How come everyone's mad at *me*?" she whispered to Seamus.

Seamus glimpsed over his shoulder. "Come here to me."

Annaliese leaned in. MacLeod strained to hear, too. Seamus whispered, "You get accused of stealing Rebecca's cross but somehow Mr. Grubb gets whipped? I'm not saying it, Miss Cameron, but Mr. Grubb's friends say it's witchy, like you cast a protection spell on yourself or maybe cast an ill wish on him."

Her eyes bulged and her voice seemed incredibly loud. "I ain't no old witch. Witches can fly. If I could fly, I'd go to the top of the mast for fun."

Jesus, Joseph and Mary, is she trying to get hung? A few passengers glanced over.

"Wheest," MacLeod snapped, and they clammed up. Annaliese withered at his glare.

The light breeze stopped completely, and the ship went dead still. Mr. Grubb's flabby skin hung like shredded meat, staining his white breeches with blood. It made a sharp contrast to the blueness of the calm sea.

MacLeod tapped his fingers on his claymore, monitoring the increasingly angry reactions in the crowd. *Damn it. I cannae fight every sailor. I need them on my side.* "Enough," called MacLeod after twenty lashes.

Members of the crew jerked their heads and whispered. Reverend Mercer seemed to nod in approval at his show of grace.

MacLeod spoke to Grubb with a sharp tone. "Next time, hold your tongue in matters of which you aren't privy."

"Aye, sir," Mr. Grubb said, eyes frosty.

Captain Adams flung Mr. Grubb his shirt. "I wouldn't have shown you such mercy."

Surgeon Johnsson handed Mr. Grubb a flask and helped him down the hatch toward the sick berth past gossiping passengers climbing down to the 'tween deck. Sailors returned to work, nodding to MacLeod in a sign of respect.

Once alone, MacLeod grabbed Annaliese and Seamus and knocked their heads together. "I want no talk about flying, spells or any witchcraft nonsense from either of you. Savvy?"

"Yes, sir." They rubbed their skulls.

"Seamus, if any sailor starts rumors about Annaliese, tell me immediately."

"Aye, sir."

"And you," he pointed at Annaliese, causing her to raise her shoulders to her ears. "Practically shouting you want to fly? Are you cork-brained? Shut your gob and stay out of trouble."

Rubbing the back of his neck, MacLeod focused on problem solving. "Go get the Bible and we'll read it on the 'tween deck where everyone can see. Off with the pair of you."

As she left to retrieve the Bible, a voice in the shadows hissed, "Witch."

Chapter Twenty-Nine

LADY MARGARET

London

"Margaret, I'll see you in my bedchamber," Lord Hallewell said.

Ugh, what does he want? Lowering her risqué novel, she glimpsed his expression and realized he was serious. *How long since we shared a bed? How old is our youngest son now? Eight?*

Lady's maids prepared her as she steeled herself. She washed off her makeup in rose water, then sat while the servants unpinned her hair extensions because Lord Hallewell preferred her to be natural. *No; he prefers me to be vulnerable.* Like the heroine in her novel, she made the tactical choice to submit.

Inhaling deeply, she placed her hand on the door connecting her room to his. *If only Percy was on the other side ...* She opened the door to a manservant plucking hairs from Lord Hallewell's nostrils.

Lady Margaret hated everything about her husband: the spread of his middle-aged male paunch, the slope of his pale shoulders, the sparse hairs scattered across his chest in search of a better home. God, his very breathing irritated her.

"Come closer," he said, waving off his servant and leaning against the bedpost. "Let me see your teeth."

Ah. He summons me for a curtain lecture. Faking a smile, she said, "How do they look, my lord?"

"Expensive. I seem to recall cutting off your allowance. Explain this phenomenon."

"My teeth were infected, my lord. Would you have me die?"

"Stop your histrionics. Have I ever denied you a single thing? Ever? At least until you went behind my back to smuggle slaves, which left us open to scandal."

She rolled her eyes. His body stiffened in reaction to her disrespect. "It appears I need to further tighten your leash."

"My lord, the *Icarus* incident happened in June. It's autumn. Do you wish to condemn your wife to rags and misery? I'm not an extravagant person, I only want what is my due."

"Oh, you'll get your due," he said coolly.

Retreating a step, she noted the firelight flickering against the wall, making his shadow taller. George seemed different, stronger. She didn't like it.

"How was Lord Percy's father?" he asked.

"What an odd thing to ask. You know he's dead."

"Lord Percy certainly didn't mourn his passing very long."

"They were estranged, apparently. Alexander would know more than I, they're friends."

Lord Hallewell took his ever-present glass and poured a drink. "A guest at Lady Granger's ball mentioned he saw you walking with the former earl at Bartholomew Fair. What were you chatting about? More ill-conceived business ventures? Disrobe."

Gazing up with just her eyes, she willed her face to stay unreadable.

"Please," he said.

Slowly she untied her robe to collect her thoughts, leaving her shift on. "My lord, forgive me. I heard rumors that the earl was going to challenge you to a duel over his son, so I spoke with him. The boy is permanently disfigured, you know."

"Lord Percy's hardly a boy, and he gives the impression of being fully functional. Was this a chance meeting with the earl, then?"

How much does he know? "No. I sought contact."

"Without my knowledge. It's my place to handle such things, not yours."

Striding toward the fire, she said, "Rather than vomit in a shrub and hide, I preferred to speak bluntly with the earl, and it worked. He no longer wanted to duel with you. Thanks to me, cooler heads prevailed."

"Well, you are an expert at coldness. Remove the shift as well."

You don't scare me. I'll be Percy's wife soon. Angling away from him, she undressed.

"You were seen with the earl the same day he was murdered, and the first I hear about it is at a card game? I laughed it off as a coincidence, obviously, but given MacLeod's overzealous treatment of Percy, that opens our family to damaging gossip. MacLeod is gone and I can't protect our family from scandal when you act surreptitiously."

"Your logic is absurd. You expect me to somehow predict a man I spoke with for five minutes at a fair will be murdered by highwaymen on the same day? I'm not Fiona."

His jaw tightened. "You don't even feign remorse about any of it? Going behind my back, exposing us to gossip, keeping secrets from me? You seem to be confused who is the husband in this relationship, but I'll remedy it. On your belly."

Bending over the bed, she felt the cold sheets on her skin. *Fine. Reassert your manhood. It will be over in two minutes and then I can have peace.*

Plucking the earl's doghead cane from beneath his pillow, he dropped it by her face.

Lady Margaret sprung from the bed. "Where did you get that?"

"I won it at Lady Granger's ball. Lord Percy's terrible at cards." Gripping the cane, he said, "Now you tell me everything you've been up to, or I swear to Christ you won't be sitting."

"Why are you so cruel?" she asked, seeking to flee. "I rescued you from a duel."

His lordship wouldn't let her pass. "Bollocks." Tossing the locket with Eleanor's portrait on the bed, he said, "Do not confuse my indifference for stupidity. Did you really think I haven't been watching you, given your recent behavior? Or that MacLeod is the only resource at my disposal? There are countless people loyal to me. Did you assume I wouldn't notice new teeth, or my missing locket—which I paid an exorbitant amount to retrieve from the barber-surgeon—or that you're parading around in a new dress I didn't buy you?" He pinned her face down on the bed as she struggled. "Or I wouldn't discover you disappeared with Lord Percy in the gardens at our Oxford estate?" Lord Hallewell swung the cane across her rump with a loud crack.

"Stop," she cried. "We did nothing but talk."

"You think I'm an idiot? I'm done letting you soil my household's honor with your misdeeds," he said, walloping her again.

"Hypocrite. You're bringing back Eleanor and your little bastard."

"My lady, are you safe?" Her maid cracked open the door.

"Get out," Lord Hallewell said. The door quickly closed. "How many times should I cane you? Five times? One for each year you let Eleanor and my natural daughter suffer through a similar fate while you kept the letter from me? Who's the cruel one?"

He hit her again, then dropped the cane on the bed, the bronze dog fangs grinning at her. Lord Hallewell backed away, and his ragged breath slowed while she battled angry tears from falling. Rising with as much dignity as she could muster, she glimpsed in the mirror. Red welts were already blooming into violet bruises. Tying on her robe, she said, "Yes, I intercepted Eleanor's letter and kept it secret. Why should you get to hold the love of your life when you killed mine?"

Lord Hallewell gaped, bewildered. "What are you talking about?"

"Wasn't it enough you bound me into matrimony and stole my son's inheritance? I loved Colonel Wilkes. You had Fiona lure him away so MacLeod could kill him, because God forbid you allow me happiness. God forbid you soil your own hands to kill my lover, you bloody coward."

"I never would have done such a thing. Is that why Lord Percy taunted MacLeod about Wilkes dancing with Fiona? Is Lord Percy slyly filling your ears with this poison?"

"Shall we discuss underhanded dealings? The gardeners found Wilkes' Order of the Garter wrapped in Fiona's shawl. You swore to me you had nothing to do with his disappearance. Will they find a full skeleton if they keep digging? Your own misdeeds soil your household's honor more than anything I ever did."

Lord Hallewell scratched his neck. "Let me explain—"

"I married a monster."

George grabbed her arm. "I swear to you, I never killed Wilkes. MacLeod said it was an accident, a fight over Fiona. It all happened so quickly. I should have burned the shawl, but my mind grew muddled. The ground was open already, and I threw them in. MacLeod's a good man. He's like my brother. I helped him hide the murder. He'd do the same for me."

"You truly are a dolt. Your *brother* MacLeod had your precious Eleanor sent to the colonies."

Lord Hallewell seemed disoriented, and a rash dotted his neck. "What nonsense are you spewing?"

"You take MacLeod's word as God's truth, but I don't. I never cared to learn why your mistress ended up in Virginia, but since you sent him off to bring her back, I made my own inquiries. That's what Percy and I were discussing in Oxford. He had his solicitor research her court records. Did you know Eleanor stole my earrings? MacLeod found out, had her arrested and shipped her off to the colonies."

"You lie." Lord Hallewell batted her words away with his hand.

"Who do you think filed the papers? William MacLeod wrote the indentured contract, signed it and sold her off."

"William would never betray me."

"Go ask your friend the Lord Mayor. Your paramour was a thief. She used you. You can verify it with one trip to the Old Bailey. Or interview Eleanor's servants, as I did."

"I don't understand." George loosened his jabot. "It can't be. You're a liar."

"I wonder how MacLeod discovered my stolen earrings? Undoubtedly during one of his voluminous visits with her, with your permission, of course. Teaching her to *read*. Your best friend sold your mistress to the colonies. Why? To protect you? Or maybe his own secrets? Is Eleanor's bastard even yours?"

His gasps grew shallow, and the rash spread across his cheeks. "You shut your mouth," he said, leaning against the wall.

She moved closer. "I warned you MacLeod is a Judas, but what do I know? I'm only the rich widow you blackmailed into marriage. You sent him off to fetch your mistress. Idiot. I'm curious how they'll pass the time on the long voyage home? Reading?"

Lord Hallewell clawed at his jabot.

"Does your skin crawl, George?"

"I'll kill him. I'll kill MacLeod," he gasped. Leaning against his night table, he struggled for air. *If only he keeled over from heart palpitations.*

"You'll kill him? Please. MacLeod will hew a valley through your brain before you draw your weapon."

His nails dug into his cheeks. "I'll find a—another man to fight in my place. Wilkes' son."

Chapter Thirty

WILLIAM MACLEOD

It took about a week, but the routine of ship life returned to some semblance of order. Captain Adams assigned Mr. Grubb and two drunken sailors the tedious task of sitting in a boat all day to scrape off barnacles from the hull and check for leaks above the waterline. MacLeod suspected the captain felt the need to keep Mr. Grubb as isolated as possible to prevent him from stirring up trouble with the other sailors prone to superstition.

Thankfully, Annaliese settled into a few hours of school each day before getting into mischief, giving him the privacy he required.

It's time. Drinking whiskey to steady himself, he rummaged beneath his clothes to the very bottom of his trunk, where he had hidden Eleanor's journal. He knew you should never keep the evidence, but he was curious. Inhaling its musty leather, he tried to remember Eleanor's scent. *French perfume, like cloves and jasmine.* Cracking open the book, he felt humbled reading his own inscription.

Remember to reflect.

~~William~~

He noted his scratched-out name. *Suppose I deserved it. What an arrogant shite I was.* Flipping through the diary, he heard Eleanor's voice jump from each page.

∽

Grimbly Manor, Oxford

'Twas the summer of 1729. Setting up the barrel near the well, I lifted my skirts high and began to dance in the water, rubbing my bare feet against the linens to ground out the spots of dried sauces and wine, when I noticed Lord Hallewell pretending to read a book but ogling me. Perhaps he'll be bolder today? "If you're going to watch, my lord, come out from behind the tree. No need to be sneaky."

His lordship's shocked face was laughable. Not many people challenge Lord Hallewell. Dressed impeccably with a powdered wig, gray velvet coat and silk hose, the man was miles above the ruffians I usually dallied with. This could be fun.

"I was just—I beg your pardon—I was reading a rather risqué novel. Perhaps you'd care to borrow it?"

"They taught me laundry in the orphanage, not letters," I said. "But you can tell it to me."

"Can't read?" he asked, stunned.

"Not everyone is highborn as you, my lord." Rich men like to be reminded of their importance, dinna they? Smiling, I continued dancing on his dirty linens. "Dinna tell Lady Margaret I'm doin' it this way. She'll have my head on a platter."

His lordship coughed at the mention of his wife. "She's in London with the children."

"And you're alone in the countryside with me."

"Indeed. Well, not with you, obviously, but we are both standing here. You know, my solicitor, Mr. MacLeod, can teach you to read. His wife was just a simple farm girl when they met. He taught her."

"Fiona, right?" Everyone had heard the rumors not to cross Mr. MacLeod or his witch wife. "No need to bother him," I said. I didna need a curse placed on my head. George must have seen some fear in my face.

"Oh, he's just gruff. He's very loyal to me. It's settled. He'll tutor you immediately."

Not even a rich lord would pay for a servant's education out of the kindness of his heart. Perhaps I could become more than a laundress. *Perhaps a mistress.* "Make yourself useful and hand me the soap." George looked startled. It was a risk to speak to him impudently, but men like novelty, too, dinna they?

"Eh ... here?" He found the slippery stuff, but it fell into the barrel. My lord would want a chase. Gentlemen like to hunt. Reaching for the soap, I smacked his hand. It felt softer than a bairn's arse. I dinna think he was ever slapped once in his pampered little life.

"My lord, the last thing I need is to have to remove water stains from your fine coat."

Bending over, I searched the soapy water, making sure to give him a good look down my bosom. Before I found the soap, he found my mouth and kissed me. Lord Hallewell tasted like wealth. Cream and sugar and wine.

Yanking down his trousers past his bum, his excitement was evident.

∞

MacLeod lowered the book. *My God, should I even be reading this? Ack, Eleanor's dead, and she wasna modest to begin with, but still, the last thing I want to read about is my employer's sexual conquests.*

Skipping ahead, he scanned the sections about teaching her to read and write, and her increasingly tumultuous love affair with Lord Hallewell. And then the violent snow. He took a deep, pained breath, moving to their last conversation.

∞

London, 1730

TO RESCUE A WITCH

Scratching at the brown serge I wore along with the other one hundred twenty-one female convicts in Newgate Gaol awaiting trial, I heard the turnkey drink a glass of spirits before inhaling the foul stench to gather us.

"Dead Man's Walk," he said, leading us through the underground tunnel past a Bible and candlestick chained to the wall.

If stealing anything over thirty-nine shillings meant death, then they're going to burn me to a crisp and sell gallows souvenirs while people cheer. No one pities a mistress who steals jewelry.

Sniffles and coughs mingled with the pelting rain as I shuffled in my irons into the courtroom. It reeked of vinegar and burned herbs, to stop gaol fever from spreading. Rickety seating creaked as people in the galleries craned to hear our sob stories while the Lord Mayor sat high above.

Then I saw him. William MacLeod wore a powdered wig and black robe, a true barrister. "Keep your gob shut, and for God's sake, look contrite," MacLeod whispered.

"George is saving me." I stupidly searched for him in the crowd.

"Eleanor, I'm here by my own accord." MacLeod caught the Lord Mayor's gaze. "She pleads guilty, your Honor." He tapped his chin with two fingers.

The Lord Mayor mimicked the gesture and nodded. "Never have I met a more proper subject for parts beyond the seas."

I stood in shock. I prepared for death, not indentured servitude. I'd be trapped in a hostile land forever. *Should I plead the belly?* When I thought I'd hang, it had been a simple decision. Let the babe die with me. I'd never put my child in an orphanage. But shipped to the wilderness? How would I raise a bairn there?

"You may be a thief, but I winnae let you die for it."

I spit in his face. Did he expect kisses? "You told George. Why?"

MacLeod wiped his face with a folded handkerchief. "My job is to protect the family. This is your half of the indenture contract. Dinna lose it."

Such a condescending man. I'd never lose papers holding my freedom. "I can ruin you. Tell the world about what you and your witch wife did to Colonel—"

He covered my mouth. "Think before crossing the person who saved you from hanging."

I nodded and he let go.

"You'll be working at Matthew Crowan's plantation in Virginia Colony. I negotiated a reduced term of four years, and at the end, you get your freedom and ten acres. If you want a clean break, this is how to do it."

"I think it's you who wants the clean break, Mr. MacLeod."

"It's for the best, Eleanor. Lord Hallewell already has a wife and legitimate children. I wager you'll want your own children someday and not have to send them away like all his other bastards."

MacLeod knew how to cut me to the core. Handing me a carpet bag, he said, "Here's a blanket, a journal, some quills and ink, smoked meat and forty shillings. You might have to bribe the guards."

How can he be awful and good to me at the same time? I didna understand him. "Can I write a letter for you to give to George?"

"May I, and no." He nodded to the bailiff to remove me.

"And if I write to him, anyway?"

William MacLeod grew serious as the grave. "Dinna contact Lord Hallewell or I guarantee you will regret it. Understood?"

"Aye." I understood completely. I ken too much about MacLeod's witch wife.

<hr />

William MacLeod slammed the book and clasped Fiona's protective charm tied around his neck. No one aboard ken anything about his wife's dabbles with magic. His heart thrummed in his chest.

He ken he should stop wearing the charm. As much as he thought himself a man of reason, Fiona's powers of predicting the future were uncanny, and she said a storm was coming to kill him. *Hold fast. They'll never see the charm beneath my shirt.*

Pulling on his coat, he slid Eleanor's journal inside the deep pockets and went outside. Cauldrons of water boiled over deck fires where heaps of soiled sheets, shirts, petticoats, breeches and sanitary napkins were getting beaten clean by sailors and womenfolk. As he hopped over the river of dirty water flowing beneath the clothes hung on the rigging to dry, he chuckled. *How appropriate to pitch the laundress' diary on washing day.* He extracted it from his pocket and tossed it overboard.

That night, he tucked Annaliese in for the night and shivered, feeling a twinge of guilt. But he needed to protect his family—and himself—more than she needed to read her mother's memories. Perhaps the shiver had more to do with the fact the temperature had dropped twenty degrees in less than twenty minutes.

Annaliese popped her face out from beneath the covers and blew on her hands. "How come it's cold all the sudden?"

"*Why* is it cold, not 'how come' it's cold," he corrected her. Lifting her trunk lid to grab a spare blanket, he jumped back. "What the devil? Damn it, Annaliese. Why are you hiding food in your trunk? Roaches are crawling everywhere."

Covering her face, she recoiled. "I ain't steal nuthin'. People leave food all the time. I just collect it from the floor."

Slamming the trunk shut, he slapped black bugs off his shirt and watched them crawl into the crevices between the timbers, then grabbed his tartan from his trunk and handed it to her. *How many days until we arrive in London? This girl is driving me mad.*

Annaliese sniffed the air and cocked her head. "Something on fire?"

He smelled it, too. "Stay put." Burning wood permeated the air. "What the devil?" MacLeod jogged into the 'tween deck. Half-dressed people collided with each other in the dark, coughing into their arms. They crowded the hatches open to the gray sky. Pushing past them, his eyes watered from the gray billowing smoke that overpowered the foggy air. Visibility was barely three quarters of a mile.

"Who's on lookout?" he asked.

"Sail ho." Mr. Grubb blew his bulbous red nose and ambled forward in a zigzag.

MacLeod scowled. "Mr. Grubb, are you drunk?"

"Blastee, I'm sober as a ..."

"As piss. Get out of my way."

MacLeod shoved him aside and his jaw dropped. A flaming three-mast ship roared less than a mile away. A sheet of fire flew into the air, revealing wooded mountains close by.

MacLeod hollered, "All hands ahoy! If we dinna stop the *Icarus*, we'll crash into the other ship or ashore. Wake the captain. Lower the sails. Heave anchor, lads."

A screech of hemp sounded as the men lowered the flapping mainsails to reduce speed. Men scrambled with handspikes to cat the massive anchor.

A sailor yelled, "Heave and raise the dead!"

The anchor fell eight fathoms below, floating them backward toward the shore.

"Look out!"

In their struggle to escape a collision, no one noticed the mountain of ice. A loud crack followed by a sudden lurch sent crew mates tumbling as chunks of slush slid across the deck. Men yelled indiscernibly. A bell rang.

"Jesus, Joseph and Mary, we scraped a bloody iceberg?"

Seamus burst above deck. "Captain's calling all hands below to bale ship."

Keep your head, MacLeod. He raced behind Seamus into a chaotic scene overtaking the 'tween deck. Children cried and men raced with buckets in both directions. Ahanu held a bleating goat over his shoulders, which he handed off to another sailor.

MacLeod climbed into the orlop and blinked into the hazy lantern light. Water gushed as he moved aft, and sailors raced to fother the leak with canvas. Icy water poured into his boots.

Captain Adams stood in nothing but his nightshirt and boots and yelled, "Lighten the load. Throw the tobacco overboard."

Sailors hauled away tobacco barrels as other men frantically yanked the chain pump to remove water from the bilge. Carpenters hammered okum and rope yarn with mallets into the cracked hull as the water kept rising beneath their feet.

MacLeod said, "We have to get the women and children off the ship."

"Aye," agreed the captain.

MacLeod returned to his cabin, finding it empty. "Damned girl."

He climbed the deck and found Annaliese wrapped in his tartan, clinging to her burned doll. Like everyone else, she stared over the rail at the ice and fire. Scooping her up, he loaded her with the other women and children clasping their belongings into longboats as sailors from the flaming ship in the distance screamed into the night.

※

"God tests," Reverend Mercer said, at dawn on a beach littered with trunks, barrels and decomposing bodies from the other ship, burned beyond recognition. A hawk flew over them and into the towering larch, maple and birch trees, bright yellow and red.

The *Icarus*, hauled onto shore the night before, lay on its side, useless as a beached whale.

MacLeod wrapped his plaid around Annaliese's shoulders and fastened his clan brooch snug beneath her chin to shield her from the wind. Passengers were cold, wet and scared, but they survived—unlike the poor wretches from the other ship—and most had saved at least some of their belongings.

From sunrise to starfall, there were no idle hands. Carpenters checked the weak spots, identifying the warped sections of the hull's skins while the crew chopped nearby trees. Fortunately, a freshwater stream ran from the craggy rocks above and the salmon and trout were plentiful.

Women and children made camp, keeping wary eyes trained on the dark forest. They put ripped sails on top of layers of pine needles and leaves to make beds. MacLeod showed Annaliese how to turn his long plaid into a sleeping bag.

Nightfall came early. A wet mist covered them all in a cold, salty film as they huddled for warmth around the bonfire.

Grubb sat tied to a tree fifty feet away blubbering, "Blastee, what a cursed voyage." His back was still raw. Captain Adams had personally lashed him until his arm grew tired.

Screeching predatory birds interrupted the rhythmic surf as the bonfire crackled.

Surgeon Johnsson said, "Good location to tell ghost stories, ja?"

As Mrs. Mercer tucked in Rebecca, she complained, "Annaliese already screams with nightmares as it is, don't scare her more."

Seemingly mortified, Annaliese retreated beneath the covers to cuddle her doll.

Please dinna dream tonight, Annaliese.

"Then how about an Old Norse story about Freyja and Odin," said Johnsson.

Reverend Mercer snorted. "Pagan rubbish."

Captain Adams came by with lots. "Who wants first watch with me?"

"I'll do it," MacLeod said. His mind was too restless to sleep.

Annaliese grabbed his arm. "Don't leave me."

"Dinna fash. I'll be near."

But her guarded blue eyes pleaded, so he sat beside her and whispered, "Do you want to hear my wife's protective saw against evil?"

She nodded.

"From ghoulies and ghosties, long-leggety beasties, and things that go bump in the night, Good Lord, deliver us."

"Amen," she whispered.

Giving a reassuring nod, he left to patrol the perimeter as Captain Adams guarded the camp. Stepping over the spongy moss sticking to the margins of the rocky shore, his mind assessed the risks closer to home. *Keep a better eye on Annaliese. Keep her busy and quiet. Make her pray publicly.* MacLeod scratched his face, annoyed at his fast-growing beard. *It dinna take long for me to look like a proper Highlander.*

Charred remnants of the other ship washing ashore made plain the dangers of the sea, and he squeezed the charm around his neck. *Is this Fiona's vision? Granted, an iceberg isna a storm, but the result is still a shipwreck. Did her charm save our ship? Please, God, get us home safe.* Picking up a black stone, he pitched it into the frothy waves.

Why did he always dismiss her second sight? Fiona begged him to avoid London all those years ago, begged him to steer clear of the colonies, but Lord Hallewell's wishes always came first. *Perhaps if I had heeded her pleadings, there wouldn't be blood on our hands.*

He walked past axes left in the stump beside the logs on the shore, coughing at the sawdust. It had been a productive day. The carpenters, to their credit, were doing a fine job fixing the hull. They estimated it would take about a month until they could raise the ship on a high tide and head home.

How can I protect Fiona from Lady Margaret's whims when we're stuck on an island in the Labrador Sea? What if the sailors become mutinous against Annaliese? Jesus, Joseph and Mary, these womenfolk are going to be the death of me.

MacLeod nodded at Captain Adams as he approached the camp, now a cacophony of snores and farts as people cuddled for warmth beneath old sails. Separated from the other children, Annaliese lay curled in a tight ball. A light breeze blew sand, and the grains stuck in her tangled hair. Tucking his plaid under her chin, he traced a finger over his clan brooch then kissed her forehead. "Hold fast, Annaliese," he whispered.

A wolf howled a lonely cry. MacLeod scanned the forest, feeling the hairs on his neck rise. Grabbing *Justice* from her sheath, he stood beside the freshly dug graves, readying to protect her from the wild things.

Chapter Thirty-One

ANNALIESE

Pa kept his hunting knife sharp as a thorn bush that pricked when you walked past. Drizzle from the evening storm tapped the greased paper window, seeping through the edges. His whiskey stunk from across the room.

"Don't flinch."

Aiming his knife, he turned her face into the bullseye in his newest stupid game that made no sense.

Pa's muscles tensed and he flung. Sucking in her breath, the steel whizzed past and bounced off the wall. A strangled cry left her lips as the knife dropped at her dirty feet. *Hold fast, Annaliese.*

Lifting the knife, he smiled. "You think a protective spell's gonna save you? MacLeod ain't care 'bout you. Ever curious what he done to me? Don't trust that man, Annaliese Birch."

Her skin grew sweaty staring at a bullet hole in the middle of Pa's forehead. Dragging a ball and chain behind him, he stood behind his imaginary toe line, then aimed at her pounding chest. "Don't fucking flinch this time."

Blinking at the flash of metal, heat rushed to her waist and a red stain spread across her shift. She jerked the handle, but it was stuck good. "Git it out. Git it out!"

Jolting awake, she found a fistful of petticoat twisted in her hand and MacLeod's arm across her chest. MacLeod whispered, "Just another dream."

Mrs. Mercer said, "Heavens. Is the child stricken?"

Muffled voices grumbled: "Not again." "Shut it, girl." "Stop screaming."

Annaliese caught her breath, feeling a wave of fear and hatred from the people press on her like a brick. Mist rolled out to the sea as the sun rose, revealing Ahanu stewing cod over an enormous cauldron on the beach.

Mr. MacLeod said in his loud voice, "All right, stop this silliness, Annaliese. We've got logs to split and sails to mend, aye? Air your bedding."

Why's he acting like it's my fault? Maybe Pa was right 'bout him. Or maybe everyone's right 'bout me. I ain't worth shit.

As Annaliese folded MacLeod's plaid, her poppet dropped in the sand. Rebecca picked up the doll, examining the blackened wood. "What happened to your baby's hand?" Rebecca stared between Annaliese and the charred bits of ship that kept washing ashore.

"Oh, she was being bad, so I burned her. I gotta learn her to be good."

Mr. MacLeod's jaw went slack, and she known she made a mistake. Reverend Mercer and his wife exchanged stares as Irish sailors crossed themselves.

Surgeon Johnsson came to her rescue. "Hm, it doesn't appear to be a serious wound, but let's bandage it, ja? Do you have a hair ribbon?" Untying her bun, she handed him her ribbon and he wrapped it around the doll's hand.

Jacqueline, grabbing her own poppet, lightly tapped MacLeod's arm. "Excusez-moi, Monsieur MacLeod, may Annaliese and I play with our babies before we break fast?"

He nodded warily. Annaliese silently thanked God for her friend. They ran partway between the beach and the forest, within adult vision but beyond their earshot.

"You still play with poppets? It's one thing to hold onto a doll at night, but actually playing with it?" *Is this what normal girls do?*

Jacqueline laughed. "Ma chère, you and I are going to have great fun together." Her brown eyes twinkled with mischief.

A shadow cast between them. Annaliese put her fists on her hips. "Stop following me, Seamus. You're worse than a mosquito on shit."

"Oh, for the love of heaven, I have orders. I'm your chaperone, and you know it."

"MacLeod's right there. The ship ain't moving. Where you think I'm going?"

Jacqueline batted her thick lashes. "Seamus, could you please step a few paces back for privacy? I'd appreciate it greatly."

His freckled face reddened. "I'll be over here." He sat in the sand.

Jacqueline hooked her lace-sleeved arm through Annaliese's, walking further away. "I see you have much to say, but cannot due to adult meddling, oui?"

Annaliese nodded.

"Without being obvious, notice how your master constantly watches?"

Annaliese looked at MacLeod, studying maps laid on a trunk. Suddenly aware of being watched, he stared back, folding his arms over his chest. Annaliese broke her gaze.

"I said *without* being obvious, ma chère." Jacqueline laughed. "If you want him to stop watching you, then you must persuade him to trust you, as my maman does me."

"How?"

Jacqueline brushed the sand off Annaliese's shoulders. "What's important to him?"

"He wants me to be perfect, like Rebecca. Obedient, quiet …" Annaliese thrust a finger down her throat and pretended to gag.

"My maman says, 'A lady knows how to get what she wants.' Our sex must be clever in general, but girls our age must be adroit in particular. Show me your baby. How exquisite. What is her name?"

"Charlotte."

"This is Amélie." Jacqueline's poppet had glass eyes, blonde hair nailed to the head, a pink satin dress decorated with ribbons, and matching shoes. "They make us invisible. My cousin Gabrielle taught me this trick. Kiss your baby."

Annaliese's ears grew hot thinking Seamus might tease her, but he was busy picking his cuticles, scanning for witches through the larch trees. She pecked her doll's cheek.

"Adults want good little girls hugging their poppets, not burning them, oui?"

Annaliese hung her head.

"Hold your poppet like a real baby. Like this." Jacqueline cuddled her doll.

Annaliese mimicked, feeling ridiculous. Five weeks ago, she had lain on her back while Mr. Daniel tried to give her a real baby.

Jacqueline kneeled, spreading her pink tulip-embroidered petticoat in a regal display. "Fluff your petticoats like so. A young lady must always act dignified and beautiful, even on a deserted island. Your hair is trying to escape your head. We must fix this."

Annaliese smoothed her wrinkled petticoat with her gloved hands as Jacqueline tied her hair in a neat bun.

"Spy your master *subtly* as you kiss your baby. Notice how he is calm now, and no longer paying attention to you?"

"He do seem relaxed." Annaliese bounced Charlotte on her knee.

"Tell me everything you know about lovemaking."

"What?" She dropped the doll in the sand.

Jacqueline laughed. "Dearest Annaliese, I know you have been with men. Clearly, you want me to know this, or you would not say the things you say."

"I ain't never—"

"You bragged you were practically married; you know all the different words for cock; and you use sexual innuendo in casual conversation. So, tell me."

Don't tell. But what if Jacqueline stops being my friend? "Well, tell me everything *you* known about lovemaking."

The bosun shouted an order, and the men pulled cables adjusting the hull on the beach.

Jacqueline rocked her doll. "Sadly, I only have secondhand knowledge, but I know a lot. My brothers tell me trifling little, obviously, but my older cousins have taken on lovers."

Annaliese jerked her head, touching her parted lips. "I thought women become pariahs if they busy at clicket and ain't married."

Jacqueline smirked. "Only if they are caught. Then it's problematic. Parisians are discreet. Hug your baby."

There's hope for me? Annaliese squeezed her eyelids shut and hugged Charlotte tightly.

"May I join?" Rebecca asked.

"No. Go away."

"Oui, ma chère, but only if you have a poppet."

"I'll get mine." Rebecca ran off.

Jacqueline cradled Amélie. "We have two minutes before she returns. Tell me whatever you want."

Annaliese kissed Charlotte, subtly checking on MacLeod, who was joking with the sailors. Jacqueline was right. They were invisible.

Jacqueline tugged the doll's toe until Annaliese met her eyes. "You can trust me."

Annaliese took a deep breath. "There was a boy named Jack. I thought he loved me but ... it ain't matter none."

"You were engaged, and he betrayed you, oui?" Jacqueline squeezed Annaliese's hand while nodding sympathetically.

Annaliese mirrored the nod, almost feeling like crying. It was the first time in her life she felt safe enough to be herself. "Yes. Reckon I should hate him, and I do, but it's confusing."

Ocean spray hung in the air, moist and sticky. She remembered Jack's warm chest against her rain-soaked skin and felt his lips brush hers, like a ghost kiss.

"Oh, ma chère, you like bad boys. Let me picture him." Jacqueline closed her eyes. "Describe him."

"Fourteen. Handsome, lean and dark like my pa. Strong, too, from working on the river. His eyes was sky blue. He had silver rings and tattoos. Boy, could he kiss." Dropping her chin to her chest, she blushed.

"And his cock?"

"Huge. Unbelievably huge."

"What's huge?" Rebecca came with her button-eyed rag doll.

"The eyes on Annaliese's baby," Jacqueline said, without missing a beat.

"Hmm." Rebecca plopped in the sand, patting her doll over her shoulder. "This is Mary, named for Jesus's virgin mother."

Jacqueline and Annaliese glanced at each other and sighed.

Ahanu rang a bell to eat.

"Annaliese," Mr. MacLeod called.

"Coming."

While passengers grabbed their makeshift trenchers, MacLeod pulled Annaliese aside and hid her poppet beneath the bedding.

"I ken you were being honest about burning the doll, but some things are left better unsaid. You'll frighten the sailors."

Annaliese tilted her head. "Why would grown men fear me?"

"When bad things happen, people want someone to blame. Dinna give them cause to mistrust you. Let's eat."

They headed toward the food line. "What's the French girl's name again?"

"Jacqueline."

"She seems like an excellent influence. You play nicely together."

Chapter Thirty-Two

FIONA

Scotland

Oh my God, no. Fiona's pulse quickened as she exited the coach. Her heart had been pounding since her newest vision two nights ago. A double-headed serpent coiled around her son, James, biting his face. Her younger sons didna understand why she packed them up and headed to Glasgow, but now her darkest fears were coming to pass.

Lachlan and Hamish ran ahead, pushing through soldiers and onlookers crowded outside her husband's law office. Broderick lingered by her side, holding her hand, fearless as a kitten.

A bell jingled as she opened the door. Fiona gasped at the utter destruction. Fallen cabinets, broken locks, ripped parchment papers and legal books littered the hardwood floor. All the strong boxes were gone.

A blond redcoat interrogated her battered son as his worried wife looked on.

"James." Fiona touched the large knot on his forehead, then hugged him.

"Ow, Mam. What are you doing here?" he asked, rubbing his wound.

"I had a feeling. What happened?"

"Robbers broke in while I was in the backroom. They bound me and stole everything." James blinked back tears, swallowing hard. She kissed his rope-burned wrists.

Nelly said, "When he didna come home at noon, I came to the office and saw the door open. I walked inside ... and found him tied ..." Nelly began to tear up and Fiona hugged her.

"Thank God she wasna here when they came. If anything happened to her ..." James scanned her growing belly and squeezed her hand. "When I track down those bastards, I'm going to bloody kill them."

The soldier said to James, "You're sure they were English, not locals from university?"

"Aye. They had London accents, at least the one with the eye patch did."

Did the robbery have to do with Colonel Wilkes' murder? But William bribed Lady Margaret to stay quiet. I dinna understand. Fiona saw black spots.

"Mam, are you all right?" Broderick grabbed a chair for her.

"It's a wee bit overwhelming," Fiona said between quick gulps, sinking into the seat. Hamish wrapped his arms around her.

"Give her some air," James said. "Lads, start cleaning."

Broderick said, "Why rob a law office when the warehouses at port are teeming with money? I thought thieves wanted gold, not papers."

"The boy makes a good point," said the soldier. "Does your father have any enemies?"

James said, "Our father is a barrister, and an excellent one. He's made many enemies."

Fiona felt nauseous. *Who else wants to hurt us?*

"We'll be on the lookout," said the soldier, slinging his Brown Bess over his shoulder.

James shook his bruised head. "I cannae believe I didna hear them. I should have grabbed my sword. I should have—"

"You're alive," Fiona said.

"I have to notify all Da's clients their secrets are missing. Da put his trust in me and I utterly failed him. Ah, bugger, what a nightmare." James ran a shaky hand through his wild red hair. "It's not safe here and I dinna want Nelly alone in the backroom when I'm at court. Well, you get your wish, Mam. We'll move back with you. Besides, we cannae pay the rent now with the business money stolen."

Fiona covered her mouth with both hands. She stared at James' battered skull. *This dinna make sense. I didna use black magic. I said, "with harm to none."*

Chapter Thirty-Three

ANNALIESE

"Don't stand close to the surf. You'll dirty your petticoat," Rebecca said, primly as ever.

"You ain't the queen of me."

A wave of burning cold water hit, coming midway up Annaliese's calf, leaving a stain on her pale blue skirt. *Figures.*

Lifting a washed-up fishing net, Annaliese jumped at the crabs scrambling back into their holes. This was the first time in two weeks they'd had any free time to wander the shore and Rebecca was ruining it. An odd noise made her spin. "Do you hear dogs barking?"

They froze, pricking their ears.

"This way." Annaliese sprinted past the doomed *Icarus* to an area full of boulders.

Rebecca called, "We shouldn't be out this far. It's not allowed." Annaliese kept going. "I'm telling," Rebecca yelled, running back to camp.

The barking grew louder. Annaliese's foot slipped on the slimy algae, but she climbed the rock right quick. Seamus and Jacqueline joined her. Turning on them, she said, "Ain't you want to tattle on me, too?"

Seamus shrugged. "I want to see the dogs."

Only they weren't dogs. On a flat iceberg fifty feet from shore, plump animals with paws on fins and a long tail instead of legs napped and played. A huge one yawned widely, then dove in, swimming close enough to show his adorable face and long whiskers.

"What are those things?" Annaliese asked, fascinated.

"Selkies," Seamus said.

Jacqueline said, "They're seals, no? Look at the babies." Her voice raised ten octaves as she cooed and pointed to the furry white blobs with big brown eyes.

Seamus said, "My cousins make good money selling their oil and skins. We should tell the captain."

"But they're babies," Annaliese said.

"Money's money, lass."

"Annaliese Cameron," called MacLeod.

Ah, hell. He's using both my names. "Up here."

"I can see that," he said, climbing with Rebecca. "You found the selkies."

Annaliese jumped to another rock a few paces away from MacLeod.

Rebecca cowered behind him. "Ew. What are those revolting creatures?"

Annaliese rolled her eyes. *Back off, Rebecca, MacLeod's mine.*

"Ack, nothing to fear, lass. They say the Fairy Queen disguises herself in seal skins."

Why is he calling Rebecca lass? I'm his lass.

Seamus said, "Well, my cousins never found a single fairy inside a selkie, and they surely would have told the tale had they done so."

Jacqueline kneeled next to Annaliese, laughing. A white-gray seal dove into the water, swimming close to Annaliese. The pup's large brown eyes and heart-shaped nose drew her in, making her giggle. Reaching out, she rubbed its soft, wet fur. The selkie splashed and barked in the pale blue water. "Can we keep her?"

MacLeod laughed. "And what would you do with a pet selkie? We need to get back. I dinna want any of you out this far until we understand our surroundings."

"Look. A shark." Seamus joined their rock and pointed.

A triangular fin cut through a dark patch near a rock thirty feet away. The seal made a break for it but realized the danger too late. In an instant, a slick gray monster burst from the water, showing a mouth rimmed with pink gums spouting six-inch dagger teeth.

"We have to help her!" Annaliese shouted, ready to dive in.

Jacqueline pulled her back. "That's nature, ma chère."

Black eyes rolled back in the shark's head as he chomped the selkie's tummy into bits. Annaliese stared into the pup's terrified eyes as it thrashed trapped in the shark's jaws.

Seamus laughed. "Wait till I write my cousins about this," he said to Jacqueline.

"Stop laughing." Annaliese balled her fist.

Dragging what was left of the baby seal below, the shark left a trail of bright red bubbles.

"Quite savage, aye?" MacLeod said.

Seamus framed his sunburned hands around his mouth, yelling, "Leave some for us. We're hungry, too, mate."

"Stop laughing." Annaliese punched Seamus's jaw, catching him completely off guard. He fell hard on the rock. Grabbing hold of his shirt, she pummeled his face.

"Annaliese," MacLeod roared. He yanked her off, but she kept kicking the air. "What's gotten into you?"

"She's crazy, that's what. Only you would get into a fight over a fish." Seamus's lip bled with a puffy bruise already forming.

"Stop laughing."

Jacqueline pressed her handkerchief to Seamus's lip.

Annaliese felt dizzy, crumpling over her knees. Her gasps grew shallow as hot tears streamed down her cheeks. Feeling everyone stare, she covered her ears and rocked. "Stop laughing. Stop laughing."

"Go back to camp," MacLeod said to the others. "I need to have a wee chat with Annaliese."

The children left, muttering. MacLeod kneeled, searching her eyes. "What is going on in that brain of yours? You've seen animals killed in the wild. Has Seamus been teasing you?"

She peered into his eyes. "That was me."

"What do you mean?"

"I ain't—I don't know how to say it."

She felt so mad she shook, punching her thighs. *How do you say it? How do you say every man in your life was a shark who wanted to drag you under while people laughed?*

MacLeod understood, even without her words, and opened his arms. For the first time, she hugged him tightly.

"No more sharks," he whispered. "They're gone now."

Knuckling away the tears, she forced her jagged breath under control. "Oh, there's plenty sharks," she said, staring at Rebecca in the distance. "I'm gonna be one."

His face darkened. "Annaliese Cameron, the lesson is to avoid sharks, not to become one."

Chapter Thirty-Four

WILLIAM MACLEOD

Reverend Mercer stood beneath a slate sky, his cold eyes narrowing as he surveyed the crowd.

As the repairs dragged into their third week, the *Icarus'* shipwrecked passengers huddled on the outskirts of the wilderness, listening to Reverend Mercer's now daily sermons.

"Why, brothers and sisters, have we been held captive? Pray, tell me."

People shifted uncomfortably in the sand as the surf foamed behind them.

"Because the ship broke?" offered Annaliese.

Jesus, Joseph and Mary, does she ever keep her gob shut? Just like Eleanor.

A few sailors snickered, but the preacher's stern face silenced them. "Just because you don't understand why the wind and the waves are crashing over us, doesn't mean God doesn't understand." Reverend Mercer kept his cold eyes on Annaliese. "God is angry with your sins."

That son of a bitch. MacLeod went rigid.

"Everyone's sins," Reverend Mercer said, now scowling at the whole congregation. "Is it any wonder we've been stuck in the wilderness for weeks, with witches, savages and wolves a stone's throw away? God has granted us the mercy of life and yet you sin, and sin, and sin, and I assure you that sinners are lower than a worm under God's foot."

"How do we get home safely?" begged a man beside his shivering wife in a marigold bodice.

Reverend Mercer answered, "Repent. Anyone who does not walk with Christ will shudder at their fate. And be alert to the daughters of Eve, prone to Satan's whispers."

Tanned sailors pressed forward, listening enthusiastically to Reverend Mercer with nodding heads. Not all men were enthralled. Ahanu leaned against a boulder with his arms folded, while Surgeon Johnsson sat quietly and exhaled through his nostrils. MacLeod sat motionless, feeling his jabot constrict his neck as Mercer seemed to circle his prey.

"I assure you; Lucifer's call is powerful to the weaker sex. Pray that we leave before we lose any souls to covens of hellbrides hiding in the woods." Glowering at the womenfolk, he said, "Watch them. Man is God's representative, and lo, God chastens. If we do not correct our women's sins, I fear God's wrath may manifest in a storm."

Ladies shifted on their feet, avoiding the reverend's gaze.

I'd like to correct Reverend Mercer with my fist. He's going to mushroom fears and provoke violence. I hate it when preachers blame everything bad on women and witches. Will reason ever prevail?

Fiona had told him about the villagers betraying her Aunt Matilda only after the preacher's sermons singled her out. MacLeod felt a tightness in his chest where the sachet dangled. Fiona always protected him, in her own way, but he didna do enough to protect her from the church when the time came. *I didna defend her, just negotiated a quiet punishment, and took my anger out on Broderick. I failed everyone. God, please dinna let me fail Annaliese, too.*

After the sermon, everyone seemed on edge. MacLeod walked along the beach with Annaliese watching her collect shells.

"You think we're stuck here because Rebecca's cross is missing?"

MacLeod did his best to keep a neutral face. "Is there something you want to tell me?"

She rolled the shells in her hand as if feeling their collective weight. "Everyone would be better off if I was dead."

"Annaliese, dinna say such things."

"Ma met my London father when he was married. She was a whore, they did adultery, and I'm a sin. I was born bad. I hate being a bastard," she said, crunching the shells in her fist and throwing them into the violent sea.

A knot formed in his stomach. *Didna I wish Broderick was never born? Does he feel the same self-hatred as Annaliese?*

His thoughts spun before he found his voice. "You're not a sin, Annaliese."

"Don't lie to me. I know my sins is the reason we shipwrecked. How come God made me rotten? Pa's right. The reverend's right. I'm just a worm under God's boot. I'm gonna burn in hell with Ma."

Heat flushed through his tensing muscles. Did this 'man of faith' have any idea how his words impacted the weakest among them? "Let me tell you about God. He made you. You're not a worm, you're His child, and I guarantee you didna cause the shipwreck. For what it's worth, I dinna think your ma's in hell. Everyone sins. People make amends and forgive each other, too."

Annaliese snorted and watched the waves break against the jagged rocks. "You think any of them will forgive me for having nightmares? Doubt it. You think I want to have them?" Clapping the sand off her hands, her tone switched to forced indifference. "Ain't matter none. They hate me, I hate them back."

MacLeod had seen girls like her at the Old Bailey—bitterness transformed into a grudge against the world, leading to a life of crime.

Their conversation weighed on him all day and kept him awake at night. *If I dinna set her straight, she'll be pregnant, arrested or dead by the time she's thirteen. But how do I help her?*

Since he was up anyway, he decided to read. A few books survived the wreck, which were shared to pass the time. Neatly stacked beside the bonfire were travel journals, Marcus Aurelius's *Meditations*, *Robinson Crusoe, Gulliver's Travels*, and Socrates.

That's it.

Shaking Annaliese's shoulder, she jolted awake. "What's wrong? Did I scream again?"

"No," he whispered, "I want to show you something."

Grunting, she rolled over. Nudging her, he said, "Hurry before we miss it."

Annaliese trudged out of her sleep sack with eyes barely opened, and fumbled in her sleepiness to attach hoses to garters and buckle her brown leather shoes. "The one time I don't have a bad dream, he wakes me," she grumbled, wrapping his tartan around herself like a shawl.

Shepherding her past slumbering souls, they ambled to the shore. A sailor on night watch tapped his knuckles to his forehead to MacLeod in greeting, then returned to standing guard.

Annaliese rolled her neck and stared into the dark water.

MacLeod said, "Have you heard of Plato?"

"He work on a plantation?" she asked, tugging his tartan tighter beneath her chin.

"Plato studied with the Greek philosopher Socrates and wrote *The Allegory of the Cave*."

Tapping her foot, she said, "Uh-huh."

Get to the point; you're losing her. "Prisoners lived in a dark cave, chained, such that they only saw the wall in front of them. Behind them was a fire and puppetmen who cast shadows on the wall, telling the prisoners these shadows were the true things. One day, a prisoner escaped. Once outside, he discovered everything the puppetmen told him was wrong. The world was more than just shadows and lies. Now exposed to the light, he'd never want to live back in a cave. Do you understand what the light was?"

"The sun?"

"Knowledge."

Dawn broke the horizon and the fiery red orb illuminating the waves reflected in her eyes, wide and innocent. He noticed the little freckles dotting her nose, the deep look of concentration. *What goes on in her head?*

"Annaliese, I can show you the light, but you have to stop clinging to the cave of your past where Rob Birch filled your head with lies. I can teach you to read. I can give you a moral compass and guide you, but I cannae make you want to become a better person. Only you can decide to change."

Blocking the blinding rays with her gloved hand, she squinted. A bell rang and sailors walked toward the *Icarus*, now repaired but still stuck in the sand.

MacLeod leaned in. "Fighting Seamus, disrespecting Mrs. Mercer, stealing Rebecca's cross—"

"I ain't steal it."

A wave crashed, spreading foam across the shore. Snatches of the captain's orders carried across the wind. Annaliese grew still, peering into the glassy sea.

This is useless. She'll never change.

"Pa chained me in the rain sometimes." Annaliese spoke so matter-of-factly it jarred him. "Mostly he kept me inside. The first time I met Uncle Hal, I was sitting on the floor with my hands behind my neck, like those prisoners in the story. Uncle Hal said, 'What you do to get treated like an *attemous?*' That means 'dog' in Powhatan. I ain't remember what I done, but I do remember Uncle Hal walking around the room, then he piled a dozen empty whiskey bottles on the table, and said to Pa something like, 'I known you got your demons but don't wreck it all like your pa done.' Pa looked shamed, like he wanted to cry—I almost felt sorry for him. But then Pa got mad, knocked off all the bottles. Uncle Hal stormed off. Pa was screaming at Ma for some reason. I ain't even known what she done." Annaliese closed her eyes, and MacLeod could see she was back there, reliving it. "He choked Ma. I pulled his arm away, but he shoved me on the broken glass." Gritting her teeth, she imitated Rob's voice, "'Hands behind your neck, bastard.'" Looking directly at MacLeod, she said, "I sat for hours, bleeding. If I moved, I known he'd beat me fierce. He kept the door open, though, like a dare. Mind games. It was—what's the word? Exhausting living with him."

A loud creaking came from the ship as the men tugged on ropes. Grunts carried across the wind.

"Annaliese, the door is open, but I can't make you walk through it. You're facing a decision that will affect your entire life. Who do you want to be? Annaliese Cameron or Annaliese Birch? You can't be both."

Annaliese grew uncharacteristically still. In her silence, it occurred to him that he'd been playing a double life as well.

Am I the honorable Scottish Highlander who loves my clairvoyant wife? Or am I just an Englishman's brute-for-hire, who's ashamed of Fiona's magic and treats Broderick cruel for no reason? What puppetmen tricked me into believing the only path to success was through denying who I am and everything I used to value? He stared at the girl. *Can either of us be fixed?*

A cheer rose from the sailors. A few minutes later, Seamus ran up to them, waving his wool hat. "Captain says the repairs will hold," he panted. "We sail today during high tide, sir."

MacLeod exhaled a sigh of relief. *Maybe Reverend Mercer will be placated now.* "Excellent news."

Seamus ran toward the camp to tell the passengers, and Annaliese tried to follow, but MacLeod stopped her.

"Until we reach London, you'll stay in our cabin. Full stop. No more dame school, no more prayer services, no more dolls with friends, no more fights. Sleep during the day and your dreams winnae disturb anyone. With any luck, we'll make it home in peace."

Annaliese took a step back. Her face blushed pink as she punched her thigh in frustration. "Door ain't sound open to me. Guess I'm leaving one cave for another."

Ah, shite. "What's my job?" he asked gently.

Annaliese chewed on her bottom lip. "Take me to my father in London."

"To protect you."

"Because Lord Hallewell is paying you to," she noted bitterly.

His voice raised in frustration. "Because I love you, you damned pain in the arse."

Her mouth fell as she peered into his eyes, clearly not knowing what to say. MacLeod felt just as startled as her, since he didna plan on saying it. He felt flustered and cleared his throat. "Just listen to me for once, lass. It's the only way."

Why would she ever trust me? I'm nothing to her, after all.

Chapter Thirty-Five

FIONA

Scotland

Fiona hadn't realized the trouble she thrust upon herself conjuring James and his new wife to move in. Oh, what she wouldn't give for enough privacy to invoke a prosperity spell. Here it was Samhain, not to mention her wedding anniversary and her birthday, and instead of doing powerful rituals beneath the harvest moon, she dished haggis and neeps onto pewter plates.

While her family seated themselves in the dining room, her daughter-in-law pulled her aside. Nelly said, "I have a bone to pick with you."

"Oh?" Fiona blinked.

Nelly whispered, "You were the one who suggested the fertility potion to me. I dinna appreciate you throwing me to the wolves to divert attention from your own cunning habits."

"My son is a wolf now?"

"James is furious. Do you have any idea how many arguments you caused? He's already troubled over the robbery. Ever since we moved here, he's terrified you'll tangle me in magic."

"The tincture worked, didna it? You've a healthy wean growing in your belly, aye?"

Nelly opened her mouth, but nothing came out. Rounding on her heel, Nelly brought the steaming plates into the dining room as the kitchen door slammed behind her.

Some way to celebrate. It's just like Auntie Matilda warned me. Even when spells work, it doesna guarantee people will be happy. I ken I should stop practicing sorcery, but it's like a dam has been broken and the magic keeps flowing from me. Eisd rium a Dhia. Help me figure out what's going on with my husband.

"Mam, can you bring a candle for the carving?" called Lachlan.

There weren't any in the kitchen, so she went into William's study. Rifling through his desk, instead she found a note.

> My dearest Mr. MacLeod,
>
> Thank you for teaching me to read, oh strict headmaster.
> Your obedient servant,
>
> Eleanor

Lord Hallewell's Eleanor? Why would William keep a note from her? Fiona remembered her own steamy lessons with William that ended up producing James nine months later. *William taught Eleanor to read?*

Fiona found a spare candle and entered the dining room decorated for Samhain. Touching the candle to another flame, she put it inside the carved turnip. Everyone looked hungry. "It's been years since I've cooked. Hope it tastes good."

Her curmudgeon brother, Malcolm, sat in William's chair. "You cooked well enough before William put on airs." He grunted. "Twelve servants for one manor. Wasted money. It's good you let them go."

Broderick pulled out her chair. "Sit, Mam, it's your birthday."

"Any word from the colonies?" her sister Mary asked, helping to serve.

Malcolm said, "The Great William MacLeod hasn't written? Not once?" He drank his beer. "Pluck off a peacock's feathers, and he's no more special than a chicken."

"Malcolm, stop," Mary chided.

Fiona said, "I've been waiting for a letter, but I only get bad news instead. Creditors circle us, demanding payment for bills I didna ken we had."

James hovered near the window, scanning into the darkness. Ever since the robbery, he obsessively checked the windows and doors. Sitting, he said, "Post is slow overseas. I'm sure you'll receive ten letters after Da arrives home."

"Aye, I suppose," Fiona said.

"Has Lord Hallewell had any news?" Nelly asked.

"No." Fiona measured time in her daughter-in-law's silhouette. William left a week after the wedding, now Nelly was quick with child. Fiona lowered her fork, looking at her younger sons. "I'm going to miss you three going to school tomorrow."

James and Nelly exchanged pained expressions, speaking in silent marital shorthand. They had argued earlier but stopped abruptly when she entered. *About the fertility potion?*

Fiona raised her glass. "A toast. These past few months have been difficult. I'm grateful to everyone. Truly. *Slàinte Mhath.*"

They drank and ate in uncomfortable silence. Left unsaid was that the harvest was paltry, inflation reduced their profits further, and their tenants were just as broke. Their circumstances grew bleak as a November sky, but at least she scraped enough to cover tuition. Education meant everything to William.

He taught Eleanor to read? Why did he never mention it?

Fiona's gaze flitted, never settling long on anyone's face. Lachlan cut off the burned bits from his haggis. Nelly had dark circles under her eyes. James barely ate.

Fiona pushed her plate aside. "What if he dinna return? How are we to survive?"

James glanced at his wife. "Da's coming. Let's go to church tomorrow and pray."

"I dinna need to light a candle with Reverend MacDonald. I need my damned husband to come home." Fiona pounded her fist on the dinner table. Everyone jumped, it was so unlike her. She fled to compose herself.

Broderick pursued her into the drawing room. William's empty chair blocked the hearth, the fire gone cold within. The chandelier remained unlit to save candles.

"I'll quit school. Save money."

"Broderick, no, I dinna wish to interrupt your education. I'm just fussing. Look at me carrying on." Fiona kept forcing a smile, but her stomach twisted in knots.

Mary gave her a hug as the others came inside the now sparsely furnished room. "Dinna fash yourself. God has a plan."

"Well, I wish He'd share it with me." Fiona angled away from her sister. "Not knowing is driving me mad. Why hasna William written? Is he punishing me? Did he die? I keep having visions of powerful storms and a lass screaming."

"Visions?" Malcolm said. "Like Auntie Matilda had?"

Shite. "Dreams, Malcolm. Visions in my dreams."

"You really think Da is dead?" wee Hamish asked.

Fiona covered her mouth, guilt flooding her face. Picking up Hamish, she hugged away his fear. "No, love. Mam is being so silly, talking about bad dreams."

"Da's alive, Hamish," Lachlan said.

"How do you ken?"

"Because I sense him. Come back to the table. It's Mam's birthday, we leave for Lottington Hall in the morning, and the haggis is getting cold. Da's probably bribing a local magistrate in Virginia or sharing a whiskey with a Mohawk Indian. Let's eat."

Fiona laughed. "Lachlan's stomach wins the debate."

James inhaled. "You're not leaving for school tomorrow."

"When are we going?" Hamish asked.

James said, "I had to use the tuition money to pay off one of the many liens against our manor. I'm trying to get a scholarship for Broderick since he's close to graduation, but—"

"But what about my friends—" Lachlan began.

James interrupted, "We're going broke."

"What about your legal work for Lord Hallewell's noble friends?" Fiona asked.

"You mean the ones suing us for not protecting their secrets? Whoever broke into the law office is blackmailing Da's clients, threatening to print their private affairs in the newspapers. And remember those loans Da guaranteed to help our tenants? A shadow party purchased the notes and foreclosed. I doubt they'll accept rabbits and goats for rent, as we do. We sold the silver candlesticks from our wedding to help, but it's a drop in the bucket of what's owed. We might lose the whole farm."

Fiona said, "We sold our valuables and still we face ruin? How can this be happening?"

James ran his fingers through his hair. "If Da doesna come home, or we dinna make tough decisions soon, this family will be bankrupt by yuletide. We have to meet with Lord Hallewell and ask for a loan. We're drowning in debt. Someone is trying to destroy our family."

"I've written to him, and he hasna replied," Fiona said.

James said, "You need to go to London. Or I will."

A vision of a double-headed snake flashed before her again, fangs sharp as knives.

Chapter Thirty-Six

LADY MARGARET

London

Posing for her portrait, Lady Margaret sat erect in a low-cut gown, red as the last bloom of summer, with a white feather bent over her hat. A West African boy about eight stood beside her, wearing a white turban and gold slave collar. His red waistcoat matched her dress, but with simpler embroidery in white. Lord Hallewell sulked in a corner with his drink.

The butler announced, "Mrs. Wilkes and her son, Lieutenant Wilkes," then bowed off.

Lady Margaret smiled. "Welcome, or welcome back, I should say," she said, showing off her trophy to her guests. "Feast your eyes on the new slave Lord Hallewell bought me. Isn't he the darkest shade you ever saw? I thought the gold choker was a tad much, but Lord Hallewell believes we must dress the blackbird worthy of our status. My lord spoils me." To the boy, "Leave. Keep your livery clean."

Buying a decorative slave was the minimum George owed her. Once she exposed MacLeod for the villain he was, her husband had become remarkably easy to manage. Her allowance flowed like the Thames to the sea.

TO RESCUE A WITCH

Mrs. Wilkes brushed a graying lock past her pale blue eyes. Age had not been kind, and her skin slid off her face in puddles. *How jealous I used to be of her pretty features while I slept with her husband. Did she even know?*

Lieutenant Wilkes, about twenty-five, resembled his father, the late Colonel Wilkes. Brown hair, brown eyes, tan skin, very handsome indeed.

"Darling, greet our guests."

Lord Hallewell grunted his acknowledgment with bloodshot eyes and port on his breath. He kept opening and shutting the locket of Eleanor mindlessly. Now aware of multiple betrayals, her husband's fleeting spark of strength had been permanently snuffed. *Pathetic.*

Mrs. Wilkes said, "I don't mean to be impolite, but I don't understand why you've invited us to call. The only reason we came is to discover what Lord Hallewell has to tell us. If his intoxication is any indication, I fear the contents of the message."

"Do have a seat," Lady Margaret said.

"I'll stand, thank you," Mrs. Wilkes said.

Lady Margaret returned to her armchair, slowly undressing the young lieutenant with her eyes, remembering his father. "I understand. We parted on difficult terms."

"Terms? Is that what you call it?"

The metallic click of Lord Hallewell's locket opening and closing grated Lady Margaret's nerves.

Lieutenant Wilkes said, "Lord Hallewell, is there something you wish to say?"

The cadence of the young man's voice struck her as uncannily similar to his father's. Forgotten conversations swirled in Lady Margaret's mind, and she blushed.

Lord Hallewell slowly advanced. "You were a boy when I met you, maybe ten? Time passes so quickly," Lord Hallewell rambled. He held Mrs. Wilkes' hand in his own, much to her discomfort, it seemed. "I've kept this burden for so long ..."

They waited, but he dropped her hand.

"He's drunk. We're leaving, Mother." Wilkes showed his arm for her to lean on.

Lord Hallewell tossed the locket on a side table. "William MacLeod murdered him."

He actually admitted it aloud.

Mrs. Wilkes' already sickly color went ashen. "Murdered? But why?"

Lord Hallewell said, "It was a fight over MacLeod's wife, Fiona. You remember her at our wedding?"

Lieutenant Wilkes stepped back from the others, covering his mouth with his hand.

"My Rupert is dead, not missing? Has not abandoned his family as you led us to believe?" Her knees buckled.

"I know it's a shock." Lord Hallewell helped her onto an overstuffed couch.

Lieutenant Wilkes stood beside her, his hands protectively resting on her shoulders.

Mrs. Wilkes said, "You'll never comprehend an ounce of my shock and grief, sir. You don't know what it's been like to live in limbo these past fifteen years. Am I a widow or abandoned? The navy cut us off long ago for presumed desertion. We've been living in a state of penury, but for the grace of my family. Shunned by society. Not able to mourn, nor move on."

"My lady," Lord Hallewell said, "I understand your anguish more than you realize."

Always parading his love for Eleanor. A long simmering rage burned Lady Margaret as she stared at her husband. *Oh, won't someone murder that horrid man?*

Mrs. Wilkes pieced together her memories. "I remember the Scottish strumpet. *Fiona.* Acted so simple and sweet. Drinking and dancing with my husband. Where was hers? She was a cunning one. All the ladies knew it," Mrs. Wilkes said. "Showing off her bracelet."

"I hear she dabbles in witchcraft." Everyone glanced up.

"Margaret, don't speak rubbish."

"They burned her aunt at the stake. You told me, darling." *Let's twist the knife into MacLeod's whole family. If Fiona hadn't flirted with Wilkes, maybe he'd still be alive.*

"People saw her reading his palm, but you're saying she bewitched my husband?"

TO RESCUE A WITCH

"A loving husband suddenly falls smitten with a low-class Scottish woman he never met before? My servants saw them walk into the library together. She could barely walk straight."

Lieutenant Wilkes stared off into the distance, leaning away from the conversation.

Lady Margaret lowered her voice to a gossipy tone. "I've heard servants say they were rolling on the Turkish rug. What an uncommon coincidence both Colonel Wilkes and the rug went missing after Mr. MacLeod went searching for his wife."

Mrs. Wilkes held her stomach and slowly shook her head. "I feel sick. My husband loved me. He would never have cheated on me."

Idiot. We fucked all the time with you in the next room. "Of course not," Lady Margaret said, moving to the grieving widow and patting her hand. "Fiona bewitched him."

Lieutenant Wilkes stepped forward with his shoulders back and chest thrust out. "Where are my father's remains? Testify to the Royal Navy so we can reinstate my father's honor."

Lord Hallewell gaped at Lady Margaret, scratching his neck. They hadn't considered this. Lady Margaret said, "We don't know where MacLeod hid the body, but we have these."

Lady Margaret pulled out the bloodied plaid shawl and emblem and handed them to Mrs. Wilkes, who took a sharp intake of air.

Mrs. Wilkes kissed the medal—Saint George on his noble steed. Quiet tears spilled down the widow's cheeks. "The king bestowed this honor." Mrs. Wilkes' blonde brows knitted tight, forming a deep line on her forehead. "My husband was bewitched and murdered? But during the investigation you vouched for Mr. MacLeod."

"I said MacLeod spent the bulk of the evening negotiating a business deal between Marquess Courtenay and me, which was true. How was I to know he found time to murder?"

"You were his alibi," Mrs. Wilkes said with a curl to her lip.

Lady Margaret said, "He believed MacLeod's lies."

"Everyone saw Fiona dancing with my husband, tipsy as sin." Mrs. Wilkes stood, her slight frame shaking with rage. "Yet you smeared my husband's name, implying any number of husbands would duel him for fornicating with their wives. You let people believe him a cad, or worse, a man who abandoned his family, knowing all along it was MacLeod? You two are the most despicable, odious, horrible people on this earth."

Lieutenant Wilkes asked Lord Hallewell, "Why now?"

Lady Margaret said, "We thought you should know the truth."

"Does your wife always speak for you?" Lieutenant Wilkes said. "Are you her puppet? Something dirty is going on here. Everyone knows MacLeod's your man. Why betray him?"

"Perhaps he betrayed me first." Lord Hallewell wandered to the decanter, poured another drink and stared into his port.

Why did he say that? God, what a fool.

"I suppose you expect me to kill him for you?" Lieutenant Wilkes kept strong eye contact as Lord Hallewell wilted under his stare.

Lord Hallewell tugged at his jabot. "No, we simply wanted to tell you ..."

"We were as surprised as you," Lady Margaret said. "We told you as soon as the gardener discovered them."

Lord Hallewell said, "Anyway, you can't duel Mr. MacLeod ... yet." He drank some more. "He's in the colonies to find my ..." Chuckling, he swirled the liquid in his crystal glass. "It's about time MacLeod faced consequences, the traitor."

Lieutenant Wilkes glowered at Lord Hallewell, speaking at an economical clip. "Where. Are. My. Father's. Remains?"

"I told you; I don't know."

Lieutenant Wilkes stood at full height, every bit the soldier. "You say my father was murdered but you can't produce his body, and the man you accuse of murder—your former friend—is across the Atlantic, indefinitely." His mouth downturned and fingers curled. "You've wasted our time and upset my mother. We're leaving." He helped his mother into the hall, then reversed. His distinctive jawline clenched. "As for you, sir, I challenge you to a duel. My second will be in communication with the day and time."

Lord Hallewell clawed at the rash creeping up his neck. "Me? Why duel me?"

Lieutenant Wilkes said, "I don't believe for one second you thought MacLeod innocent. Protecting your now former friend cost my family dearly. Your hands are as bloody as his wife's shawl."

Lady Margaret felt heat rise to her face and did her best to stifle her joy. *Young Wilkes must be an excellent shot—he is a soldier. All my plans are aligning perfectly.*

Chapter Thirty-Seven

ANNALIESE

Annaliese had to admit it—MacLeod's plan worked. For the past two weeks she had stayed in their cabin, sleeping during the day—trying to, at least—and learning to read at night. While she missed Jacqueline something fierce, spending time with MacLeod was ... No one had ever shown her kindness like him.

They sat on the floor beneath the windows, and he read her *Gulliver's Travels* while she rested her head on his chest. "Pa? I mean, Mr. MacLeod?" Her cheeks felt on fire. *Why did I call him Pa?* "Will we get to London soon?"

"Aye."

"Then what?"

Seamus knocked on the door. "Excuse me, sir, but you're needed at the captain's quarters for an urgent matter. Surgeon Johnsson and the officers are already there."

"Grubb, too?" he asked.

Seamus peeked over his shoulder, holding onto the doorframe as the ship heaved starboard. "Mr. Grubb is the reason the captain's having the meeting. He's talking mutiny, sir."

"Stay put," MacLeod said to Annaliese and followed Seamus.

After what felt like nine hundred hours, Annaliese wandered aimlessly in the cabin. Slumping at his desk, she played with his feather quills and kept thinking about their talk. *I'm Annaliese Cameron.*

But she kept hearing Pa's voice, "MacLeod ain't care about you, Annaliese Birch."

Rising on her tiptoes, she picked her shell jar from the shelf and fingered out Rebecca's cross from the sand. Blowing the dusty grit away, it sparkled in her palm. She closed her fist.

Who am I? Annaliese Cameron or Annaliese Birch?

Pa stood behind her, the bullet hole bleeding from his forehead. "Go ahead. Give the necklace back, so everyone knows you a liar and a thief."

Annaliese felt sick to her stomach. *Leave it by Rebecca's bed? Throw it overboard?*

Pa laughed. "What if someone sees you, stupid?"

Confess?

"They ain't never gonna forgive you."

It felt like the room kept shrinking and it got harder to breathe. Pa's whiskey breath was right on her neck. He whispered, "People only love perfect girls like Rebecca. You ain't never gonna be perfect, so why try?"

Her head lowered as she thought things through. *MacLeod is a good man, but he ain't my pa and he ain't gonna be around much longer, even if he lies and says he loves me.*

"Sharks may be bad, but sharks survive," Pa said.

She nodded. "I'm Annaliese Birch."

Burying Rebecca's cross back in the jar, she twisted the lid tight and left the cabin, not wanting to see Pa's bleeding bullet hole no more.

Peeking into the 'tween deck, the hairs on her neck pricked. A woman in a marigold bodice was dragged by her husband to the reverend. The woman's cheek was pink, like Ma's after a slap. "My wife needs redemption."

Mrs. Mercer stood by her husband's side, nodding passionately.

Jacqueline stood away from the crowd. Annaliese grabbed her hand and whispered, "Come on."

They headed toward the forecastle when Seamus pounced on them. "There you are. And a good thing, too; MacLeod sent me to check on you. He wants you in your cabin."

"Seamus, please," Annaliese begged.

He crossed his arms until Jacqueline placed a delicate hand on his forearm, the lace at her elbow brushing against his blond hairs. "Seamus, the adults are in a fever. It seems like every husband is fighting with his wife. No one will notice our absence. Besides, I have come up with a wonderful game for us to play. Questions and Commands. But we need to be hidden. This is an *adult* game."

Seamus melted quick as butter in the pan. It took two seconds for him to say, "No one will look for us in the orlop." Grabbing a lantern, he said, "Mind your step. The tobacco is gone but the food barrels and trunks they saved are still there."

They climbed unnoticed down the worn ladder into the darkness. Lantern light cast shadows over a maze of numbered pork casks, barrels of hard tack, carpentry tools and coiled ropes. Annaliese touched the newly repaired walls as they moved near the brig.

"How come it stinks?" Annaliese asked.

Seamus said, "All the piss and shit from Viscount Percy's smuggled slaves is stuck in the bilge sand. There's no way to reach it."

They sat on hogsheads barrels.

Annaliese asked, "How do you play the game?"

Jacqueline said, "The commander will ask an incredibly embarrassing question which you must answer honestly, otherwise you have to do whatever she commands you to do."

Annaliese's stomach knotted. *Don't tell more secrets. What am I even doing here? MacLeod's gonna be furious.*

Jacqueline said, "Seamus. Have you ever kissed a girl?"

He nodded. Even in the dim light, his cheeks shone rosy from embarrassment.

"I don't believe you," Annaliese said.

"You don't know anything, Miss Cameron."

Annaliese tapped her dangling legs against the barrel. "Jacqueline should command you to kiss her, to prove you ain't lying."

"What?" Jacqueline said.

Seamus saw the game's potential. "If ... if that's what you command, I'll kiss her."

Annaliese smiled, flicking mouse scat from the barrel top. *I known they like each other.*

Crew mates' voices hollered above as the ship made a quarter turn into the wind. Light footsteps came down the ladder.

Rebecca called, "I know you three are here. I see the lantern light. I want to play, too."

The trio rolled their eyes.

"Back here," Jacqueline called, then whispered, "Annaliese, I command you to be nice to Rebecca."

Annaliese groaned as Seamus laughed.

Rebecca stumbled in the darkness, climbing over crates. "Why are you laughing?"

"Shouldn't you be praying with your parents?" Annaliese asked.

"They're busy helping people reach salvation. I'm sure we'll reach port safely now. What are we playing?" Rebecca adjusted her mop cap over her perfect hair.

"Questions and Commands," Jacqueline said.

Rebecca squealed. "That's an adult game. I'm going to tell Mother—"

Jacqueline wagged her finger. "If you tell, I will never play with you again. We will all get in trouble for this game, ma chère."

Rebecca exhaled. "Fine."

"Miss Mercer, question or command?" Seamus asked.

"Question," Rebecca said, sitting prudishly atop a trunk with rusty metal hinges.

Seamus asked, "What's your deepest, darkest secret?"

Everyone leaned in. Rebecca pressed her hand to her heart. "I hardly think that's an appropriate question for an indentured servant to ask his better."

"Play the game, or hush up and leave," Annaliese said. Jacqueline nodded.

Rebecca huffed before confessing, "I once spit in Father's porridge."

Seamus laughed. Jacqueline covered her mouth in mock horror. "Ma chère."

"You're so boring." Annaliese picked the dirt from her fingernails.

"I spit in *your* food," Seamus said. Annaliese punched his arm as he laughed.

"My turn," Rebecca said. "Annaliese. Question or command?" Her sly smile made Annaliese nervous.

"Question."

"Where's my cross? I know you took it."

Annaliese's lips went tight. *I hate that stupid cross. I wished I never saw it.* "Command."

"Kiss Seamus," dared Rebecca.

"Ew. No."

"I don't want her kissing me," he said, as though Annaliese was a stuck pig.

Jacqueline said, "Why are you trying to get Annaliese into trouble? Kissing is forbidden."

"Then climb the rigging," Rebecca taunted.

Jacqueline grew exasperated. "You know she can't. Do you want to get her whipped? I thought you were Christian."

"I thought Annaliese wasn't afraid of anything, especially not her guardian."

Annaliese's hands balled into fists. No one was gonna call her a damn coward. She kissed Seamus's chapped lips, and he blushed purple-red to his ears.

Rebecca yelped, "I can't believe you did it. Now I'm telling Father how lewd you are."

"You commanded me to," Annaliese said, rising.

"Satan tempts people all the time. The good ones never fall for it."

Quick as lightning, Annaliese knocked Rebecca off the trunk and twisted her arm behind her back. "You think you gonna trick me? I'll break your damned bones if you tattle on me again."

Rebecca writhed in agony, her mop cap falling to the dirty ground. A rat scraped over it.

"Miss Cameron, stop." Seamus elbowed Annaliese aside, then searched Rebecca's arm for breaks. "Are you all right? Can you wiggle your fingers?"

Jacqueline yanked Annaliese's arm. "What is wrong with you?"

Annaliese faced off against Jacqueline. "Rebecca started it." Musty air filled her lungs as she breathed heavier.

"You didn't have to hurt her," Jacqueline yelled.

The ship tilted again, sending loose sacks of oats to scatter across the damp floor. "You think I'm stupid? You all tricked me to play this game to get me in trouble."

Rebecca sobbed. "I'm telling my father on you, Annaliese. Your guardian is going to whip you while I laugh, you dirty bastard."

Annaliese went still. "What did you call me?"

"That's right. I can figure things out. Mr. MacLeod works for your father, Lord Hallewell, but your name's Annaliese Cameron. Only bastards have different surnames. No wonder you're so bad—your mother was a whore, a Beelzebub. You're a witch like her."

Fury coursed through Annaliese's veins, and she pointed two fingers at Rebecca's forehead in slow motion.

"What are you doing?" Rebecca's eyes widened.

"Aye, my mother was a witch, and she taught me. Rebecca Mercer, I curse you. *Nimatew Maheegan Attemous Keshowse.*"

Rebecca walked backwards, pale as ice, bumping into hogshead barrels. "What—what are you saying?"

Seamus blessed himself, "May the Lord be between us an' all harm."

Annaliese moved forward, menacing her. "*Nimatew Maheegan Attemous Keshowse.*"

Jacqueline hissed, "Stop scaring her, Annaliese. You're not a witch."

Rebecca tripped over a crate, then escaped up the ladder. "Father, she put a curse on me!"

Jacqueline jabbed her finger at Annaliese. "Shame on you."

Annaliese shoved her. "If you like her so much, go run after her. You told Rebecca what I told you about Jack. Why else would she command me to kiss a boy? Why else would she say I'm like my whore mama?"

Seamus pressed his fist to his mouth.

Jacqueline said, "I never told her anything."

Annaliese stepped closer, getting right in her face. "Liar."

The ship heaved forward, sliding the lighter crates and trunks. They struggled to steady themselves.

"You betrayed yourself. Why do I waste my time? Adieu." Jacqueline stormed up the ladder. Seamus followed quickly with the lantern. Darkness closed in, like the cave in MacLeod's story.

Annaliese kicked a barrel, then lobbed a small crate across the orlop. Covering her ears, she struggled to catch her breath. *What would MacLeod tell me to do?* Apologize.

Racing upstairs, she realized she was too late. Everyone had gathered around Rebecca sobbing on the 'tween deck. Surgeon Johnsson mended her arm.

"MacLeod," Reverend Mercer hollered.

Blast it. She only had a few minutes before she'd be hunted again. *Go back to the orlop and hide? No, they're going to search there first. Why didn't I stay in my room?* Sneaking toward her cabin on the quarterdeck, she was shocked to see Grubb and a sailor digging through her trunk. *Oh no. This cain't be happening. It wasn't even a real curse. I'm so stupid.*

Kicking off her shoes and hose to walk softer, she climbed the ladder to the empty deck. The crew crowded near the aft hatch to listen to the drama below. Leaning over the rail, she considered stealing a longboat, but how would she lower it? And then what? Row to England?

Salt air burned her lungs. *Everyone hates me.* Time slowed, as though her body guided her without telling her why. Annaliese pulled loose the ribbon from her hair. Gripping the angled shrouds coming from the mast, she took a step on the ratline. A final act of freedom. *No turning back now. Annaliese Birch ain't scared of nuthin'.*

Up she went, at least twenty feet high before anyone even noticed. The air grew colder, but the sunlight made the ropes warm on the soles of her feet. It felt good to be barefoot again, like home.

"Miss Cameron, get down before you get hurt," a sailor called.

Ain't they known I'm Annaliese Birch? A bell rang and she climbed faster and higher. Thirty feet, forty feet, fifty feet, she climbed higher still. Her hands were raw with rope burns but she kept going until she reached the top.

I did it. She laughed, feeling alive. A cloud passed over the sun, blocking the glare. Gray ocean stretched endlessly, like purgatory.

The whole ship rolled leeward, and she made the mistake of looking down, seeing nothing but the sea directly beneath her, with sharks circling below. Shutting her eyes tight, she felt the wind shift. When she opened her eyes, the deck came back in view. An angry mob had gathered below. *Oh, what the hell did I do?*

A sailor cried, "Witch!"

"Come down," MacLeod hollered as he climbed. *He's gonna kill me.* He was already halfway up.

Should I jump? Her face itched something fierce. Her skin felt like it was being stretched across her skull. Crawling out on the crossbeam, Pa's voice in her head screamed at her. "You ain't never gonna be anything, Annaliese Birch. Jump."

MacLeod came within arm's grasp. His face shocked her. Annaliese expected anger, not fear. "Come to me."

She shook no. Her loose hair whipped in the wind.

Reaching out his long arm, he shouted over the wind, "You have to trust me."

She closed her eyes, desperately wanting to feel safe. Pa whispered in her ear, "Jump, Annaliese."

Frozen, she couldn't figure out what to do. Her muscles locked as she whispered, "No, I don't want to live in your cave, Pa." Taking a steely breath, Annaliese reached out.

"Mac's got you," he said, plucking her into his arms and hugging her tight. "I'll not let you go."

Wind blew ferociously, like a lion roaring in her face. MacLeod squinted at the sun as she wheezed. She felt his beating heart, and the brush of his beard against her cheek. "Easy now. Easy does it."

Now secure in his arms, his face changed from terrified to furious. "Are you out of your bloody mind? Do you have a death wish?"

Tears spilled down her cheeks. Even holding her in one arm, he flew down the ever-rocking mast. "I told you to stay in the damned cabin. I told you it wasnae safe. You disobeyed me and put a bloody curse on the reverend's daughter? Are you stupid?"

She cried harder.

"You wicked child. I'm going to give you a whipping to cry over, Annaliese Birch, since that seems to be the only thing you understand."

"I'm sorry, Mac. I'm sorry." Her skin felt on fire and itchy as her throat closed off. *Pa was right?* "Please," she gasped, "stop hating me."

They went into the chaotic mob of claps and jeers. *Stop laughing.*

Captain Adams said, "What's wrong with her face?"

"Annaliese, breathe." MacLeod lowered her to the deck, slick with saltwater.

It felt like the Devil was choking her and she clawed her neck. Sailors and passengers grabbed each other's arms, backing away from her. Grubb said, "She's bewitched, she is."

Just before she blacked out, the reverend said, "I know a witch when I see one."

Chapter Thirty-Eight

FIONA

Scotland

Fiona rode her stallion over the drawbridge, past the once formidable stone gatehouse stained with mold. James was right; she had to go to London, but she needed to steel herself first.

Glancing over her shoulder, she felt confident no one followed. Dismounting, she grabbed her satchel and strode beneath the archway to the water gate and ascended the winding, pitted steps to the cliff overlooking the shore.

Pouring the salt circle, she lit a candle and burned the mugwort leaves while the glassy loch reflected threatening skies and barren alder trees.

Eisd rium a Dhia. Auntie Matilda, guide me through the past. Help me overcome my fears. Fiona closed her eyes, deeply inhaling until the memory resurfaced.

∞

London, 1724

Fiona rubbed her aching feet beneath the polished oak table, staring at the stuffed pig and truffle platters. Music from the wedding orchestra penetrated the long dining hall crammed with London's elite. "Tiaras," she muttered. "Only the British aristocracy would wear diamond hats to dinner."

William snickered. "What are you looking at, love?" He followed her line of vision.

"The duchess's diamond and emerald bracelet. Think of the healing properties alone, not to mention the magical purposes. It's stunning."

Sauntering to Countess Eldsworth, he whispered until the old dame chuckled. He handed her money from his waistcoat, unhooked the bracelet, came back and clasped it on Fiona's wrist.

"William." Guests clapped and raised their glasses as she brushed her finger over the glittering stones. A farm girl wearing a duchess's gems.

He burst with love, and perhaps pride at having money for such extravagant spontaneity, but she noticed jealous ladies darting their narrowed eyes from her wrist to their own husbands. Lords crossed their arms, blowing out noisy breaths in annoyance. An invisible rule had been broken and she hunched in her shoulders. "Will the wedding last much longer?"

"They'll celebrate until sunrise. I'm nearly done negotiating a deal between Lord Hallewell and Marquess Big Wig if they dinna kill each other first. So many potential clients here. See, love? Nothing to fear in London. 'Twas just a silly dream."

"Dead ravens aren't silly. My predictions for you manifested, aye?"

"Aye, you were right I'd be wealthy. Arranging Lord Hallewell's marriage has proven profitable. Stop worrying so much, Fiona, everyone is impressed with you."

"Me? No."

"I wish you hadna brought your plaid shawl. Your English dress looks so bonny on you."

"It's cold."

"Let's warm you up then." William led her to the ballroom. Couples danced the latest minuet. William's penchant for stepping on her toes made the endeavor unpleasant.

"Sorry." He cringed in apology.

"MacLeod, you old dog, where have you been hiding this beauty?" asked a darkly handsome soldier, kissing her hand. Blood rushed unbidden to her face.

"Colonel Wilkes, this is my better half, Mrs. William MacLeod."

She chuckled. All night he had introduced her as Fiona. Suddenly an attractive man appeared, and it was Mrs. William MacLeod?

A servant offered drinks. Colonel Wilkes tossed his blue velvet cloak over his shoulder and grabbed a goblet. A pendant of Saint George on horseback hung around his neck over a red sash. "We all thought you were a figment of MacLeod's imagination—the lovely Fiona, hidden in a fairy tower in Scotland."

"Where's your wife, Wilkes?" William wrapped his arm around Fiona's waist. "I'm sure she'll enjoy the extra time you'll have for her now."

The men locked stares before the colonel eyed Fiona's bracelet and left.

"What was that about?" Fiona asked.

"Nothing important."

"MacLeod," Lord Hallewell shouted from across the room, arguing with Marquess Courtenay. William called him "Big Wig" behind his back because his peruke rose a foot above his head, yet he still seemed short.

"I'll only be a moment." William kissed her knuckles and headed toward Lord Hallewell, who threw down his expensive silver coat in a rage. The bride, Lady Margaret, looked stunningly miserable, drinking wine alone in the corner.

Fiona retreated toward the dining room, but Colonel Wilkes intervened. "Leaving?"

"I'm no' much of a dancer, I'm afraid."

"That depends on your partner. A strong lead can make any woman appear graceful. I've watched you dance, though. You rival the queen's elegance."

Fiona laughed. "My goodness, you lay it on thick," she said, finishing her drink and giving the goblet to a passing servant.

His eyebrows raised. "A thousand pardons. Was I being too complimentary?"

"Em ... no. I suppose not."

"May I get you another drink? Punch, perhaps?"

"Oh, lovely, thank you."

Fiona stood on the dance floor's outer rim, watching William do his best. Lord Hallewell was red-faced and flustered. *How ridiculous to cause such a commotion at your own wedding.*

"One punch for the bonny Scottish matron with the new emerald bracelet."

She blushed. "Thank you, Colonel Wilkes." It tasted strong.

"What a racket," Wilkes said. A crowd gathered as William corralled the spoiled aristocrats into another room. "Lord Hallewell has a family history of losing money. Your husband has his work cut out for him, being the trustee of young Alexander's inheritance. I'm sure he'll guard the money well," he said, glancing at her bracelet again.

"I dinna ken his business dealings, sir. I best retreat to dinner."

"Undoubtedly, you don't. What wife does?" Wilkes blocked her, smiling disarmingly. "Lady Margaret tells me you're a soothsayer. I must admit, reading *Dr. Flamstend's and Mr. Patridge's New Fortune-Book* has been a guilty pleasure."

"Ack, I dinna believe such nonsense. Why trust cards when nature reveals true secrets?"

"Why, Mrs. MacLeod, you are a mysterious creature, aren't you? What's your specialty then—palmistry? Dreams?"

The heat of the crowd, or perhaps the punch, made her face warm. Walls lined with ornate mirrors in gold leaf frames distorted the room and multiplied the people. Fiona peeked over her shoulder. William wouldna approve.

"Shh. I won't tell your husband if you don't." Colonel Wilkes opened his palm.

"Ack, it's just a parlor trick." Fiona downgraded her skills, as she always did. Putting her drink on a nearby table, she examined his outstretched hand, noting the rough callouses of a man accustomed to yielding a sword. His skin scorched hers as she traced the textures and lines, but she flinched at the coldness of his wedding band. "This is your love line. It splits. You're a laddie who's broken a few hearts."

His eyes popped open. A sudden thrill danced up her spine as she saw color rise to his cheeks. Fiona hadn't flirted with anyone since she met William. Until now. He leaned in with genuine curiosity.

"Close your fist." Bending his hand to the side, she counted the protruding bumps. "One child from the main love line, but it branches into two lighter lines."

"You're saying I have multiple bastards I'm unaware of? Your husband is a brave man to be married to a woman with second sight."

Fiona half-smiled, releasing his palm and retrieving her drink. Lady Margaret fumed in the corner next to a nursemaid holding wee Alexander, barely one. The boy had thick black hair and brown eyes. Lady Margaret glanced daggers at her. Fiona took another sip and returned a wicked grin. Sweet punch slid down her throat, and she felt flushed everywhere.

Fiona glided a finger across his golden pendant. "It seems you're the courageous one."

"Mrs. MacLeod, are you stroking Saint George?"

She pulled her hand away quick as a slap.

Wilkes laughed good-naturedly. "It's rather embarrassing, wearing your reputation on your chest, but the Order of the Garter is quite an honor His Majesty bestowed upon me."

Fiona admired his humility. Her eyes drunk in his tanned skin. He wasn't pale like these lords William admired, hiding in their heirloom castles. No, Colonel Wilkes stormed castles.

"Care to dance?" he asked.

Fiona MacLeod, you're married. "I'm still finishing my punch," she demurred.

"Well, drink. The orchestra waits for no one."

What's one dance at a wedding? William will be back soon enough. She drained the cup. Colonel Wilkes was quite a dancer. And dashing in his uniform. He spun her round and round, keeping her laughing at his little quips about Lady Margaret and the other nobles, and she caught herself smiling in mirror upon mirror, beaming in another man's arms.

"My goodness, I need to sit. The room is whirling."

"Let's get you some air, Fiona."

Colonel Wilkes led her out of the ballroom, past gossiping guests in flowing gowns drinking champagne, their perfume expensive and suffocating. The hall seemed endless. They entered a quiet chamber, unlit save for the moonlight streaming through the windows.

Her vision blurred. Portraits of generals and ladies stared from the walls. "Where are we? I think—Where's William? He must be searching for me."

"William is busy." Wilkes closed the door and locked it with a definitive clank.

Her wits were unclear. Her limbs felt heavy. Wilkes kissed her. Fiona kissed him back before coming to her senses and slapping his face sloppily, missing her mark and hitting his chin. He laughed, dragging her to the Turkish rug. Black leaves—or were they ravens?—clustered around stylized flowers on the carpet. The room kept spinning; the murder of ravens swarmed her head.

"What's a Scotsman doing letting his little lamb wander so far from the flock?"

Colonel Wilkes climbed on top, pinning her with his weight. His pendant's metallic scent made her bristle. Lowering his breeches, she glimpsed dark hair and his aroused condition, forcing her mind to sober.

"No." She tried to break free, but her arms barely worked.

"Tell your meddling husband to stay out of my affairs. A wedding ring means nil to me. If I want to fuck Lady Margaret, I will. And I control my bastard's trust, not him."

In her peripheral view, she saw shadows passing under the door. Fiona wanted to scream but no sound came to her throat. His calloused hand was clapped over her mouth anyway. Cold air slapped her legs as he lifted her petticoats.

"Stop," she mumbled beneath his hand. Fear surged power to her arms, and she tried to scratch his face, but only ripped off his pendant instead. Fumbling for her knife from her leg garter, he easily disarmed her.

"What's this, little lamb?" he sneered. "A dirk?"

His body overpowered hers. The colonel's face moved in and out of focus as he pressed on her neck, choking her, his red silk sash softly brushing her face.

"Did you see this in your tea leaves?"

∞

Fiona sobbed in her salt circle, surrounded by weatherworn stones and clumps of dead grass. Her memories left her in ruins.

Chapter Thirty-Nine

LADY MARGARET

London

What happened at the duel? It had been weeks since she last saw anyone: not her husband, not her son, not even her lover. Alone in her private box, Lady Margaret suffered through a dreadful rendition of *The Beggar's Opera* when she spied Lieutenant Wilkes on the mezzanine level, strenuously avoiding her gaze. *That's promising.*

Focusing her golden binoculars on his lips for clues, she was thwarted by the chandelier, which cast more shadows than light. *My husband must be dead. He must be. But why is Alexander missing?*

Lord Percy sat next to her, and she exhaled, relieved. Fanning her mouth to hide her own lips, she asked, "What news, my lord? Am I a widow?"

"I just spoke to Wilkes in the hall. Lord Hallewell lives."

A frustrated moan escaped her. "Where is he then?"

"Drinking port, no doubt."

Act II started as all the actresses dressed as strumpets entered on the stage with puffed-out petticoats and feathers in their tresses. Lord Percy said, "I hope a chorus girl sets herself aflame on the stage candles."

Shaking her head, she laughed. "Such villainous musings."

Percy shifted in his seat. "Margaret, there's something I need to tell you."

"I was afraid George might live. Don't worry, I've come up with contingency plans to eliminate both my husband and MacLeod—"

"I appreciate your efforts, but I can handle MacLeod."

Taken aback by his sudden air of authority, she said, "Oh? What's your plan?"

"Remember the highwaymen who helped your mantua-maker see the error of her ways?"

Lady Margaret giggled. "I still roll around her eyeball in my gift box, although the iris is considerably distorted since it dried."

"Highwaymen cut deadbolts even better than eye sockets. They broke into MacLeod's law office and took every single paper from his strong boxes. It's wickedly fun reading about people's private indiscretions. Gambling debts, secret accounts for mistresses and bastards, bribes paid to conceal unnatural love. I should rob barristers more frequently. Anyway, I threatened his clients with blackmail if they didn't abandon all payments to him forthwith."

"But what happens when he returns?"

"My solicitors are finding creative ways to put liens against his properties. He'll be bankrupt in weeks. Once everything is set, I plan to personally ride up to Scotland with my men. I want to watch his family sob when I throw them out."

"Lovely way to spend the holidays," she smirked. "Well done. His weakness is his wife."

His smile faded and he sat quietly for a moment, shifting in his seat.

Lady Margaret said, "What is it, love? You're distracted."

"I have good news and bad—well, not bad really. First the good news. Eleanor is dead."

Lowering her fan, she asked, "MacLeod did the deed?"

"Hardly. I intercepted letters he sent to Fiona and your husband. Apparently, postboys are easy to bribe. MacLeod's love letters are rather poetic. I'll have to steal his best lines."

"Percy, stop carrying on. How did Eleanor die?"

"Childbirth. She died soon after sending the letter to your husband. MacLeod didn't mention the girl, so maybe she died, too, from the pox or some similar illness."

Lady Margaret pouted. "I had hoped for a more violent ending for Eleanor. But still. Huzzah," she said, tapping him with her fan. "You know, even if the bastard lives and MacLeod's fool enough to bring her here, once you kill George, that will make Eleanor's girl *my ward*." A laugh escaped her. "I don't know if I'd rather have her dead or alive. My mind is positively racing with ideas. Perhaps we should celebrate with a romp behind the stage? I have such fond memories from the last time we were in an actors' tent."

Percy frowned. "There's no need to bring up my father."

"Quid pro quo, love. The Wilkes' plan failed. Duel my husband so we can wed."

Lord Percy fondled her arm. "Margaret, there's something I have to tell you—"

Lord Hallewell plunked into the red velvet seat next to her. She gasped.

"You don't look happy to see your husband." He lifted the binoculars from her lap, scanning the audience. "Oh, look, there's Lieutenant Wilkes. Fine young man."

And a terrible shot. Lady Margaret waved her fan, eyeing both men. "Thank heavens, I've been worried. You resolved your dispute with Lieutenant Wilkes? Will he duel MacLeod upon his return from the colonies?"

Lord Hallewell took a long drink from his pocket flask, then sang along with "How Cruel Are the Traitors."

"My lord, stop being so cryptic. What happened?"

Lady Granger and Plump Catherine craned their jeweled necks to dissect her expressions with other society women, no doubt. God only knew what would end up in the scandal sheets.

"Thank you for warming the seat, Lord Percy, but your young wife must miss you."

Wife?

Lord Percy nodded and left, sans explanation.

Lord Hallewell drank from his flask. "I know you're fond of your new teeth, darling, but close your gaping mouth."

Fluttering her fan, she said, "Your drinking is heroic. I thought winning a duel would make you happier. Will Alexander be joining us?" She searched the vacant rows behind them.

"I doubt it, as he's currently enjoying a Grand Tour. He'll be home in a year or two."

"Grand Tour? He didn't even say goodbye. How did this come about?" *Stay calm.* Lord Hallewell was playing with her emotions.

"How appropriate we should watch this opera together," he said with a drunken chuckle.

Lady Margaret stared at Percy pecking Plump Catherine's cheek and glowered at him. *I killed for him to get everything he desired, and now Percy condemns me to a monotonous marriage in a drafty old house?* Since her husband was the only one who knew Alexander's location, she couldn't even poison him.

The audience clapped as the set changed into Newgate Gaol.

"Our marriage is a prison," he said. "When did we become enemies? I had hoped we would grow to love each other, as my parents did."

He hasn't outgrown his idiocy. Percy and Plump Catherine were giggling like school children. She stopped pretending. "You play-act to have wanted my affection. I was but a treasure chest for you to rob."

His lordship snorted. "So, tell me, Margaret, what attracted you to your first husband, the filthy-rich eighty-year-old with no living heirs? Love?"

Snapping her fan, she said, "I did as my parents bade me."

"Let's be frank. You're lucky I married you. I saved your reputation and Alex's inheritance, so I'll thank you to silence your complaints. By the way, Alex seemed unhappy I survived the duel. Perhaps he envied Percy's spectacular rise in social standing since the old earl's untimely passing. God knows what ideas you've planted in Alexander's brain."

"You sent away my son to hurt me. Is it a surprise he hates you when you cut off his own inheritance for months and you treat me with such cruelty?"

"He does hate me and it's my own fault. I've taken a hands-off approach to my household, happy to leave all the burdens to MacLeod. Perhaps if I were more involved in directing Alex's upbringing, we wouldn't have such frequent problems for MacLeod to fix. Don't worry about Alex—he won't be alone on the continent. I've hired the best tutors to accompany him. Though you may find this shocking, I honestly want to do right by you and our children."

"How noble." Fluttering her fan, she surveyed the room overflowing with men and their mistresses. Diamonds, peridots and aquamarines adorned every harridan's ear, wrist, finger. *Time to recalculate my next steps.* "Perhaps you want Alexander gone, so he won't object to spotting you traipsing around London town with your Virginia whore." *Dead Virginia whore*, she thought, internally grinning.

Lord Hallewell lowered his flask. "Staring into a pistol is a most clarifying experience. At the last instant, Wilkes aimed at the sky and fired. An act of mercy I didn't deserve but won't waste. The only thing that matters is love. Margaret, why continue to live this farce of a marriage? If you want to stay in Astwick House, stay here. If you want to move to Grimbly Manor, go there. I simply want to live in peace with Eleanor and my daughter when they arrive. I love her, no matter what she's done. I don't want to squander this second chance for happiness."

Lady Margaret was startled by the hurt she felt at his rejection and considered telling him right then Eleanor was dead, to hurt him, but stopped. *How should I play this to maximize damage? Let him believe his lover is coming home.* "If I were to consider your proposal, I want assurances. You can't arbitrarily cut off my funds anymore."

A surprised smile crossed his face. "I can arrange a trust for you, with a guaranteed monthly allowance. You may appoint your own solicitor to be trustee, to feel a sense of confidence."

"All I ask is for you to be discreet with your mistress, as will I, when I take on my own lovers."

His jaw dropped. *Didn't expect that condition, did you, George?*

"As you wish." Tugging at his jabot, he said, "I suppose you'll want to stay in London? If I bring my new family to Grimbly Manor, our noble peers will be none the wiser. I'll move out as soon as MacLeod returns with them if you'd like."

My God, his love for Eleanor must be boundless to agree to such a scandalous arrangement with me. What was so incredibly wonderful about Eleanor? At least Plump Catherine is fabulously rich. Eleanor washed our soiled linens, for God's sake.

The audience kept laughing and cheering, singing loudly off-key. Lady Margaret smiled gamely at Lord Percy as he draped his arm around his brainless and appallingly fat new wife. *You men want to cast me as a monster? Loot my money and my heart? Fine. The monster is ready to collect her debts.*

Lady Margaret brushed his cheek with her fingertips, shocking the nosy public with a gentle kiss to his lips. "It may surprise you to learn that I do love you, George, in my own way," she said, eyes welling. "I'm sorry I never became the wife you longed for. At least one of us should be happy."

Oh, George, let me fill your head with lovesick dreams, so I can crush them all.

Chapter Forty

FIONA

Scotland

Fiona wiped her tears as a quiet rain fell on the loch and wrapped her shawl tighter around her shoulders. Cold drops fell on her skin as she stared at the half-crumbled buildings filled with bullet marks from old wars.

Inhaling the smoldering incense, she readied to fall into another trance.

"Mam!" James stood ash-faced outside the salt circle, holding her stallion's lead.

Curled brown leaves blew past her, crossing into her salt circle. "It's not what you think."

Fiona reached for him, but he stepped back.

James yanked her arm, pulling her outside the circle, kicking the salt toward the shore. "What the hell are you doing? No wonder you didna go to church. You wanted me to be the man of the house? Well, I am now. I want zero to do with Lucifer's dark magic."

Her voice raised. "I dinna follow Satan. I believe in God. This is different. There's nothing wrong with what I'm doing."

"Then why are you hiding it?" he asked, revealing her book of spells from a satchel. "Because you ken it's wrong." He hurled it over the cliff.

"James, no—" It felt as if she would never move on from this moment. How long would she face the world's eternal misunderstanding of her embrace of healing magic?

James said, "Heaven and hell aside, listen to me, not as your son, but as a barrister. Witchcraft is a crime. Maybe it's only a misdemeanor now, but—"

"You think I dinna ken? I watched my Auntie Matilda burn."

"And still, you do this?"

"Two things can be true at the same time. I believe in God and the spirits of our ancestors. I'd love to pray in public, but it isna an option for me, is it?"

"You're losing your senses. Mam, listen to me. Answers aren't found through magic, but through Christ and hard work."

"How's hard work going to bring your father home?!" she yelled. "You dinna understand. None of you do."

"Just because I was only five years old, do you think I dinna remember your wearing burlap for penance? You think I didna hear the screaming matches you had with Da over witchcraft? I might have been hiding under the bed with David, but I heard everything."

His words landed like a punch. "I didna ken you heard us." Fiona's arms crossed over her knotted stomach. "We weren't fighting over my visions; we were fighting over Broderick."

James tilted his head. "What are you talking about?"

Heaviness fell over her. "I thought it would be easy—if you were raped, drink the pennyroyal tea and move on. But hypotheticals mean nothing once you become affected personally." Her eyes cast down.

He laid his hand on his mouth before quickly dropping it. "Oh, Mam."

"I thought the wean might be your father's, but what if he wasn't?" Shutting her eyes, she pinched the bridge of her nose. "Should I risk killing the bairn, for fear it was another man's? It wasn't the bairn's fault. But what if it actually was the rapist's baby? Would the child be a monster, too?"

James looked at her sideways, not quite able to meet her eyes. "What did Da say?"

Fiona snorted. "He avoided me. Hid in his work. I felt utterly alone. Cursed. I moved to the courtyard garden and performed the rituals. Anything to feel safe again. *Eisd rium a Dhia. Auntie Matilda, hear me.*" Fiona gave a bitter laugh. "Your father and Reverend MacDonald heard me instead." Staring into the past, she relived the moment. "'What witchcraft is this, madam?' the reverend asked, shaking me. He forced us to keep the baby and your father's never forgiven me—or Broderick—since."

"Oh, Mam." James pulled her in for a helpless hug. "You shouldnae be alone. I'll ask Uncle Malcolm to come while I go to London."

Power returned to her voice. "I'm not a child." Fiona broke free, storming toward her stallion as he followed. "I'm tired of living in fear with secrets and lies." Facing him, she said, "I'm a wise woman. I ken spells to make Nelly fertile and herbs to heal people if only you, your father and the Church would let me do good. I foresaw your father's voyage, but he didna want to believe me. This time it's my choice. I'm going to see Lady Margaret for some answers. A storm is coming and it's coming from London."

Chapter Forty-One

Annaliese

Annaliese bolted upright in the darkness as a rat scraped its hind claws against her to scurry off. Every muscle in her aching body tightened as she coughed at the vile stench.

A hazy light floated in the distance. Taking a cold step forward, she found herself locked in a rusty cage. The ground swayed as she rattled the bars, unsure if this was another dream or a living nightmare.

"Pa?"

Her voice echoed. The lantern closed in, glowing yellow from above. Surroundings came into focus on the other side of the bars. Stacked chests, barrels of biscuits, boxes of liquor. *I'm in the brig?*

Her ears pricked. *Footsteps.*

"Mac? I won't never be bad no more. Please let me out."

Shadows advanced through the orlop. She gripped the bars so tight her knuckles turned white. "Who's there?" she called, wiping her clammy hands on her shift.

"Is it true, child? Are you a witch?"

"Mrs. Mercer? I ain't no witch, ma'am. I was just trying to scare Rebecca. I cain't see you. Where's Mr. MacLeod?"

Reverend Mercer said, "Mr. MacLeod is uncommon tall for a man of this world. Did he take you to the Dark Man in the forest to sign his book?"

Sign a book? Flames in the lantern flickered and she squinted at the light. *How many people are watching me?*

"Do you remember what I told you? Hell is real, Annaliese."

A cold sweat broke out on her forehead. Twisting her tangled hair around her fingers, she whispered, "Please don't burn me."

"Burn you? What an exceptional fear," the reverend said. "Open the cage."

Mr. Grubb's thick silhouette came forward as he jingled through the key ring.

Annaliese backed into the corner, raising her arms. "You stay away from me."

"Shut your jaw, girl. You're lucky you ain't lying in irons," said Mr. Grubb.

Reverend Mercer said, "Shh, child. Take off your clothes, so Mother can examine you."

The ship sailed faster. Another lantern shone from the hatch. MacLeod called, "Mercer?"

Annaliese yelled, "Mac—" Mr. Grubb's calloused hand slapped over her mouth as she struggled against him.

Reverend Mercer called back, "We have a right to examine the accused, Mr. MacLeod."

"I'll have *Justice* cleave a gorge through your skull if you lay a finger on my ward." With remarkable speed, MacLeod made his way to the gaol. Mr. Grubb backed off, hands up, as MacLeod lifted Annaliese into his arms, and she buried her face in his neck. Captain Adams and Jacqueline's mother soon caught up.

Captain Adams said, "Reverend Mercer, no common men should be present during an examination—surely you know this. Mrs. Gauthier will assist your wife in the examination."

Nothing the adults said made any sense. *What are they talking about?*

Mr. Grubb snorted. "This is bollocks. MacLeod's handpicked lady friend saying all's well? This witch trial had better be fair, Adams. It's not only me saying it, neither."

Witch trial? She gulped down her breath, peeking at the angry men around her. The ship groaned as it shifted, rattling the guts of the orlop.

Captain Adams thrust out his chin. "Are you threatening mutiny, sir?"

"It ain't a threat." Grubb stared in the captain's eyes before shifting his gaze to MacLeod. "You'll have to cut off more than one hand if you try to bribe the jury. Near every crew mate is ready to make her walk the plank; only the reverend here is making us wait until the girl gets a trial, even though she don't deserve it."

Annaliese hugged Mac tighter, wishing to go home.

MacLeod said, "Look, with any luck, we'll arrive in London in a week, and you can seek the magistrate there."

He's sending me to gaol in London?

"If we don't get rid of this witch, we may never reach safe harbor," Grubb said.

"Oh, so you just want to throw the lass overboard?" MacLeod glowered.

What? Annaliese clasped his neck, trembling.

Reverend Mercer said, "Obviously not. We are reasonable men pursuing justice. There's no need to delay a trial. Nay, Ecclesiastes tells us if we do not punish evil work with full speed, other hearts will leap toward wickedness. We must fear God's word and have this trial today lest more women join Satan's ranks."

MacLeod did his best to appear calm, but Annaliese saw how his jaw tightened.

Captain Adams said, "The trial begins at three o'clock. You're a noble's barrister. Surely the girl is in capable hands for her defense. Let the women do their work."

Mrs. Mercer plucked Annaliese from Mac's arms and began untying her bodice. "We need to check your body for the Devil's mark, so I'll administer the pricking test. We're going to blindfold you, and I will prick any marks seeming unnatural."

Mac's eyes looked feverish, darting around. He grabbed the captain's forearm. "The pricking test is hardly used anymore."

"What are you hiding?" asked Reverend Mercer, knitting his eyebrows together.

Mrs. Mercer shimmied Annaliese's petticoat down. MacLeod moved to stop her, but Captain Adams blocked him.

"Stop, you won't understand—" MacLeod said, as Mr. Grubb and the reverend dragged him away.

Annaliese stood alone with the women, shivering in the cold. Mrs. Mercer pulled off Annaliese's shift. Lantern light heated Annaliese's torso and limbs as it exposed all the marks she tried to keep secret. The women inhaled sharply.

"Oh, mon Dieu," Jacqueline's ma whispered.

Mrs. Mercer said, "Just as I thought. The hounds of hell are drinking her blood."

Chapter Forty-Two

WILLIAM MACLEOD

Uniforms provide the shorthand of authority. Fortunately, William MacLeod had packed his barrister's attire: black robes and a white wig. Unfortunately, they now resided at the bottom of the sea with all the other trunks thrown overboard. It was time to don a different garb.

Laying the long tartan plaid on the floor, he meticulously folded it into crisp pleats.

By all measures she's guilty under English law. Perhaps if I look to the old ways I'll come up with a clever defense. Annaliese doesna have a witchy bone in her body, and I ken it because I'm married to a real one.

Sitting on top of the plaid, he gathered the fabric over his waist and buckled his belt. Standing, he put the excess material over his shoulder, then pinned his clan brooch to it. *Will the men on the jury be able to look past my clothes to see the truth?* Glancing in the mirror, a Highlander with wild red hair and beard smiled back. *Hold fast, MacLeod.*

Striding down the hall, he noted sailors had transformed the 'tween deck into a makeshift courtroom with tables and chairs on opposing sides for him and Reverend Mercer.

Unfortunately, he didna argue much in court. MacLeod notoriously negotiated deals for his noble clients before they got there, and bribed the right officials if they did. But today, God apparently demanded a witch trial.

Like the one he avoided for Fiona all those years ago.

Spectators crammed on benches with bated breath. Mrs. Mercer and Rebecca sat behind the reverend, encircled by Mr. Grubb and his crew. While *Justice* hung on his cabin wall during trial, he hoped legal justice would appear and he could put this nightmare behind him.

MacLeod feigned confidence, venturing to smile as he assessed the twelve jurors. All were literate, rational and moderate gentlemen of means, but some were quite swept away with Mercer's sermons. No doubt, it would be a challenge to exonerate Annaliese.

Ushered in from the brig, Annaliese looked like a puddle after a hard rain—trembling and dirty. Jacqueline and her mother joined him, blocking her from the nosy crowd's view. Before Annaliese even opened her mouth, he cut her off. "You're going to listen."

As he spoke, Jacqueline wiped Annaliese's face with a damp rag, while her mother pulled her church dress over her dirty shift. It was a white gown with two flowing ribbons.

MacLeod said, "Reverend Mercer is going to start. He'll question multiple people. Keep your temper cool, and your gob shut. Best behavior, aye?"

Annaliese nodded, chewing her bottom lip.

Jacqueline twisted Annaliese's hair into a tidy bun with several ringlets to soften her features. Anything would help.

Pounding a cane on the floor, the bosun said, "All rise. Captain Adams as judge."

The crowd rose along with bile in MacLeod's throat. With hardly any time to prepare her defense, he had to rely on the few questions he asked the children before Annaliese scampered up the damned mast.

In London, he could make the charges disappear, but Mercer and the sailors didn't give a tuppence that the Witchcraft Act of 1736 reduced the crime from a capital offense to a misdemeanor. They made their own rules at sea, and they wanted blood for wind.

The bosun pounded his cane again. Everyone sat but Annaliese.

Captain Adams said, "Annaliese Cameron, you have been accused of witchcraft with witnesses and evidence against you. Do you wish to plead guilty to this charge?"

Dust particles floated in the light from the hatch over Annaliese, looking like a fallen angel. MacLeod gave a reassuring nod.

"Not guilty."

Chapter Forty-Three

Annaliese

I'm guilty. Maybe not for witchcraft but for stupidity, that's for damned sure.

Reverend Mercer stood in front of everyone. Silence fell, such that the creaking of the ship and the tug of ropes twisting echoed unbearably loud in Annaliese's ears.

"Gentlemen, I stand before you with a grave heart. My deepest fears, my staunchest warnings of the Devil's dangerous temptations, have born poisonous fruit. Today I will prove, beyond reasonable doubt, through witness testimony and a preponderance of evidence, that Annaliese Cameron is a witch who attempted to curse my innocent daughter. She must be found guilty and hung for her most vile crimes."

Dryness filled her mouth and her skin felt itchy. *Please not again.* She looked to Mac, who seemed to say, *Breathe, Annaliese.*

Men in expensive wigs saved from the wreck clumped together toward the side. Women holding weathered Bibles against their bodices sat behind and dirty sailors wiping their necks with soiled bandannas stood around the edges. No matter where they sat or what they wore—they all knew she was guilty before the first word. *Why have a trial?*

MacLeod stood, towering in his kilt. He looked like a different man. "Gentlemen," he said to the jury, "Ladies," he nodded to the women in the crowd. "Have you ever said something stupid? I ken I have. I dinna dispute the lass said some gibberish in a moment of anger, but I guarantee she isna a witch. You see, I come from the Isle of Skye, and I've met wise women in my travels."

Sailors and passengers shifted in their seats, whispering to each other.

"In my capacity as barrister, I've attended numerous trials to root out witchcraft, and like many of you," he said, looking directly at crew mates wearing talismans around their necks, "I understand the fine line between healing charms and something sinister. Annaliese can be prickly, and impulsive, but that doesna make her a witch. She's a scared girl facing an incredible punishment over a misunderstanding between school children. I ask you to keep an open mind as you hear all the evidence and let wisdom and logic prevail."

As MacLeod sat, Reverend Mercer said, "I call my daughter, Rebecca Mercer."

Ah, shit. Naturally, perfect Rebecca made a show of being afraid to step near Annaliese when she took the stand. Oh, how Rebecca cried big, wet crocodile tears, and dabbed them politely with a handkerchief as she told of being cursed while the crowd gobbled up her story. Poor, perfect Rebecca. Annaliese stopped paying attention. What was the point?

"Hang Annaliese!" someone shouted.

Hang me? A wall of hatred pressed toward her, wanting to crush her from existence. *MacLeod didn't ask Rebecca any questions because he loves her more than me.*

Reverend Mercer said, "I call Seamus Murphy."

Seamus clearly hadn't expected to be called. Wilting before Captain Adams, he tugged off his navy woolen cap and gaped at the crowd. Static made his blond hair stand on end.

The reverend's thin lips spread over his crooked teeth. "In your capacity as ship's boy, you are steward to Mr. MacLeod, correct? You sleep outside his cabin?"

"Aye, sir."

"Tell us, Seamus, what do you hear at night?"

Ah, hell, here it comes.

Fidgeting while glancing at MacLeod, Seamus said, "Miss Cameron has an awful dose of nightmares, the likes of it I've never seen, sir."

"Specifically, what do you hear?" Reverend Mercer's lanky frame paced slowly, dividing his attention equally between Seamus and the jury. "Does she shriek?"

"Aye."

"Does she throw fits? Kick?"

"Well, she kicks when she's awake, too."

Everyone chuckled.

Ha, ha. Keep laughing, Seamus. Some friend you are.

Seamus smiled until he caught MacLeod's eye, then wrung his cap again. "One stormy night, I heard her call, 'Run,' and she tried to come out the door, don't you know, but Mr. MacLeod kept her quiet. He said ..." Seamus glanced at the captain. "He said a swear word." The captain nodded, and Seamus continued. "He said, 'Damn it, Annaliese, wake up.' When I came in, Mr. MacLeod's hand was bleeding and there was blood on the lass's mouth."

Her stomach dropped. *I forgot that.* People murmured. Captain Adams rapped his knuckles on the table for quiet.

Reverend Mercer nodded. "So, she demonstrates signs of nightly possession? You're doing a fine job, son."

Son? Reverend Mercer, who hates Catholics as much as witches, calls him son?

Seamus avoided Annaliese's eyes and swallowed. "I don't know the ways of Church enough to say about possession, sir. She has powerful bad dreams."

Reverend Mercer preached to the crowd, "Well, I am schooled in the ways of the Church." Grubb and his friends clapped in agreement. "And anyone awakened by her shrills can attest to her possession as well."

People babbled in agreement. Annaliese stared at MacLeod in a panic, but his quick head shake kept her silent.

"Objection," MacLeod said.

Captain Adams, not used to being a judge, looked startled before saying, "Stick to your questions, Reverend."

Reverend Mercer paced, steepling his long fingers. "Have you ever heard Annaliese speak about flying?"

Don't say it. Please don't tell.

"When Mr. Grubb got flogged, she told me it would be fun to fly to the top of the mast."

Reverend Mercer spun sharply. "Fly to the top? She actually said that?"

"Order," Captain Adams said.

Seamus's freckled face flushed. *At least he's ashamed for sending me to the gallows.*

Reverend Mercer scowled in disgust. "Tell me, Seamus, when you were chaperoning Annaliese, what did she do to my daughter, in a fit of rage?"

Seamus shifted uncomfortably from foot to foot, staring at Rebecca. "Annaliese—Miss Cameron—twisted Rebecca's arm until it popped out the socket. I tried to mend it, sir. And I elbowed Miss Cameron off, but she's so quick."

A cloud passed over the hatch, momentarily darkening the room and sending chills down Annaliese's spine.

"Did Annaliese confess her mother was a witch?"

Seamus glanced between Rebecca and Annaliese, swallowing hard. He wrenched his hat as though he were trying to squeeze milk from a stone.

Annaliese rubbed her scarred hand and didn't even blame him for tattling. *I'm wicked.*

"I don't think it was a confession, sir, more like a lie?"

Annaliese peeked up. *Seamus is defending me?*

"See, Rebecca called her mother—"

Reverend Mercer interrupted, "What I want to know, nay, what we all want to know, is did you witness Annaliese casting a spell against my daughter? A curse she admitted her mother taught her?"

Seamus stared at Annaliese a long second before glancing down and mumbling, "Begging your pardon, sir, I don't know spells, but she did point her finger at Rebecca's forehead and say, 'I curse you,' and said some words I don't know."

As the crowd exploded, Mr. Grubb stood. "How much evidence do you need? She's a witch."

Captain Adams said, "We will have order, or I'll hold the trial in my quarters."

Everyone hushed. Her stomach felt worse than from a punch from Pa. *What will rope feel like around my neck?*

Sitting triumphantly, the reverend said, "I have no more questions. Do you?"

"Aye," MacLeod said, rising. Sunlight streamed through the open hatch and warmed her face. "Ever had a bad dream, lad?"

"Aye, sir."

"Would you consider yourself possessed by the Devil?"

Reverend Mercer complained, "It's not the same thing, and Mr. MacLeod knows it."

"I believe it's my turn to question the witness, is it not?"

The reverend mock bowed, presenting Seamus as though he were a gift. MacLeod stood beneath the hatch, palm in palm behind his back, looking like a school master. Annaliese studied the jury. They seemed to pay Mac a fair amount of respect.

Seamus said, "No, sir. It's a bad dream is all, not possession."

"Let's talk about the game all four of you were playing. What was it called?"

Seamus glanced at Jacqueline and swallowed. "Eh, Questions and Commands?"

Three scallywags snickered, "Atta boy, Seamus."

A swell made the deck heave and Annaliese stumbled, flexing her knee to stay grounded.

MacLeod said, "What did Rebecca command Annaliese to do?"

Tingling all over, Annaliese locked stares with Rebecca.

Reverend Mercer rose. "Objection. Schoolyard games have naught to do with witchcraft. Focus on the crime, sir."

"Goes to provocation. Annaliese isna a witch but does have a temper when baited."

Captain Adams said, "I suppose I'll allow it, but not too long. I've no interest in childish things. Answer please, Seamus."

Seamus tinted red as a boiled lobster. "Rebecca ordered Annaliese to kiss me, sir. But neither of us wanted to, so Rebecca commanded Annaliese to climb the rigging. Jacqueline said Rebecca was trying to get Annaliese in trouble on purpose, which wasn't Christian."

A woman griped, "Hypocrite, just like her preacher father."

For the first time, adults gave disapproving frowns to perfect little Rebecca, who shivered in her seat. Feeling lightheaded, Annaliese wet her lips. *How does it feel to be hated, Rebecca?*

Seamus continued, "Eh, Annaliese kissed me, then Rebecca said she was telling her father. She called Annaliese a dirty bastard and said her mother was a whore and a witch. So, Annaliese cursed her."

Passengers gasped louder than the creaking hull. A flush crept across the Mercers' cheeks as Rebecca glowed whiter. Annaliese's slow grin spread. *That went better than I thought it would.*

"I rest." He sat and Seamus scurried back to his seat.

Reverend Mercer looked angry as he brushed his palms down his coat to smooth it. "I call Mr. Cornelius Grubb."

Staring at MacLeod with pure hatred, the old salt squared his shoulders and ambled forward, not even bothering to glance at Annaliese.

"Mr. Grubb, do you know Annaliese to be a godly child?"

"I dursen't but she certainly is not. The very first day, she ran wild as a savage, and cursed God."

He's still talking about that?

"What else did you observe that leads you to believe she bows to Satan?"

Mr. Grubb glanced at the jury. "God strike me down, but it's uncommon irregular for wind to blow us north. Only a witch could blow us this far off course. Then she cast a fog to keep us blinded, trying to lure us to our deaths into an iceberg. Calling the wind, she was."

"Objection," MacLeod said.

"That's crazy," Annaliese said, voice rising. "The only wind I make is from my bum."

Captain Adams said, "Quiet," as much to her as the laughing seamen. MacLeod's frown made her suck her lips between her teeth.

"Continue," Reverend Mercer said.

"And if you please, sir, it's powerful uncommon for a child to be shrieking every night, like the Dark Lord possesses her. Then she flies up the mast—"

"Objection."

"And when she gets brought down, it's like God himself cursed her face. There's your evidence. She's bewitched. Oh, and the puppet. She burned its hand the same night we came acrost the burned ship. You do the math."

"Objection."

Oh, no, this is bad. Her fingers twitched as she noticed the men in the jury avoiding her gaze. Then Reverend Mercer raised her doll from his table high in the air for everyone to see. Annaliese looked to Mac, but he refused to glance back. *This is really bad.*

"Even if she didn't burn the other ship, I'd bet my life the puppet harmed your little angel Rebecca's arm. I don't care what the Irish boy says about Rebecca taunting the girl. It's made up. There's no trusting a wicked Papist." Some of the Irishmen booed, and Grubb spoke over them. "If Rebecca had said those bad things during the game, it was only because she was under the little witch's spell."

"I rest," the reverend said.

Mr. Grubb started walking back to his seat.

"Where do you think you're going?" MacLeod said. "Come back for your cross-examination."

Biting back a smile, Annaliese steepled her fingers in front of her mouth, enjoying watching him squirm. Sailors chuckled as Grubb tugged his coat sharply and returned to the witness stand.

MacLeod stood with palm in palm behind his back. "Mr. Grubb, prior to this journey, how long had you been a ship's master?"

"Viscount Percy Monroe promoted me six months ago. But I've been a sailor since I was younger than the Irish boy, some fifty years at sea," Grubb said, with a pompous grin.

"The voyage prior to this one—the one where you helped Viscount Percy Monroe illegally smuggle slaves—was it smooth sailing?"

Grubb shook his head a bit, playing with his coat buttons. "We had a hard trip, sir. The ship's master died, that's why I got promoted to steer."

"In your six months experience, did anyone teach you how to read a bloody sextant to navigate a proper route from Virginia to London?"

Sailors hooted and Annaliese smiled to see other people laugh at Grubb for a change.

MacLeod continued, "Newfoundland is as far off course as you could get, which is why you are no longer ship's master, aye? That and your drunkenness, correct?"

Men in the jury leaned in as Grubb broke into a cold sweat. "Strange winds are out of my control, sir."

MacLeod faced the jury. "You said your previous passage was rough. How so?"

"Slave rebellions, sickness, storm upon storm. Terrible gales."

He faced Grubb. "Was Annaliese on the ship?"

The jury chuckled. Mr. Grubb's lips went tight. "No."

"Well, I'm confused. I thought Annaliese caused the wind?"

"An African cursed the ship, he did."

Snickers and groans came from the crowd. Rope cracked above as midshipmen called orders to adjust the rigging.

"Is anything your fault, Mr. Grubb? You dinna understand how to do your new job, but rather than ask for help you get drunk and when things go wrong, you accuse a wee lass hugging a damaged doll of performing witchcraft. This girl is facing execution for your blundering incompetence and I'm furious at the stupidity of it all."

Some members of the jury nodded, but the word execution hung in her mind.

"Is there a question, or is this a sermon?" Reverend Mercer asked.

"I'm done with this witness."

Mr. Grubb's jaw clenched. "I ain't done with you." He stormed off and one of his drinking buddies followed him, glancing around nervously.

A sour taste formed in her mouth. *What is Grubb planning?*

Chapter Forty-Four

FIONA

Astwick House, London

How strange to be here again. Astwick House felt as cold as the British aristocracy. Fiona's steps echoed against the marble floors as she followed Lady Margaret's long-suffering butler into the vacuous hallway. The thirty-foot-high ceiling had been painted in the manner of Michelangelo, with God touching Adam's finger. *I'm surprised they didna paint Lucifer thrown from heaven.*

Even wearing her diamond and emerald bracelet, her last unsold valuable, Fiona always felt like a poor farm girl in London. Memories came in a flash.

Ladies in silk gowns and sparkling jewels passed her—laughing, dancing, crystal glasses clinking. She stared at her bloody hands—William touching her cheek.

"What a delightful surprise," said the butler, Mr. Belmont. "How is Mr. MacLeod?"

"That's what I'm hoping to discover."

Ever the proper servant, Belmont remained silent as he escorted her into a round room painted teal with family portraits and oil paintings of ships weathering storms hung on golden chains. Lady Margaret was ripping a newspaper to shreds as Mr. Belmont announced Fiona. Com-

TO RESCUE A WITCH

pletely startled by the interruption, Lady Margaret put the pieces on a nearby table, glared at the butler, then rose and kissed Fiona's cheeks.

"Fiona, don't you look gothic? What a surprise. How lucky I was home to receive you. Are you on your way elsewhere?"

How can I look her in the face? "My lady, forgive my intrusion." Fiona curtsied. "You haven't aged a bit."

Lady Margaret smiled at the flattery, and indicated for Fiona to sit opposite, eyeing her bracelet. A servant poured the scalding tea. Composure fully regained, her ladyship's face became unreadable. "Relax, darling Fiona. We're old friends, aren't we? Are your sons well?"

Friends? They hadn't been in the same room since the incident. "Our oldest, James, is expecting his first wean."

"A grandmother already, Fiona? You hide your years well." Lady Margaret patted the table between them in a pseudo gesture of camaraderie.

"My lady, I winnae take much time. William left in early summer. It's mid-November and I haven't received a single letter. Surely, he would have updated Lord Hallewell on his progress. I've written multiple times to my lord, but he hasn't replied."

Lady Margaret politely sipped her tea to hide her grin. "I understand your worry. It's unlike your husband to be mute. I often tease his surname should be Mac Loud."

Fiona cringed at the barb.

Lady Margaret took a polished silver spoon and added four sugar scoops to her tea. "There, there, my dear creature. These overseas posts are slow. My first husband used to complain about it all the time."

"Lord Hallewell has had no word, either?"

"None he has shared with me, I'm afraid." Lady Margaret lifted the bone-white teacup rimmed with red thorns and rosettes to her lips, blowing away the steam. "You'll have to read my tea leaves when we're done. I'm very curious about my future."

The Rococo chair felt hard and uneven, as if designed to make people uncomfortable. "I've not done readings in years, my lady." *Not since the wedding.*

Fiona had once considered Lord George Hallewell a friend, back when they were all young and George was sick of being penniless. Marrying

Lady Margaret was the cure that poisoned the patient. "Perhaps his lordship wishes to join us for tea?"

"He's out, doing who knows what."

Fiona poured a spot of cream to soften the bitterness, stirring the silver spoon around the teacup like a cauldron. *If only I could cast an honesty spell over Lady Margaret's brew.*

Lady Margaret said, "I'll put in inquiries for you about William. Which ship did he use?"

Fiona sipped. "The one he commandeered for Lord Hallewell."

"Ah, yes, Lord Percy Monroe's ship. Have you checked the newspapers? Ships wreck all the time." Lady Margaret sipped casually, as though William's potential death was insignificant gossip.

A tightness in Fiona's stomach spread. "Aye, my lady. I scan the papers constantly, but thankfully haven't read of any disasters. Perhaps there was a delay in departing?"

"My darling Fiona, I apologize you came such a long way for naught." Lady Margaret stood, her red gown spilling like slaughter as she passed gargantuan windows and ventured to the balcony. "You must view the landscape before you go."

Fiona glanced on the table at the ripped society gossip pages piecing phrases together, 'Lord Percy ... wife's delicate condition ... hopes for a son.' *Hm.* Fiona stared into Lady Margaret's teacup to study the leaves. A blurred anchor fastened to the rim, revealing trying times—or did the anchor symbolize William's trip? In the brown liquid at the bottom, the near future, lurked a double-headed serpent, just like in Fiona's visions. Were enemies multiplying or fighting against themselves? Fiona rubbed her temples as she joined Lady Margaret.

Lady Margaret said, "I know you Scots shun Christmas, but you simply must attend our yuletide ball this year. I recall how passionately you danced at my wedding with Colonel Wilkes. He was so handsome and debonair. Such a shame about his disappearance."

And now we broach the subject. Does Lady Margaret think I dinna ken about her blackmailing us? Is this conversation an amusement for her?

Lady Margaret said, "His widow and son recently visited."

"You still keep in touch? Why?" Fiona felt her face burn. "Beg pardon, my lady. 'Tis none of my business."

Lady Margaret shrugged gamely. Beyond the windows, groundskeepers busied themselves pruning rose bushes in the intricate garden. London street noise did not venture this far back. *These nobles control everything, dinna they?*

"My gardeners have been digging up old roots. The things they unearthed would surprise you. Or not."

Lavender from Lady Margaret's meticulously molded curls mingled with her overwhelming narcissus perfume. Fiona closed her eyes, trying to breathe. "Aye. William told me before he left for the colonies."

Eisd rium a Dhia. Ancient gods, protect my family, wrap me in your safe arms. "My lady, William has spent his life demonstrating loyalty to his lordship and your family. I'm grateful you're doing the same for our family, stopping all the malicious rumors about Colonel Wilkes."

Lady Margaret took the measure of Fiona. "You truly love your husband, don't you?"

"Aye, my lady. And he loves me." *But William is missing, and pride winnae feed my boys.* "I dinna—I'm embarrassed to have to ask, but—it's been over five months with no income. I'm not here to ask for all the money William gave you, but just a wee bit back to help us get through until William's homecoming."

Lady Margaret placed her ice-cold hand over Fiona's. "And if he doesn't return?"

Fiona's skin became clammy. "William is alive."

Lady Margaret slid away her hand, casually returning to her chair. "Well, let's speak frankly. I'm surprised your husband handled his finances so poorly. I only asked for a small sum to keep quiet about your husband's involvement in Colonel Wilkes' *disappearance*. William makes a great deal of money as trustee of my son's inheritance."

Fiona sat. "Truth be told, my lady, we're in a terrible spot. Robbers ransacked William's law office, and all the strongboxes were stolen. His clients—Lord Hallewell's friends—have abandoned us. The famine grows worse, ruining our crops, and my son recently discovered someone is foreclosing on farms William signed loans for."

Ask her. "Are you—that is to say—"

"Surely you know your husband's brashness creates enemies?"

"Brash in service of your husband, my lady. William told me before he left, he settled matters with the Earl of Cheshire over his son, so I dinna understand—"

Lady Margaret steepled her hands to her lips, as if contemplating her next chess move, until her eyes fell on the ripped society pages. "Perhaps Mr. MacLeod fixed things with the fifth Earl of Cheshire, but the old earl is dead. The sixth Earl of Cheshire is Lord Percy, who apparently seeks his own restitution."

No wonder! "My lady, Lord Hallewell must intervene on our behalf. With William gone, I'm at a loss for what to do. Lord Percy is hurting more than just William. I have young sons, we have tenants, field hands to pay. If we become bankrupt, dozens will suffer as well."

"I had no idea you were in such dire straits or that a mere two thousand pounds would hurt your sons. Of course I'll give some back—only I've already spent the majority."

Fiona's sense of hope—and pride—was crushed.

Lady Margaret said, "I'll speak to Lord Hallewell on your behalf, but I don't know how inclined he'll be to intervene."

"I dinna follow?"

"Apparently, our spouses had a falling out."

Fiona felt queasy. "You mean over finding Colonel Wilkes' emblem in the courtyard?"

"You mean the one wrapped in your bloodstained shawl?"

Fiona's cheeks scorched. *How much did Lady Margaret ken? Lord Hallewell wouldn't tell her, would he? Did he even ken the whole truth?*

Lady Margaret pursed her lips. "In all honesty, my lord acted conspicuously incurious about evidence of a murder in our home. No, I heard them arguing over ..." Glancing over her shoulder, she whispered, "It pertains to the mistress in Virginia. Ever since Mr. MacLeod left, my lord has been questioning former servants. If I discover why, shall I tell you?"

How can I trust anything Lady Margaret says? But I ken William is hiding something, too, like the flirtatious note in his desk from Eleanor. "If Lord Hallewell is upset, where does that leave my husband? He's in the colonies at your husband's command."

Lady Margaret stood, smoothing her petticoats with ruby-ringed fingers. "I'll see you out." Wrapping her arm through Fiona's, they strolled into the great hall. Servants with feather dusters scrambled up the grand stairs to hide themselves, past centuries of dominant tyrants smiling in their golden frames.

Fiona stopped. "My lady, Lord Percy pursues the destruction of my family. Are we to be abandoned?"

Lady Margaret stood in the long hall flanked by centuries of weapons. "Not by me." Her ladyship smiled with mismatched teeth. "I want to help you financially, but I'm limited. When my husband cut off my allowance, and I sought help, your husband said, 'Who am I to interfere when a man disciplines his wife?'"

Fiona shrank. William's arrogance kept coming back to harm them.

"Still, I have a little money set aside. Why not sell me something?" Lady Margaret eyed Fiona's bracelet.

Fiona covered her wrist. "This is my only—"

"When are those notes due? Debtors' prison is not pleasant, I hear. Be sensible."

Fiona saw black spots and sank into a red velvet armchair between two suits of armor, feeling like a victim of multiple violent conquests.

Lady Margaret patted Fiona's hand. "There, there. I'll buy the bracelet. It's a trinket I don't need but let me help you."

What choice remained? "Thank you, my lady, you are kind." Fiona's fingers shook as she unhooked the bracelet. "You'll let me buy it back when William arrives? It means so much."

"I'll get it appraised and send you the money this week."

Fiona stood with as much dignity as she could muster. "Thank you, my lady. If Lord Hallewell gets a letter from William, you'll tell me?"

"You'll be the very first to know."

They kissed cheeks goodbye. James sat waiting to drive the coach home. Fiona climbed silently inside, wiped the kiss off her face, put one hand over her mouth and covered it with the other so her son wouldn't hear her cry. Her wedding band spun wildly.

Good God, what am I to do?

Chapter Forty-Five

WILLIAM MACLEOD

Good God, this next witness is going to be tough.

Reverend Mercer said, "I call my wife, Mrs. Constance Mercer." Mrs. Mercer stepped up and swore on a Bible. "In your capacity as the accused's tutor, do you believe the girl to be under Satan's power?"

"I know it to be true. Annaliese says things a little girl wouldn't say. She knows things a little girl should not know. She targets my daughter constantly."

Reverend Mercer laid a hand on his wife's bony shoulder. "Do you seek revenge?"

"No." Mrs. Mercer stared at Annaliese. "I pray for the girl's salvation daily. I know she despises me for being strict, but doesn't God command us to chasten those we love?"

MacLeod surveyed the jurors nodding in agreement. *Shite.* Mrs. Mercer made a powerful witness. Studying her features, he searched his brain for the best way to cross-examine her without provoking anger. Jurors seek to punish people for their crimes. They wouldna take kindly to a barrister attacking the mother of the victim.

"Hearing her nightly torments rips my heart. I feared Satan had claimed her soul and her examination proved it. The Devil bites her."

"That ain't true," Annaliese squealed.

Reverend Mercer pulled off Annaliese's glove, exposing her scarred arm to gasps. "Observe the markings of Satan's tongue."

Hold fast, MacLeod. Benches creaked and clothes ruffled as everyone leaned in for a better view, causing a wave of odors from unwashed bodies to flood his nostrils. Annaliese's cheeks burned as she shied away from the gawking crowd. Crumpling into herself, she dropped her chin to her chest.

"Order."

"Do you rest? I have my own witnesses." At the reverend's nod, MacLeod said, "I call Surgeon Johnsson."

Walls and floors shifted with the heave of the ship, their support forever inconstant. Walking forward, the doctor tied his blond hair neatly back with a white ribbon.

"Surgeon Johnsson, how long have you practiced medicine?"

"Fifteen years, sir."

"We'll get to the marks on her body in a moment. But first, Mr. Grubb would have us believe Annaliese became bewitched while climbing the mast. In your expert opinion, can you medically explain why Annaliese's face became blotchy red and itchy?"

"Hives, sir." The Swede stared at the confused seamen. "A rash, you would call it."

"Not bewitchment?"

Surgeon Johnsson smiled. "Nothing magical about hives. They come when the humors are imbalanced due to extreme fear, cold or wind. She most likely experienced all three."

"Thank you, sir. You've examined Annaliese today as well, aye?"

The doctor nodded. "Her anatomy is an exhibition of cruelty. The child was beaten until her bones broke, scarred from the lash, stabbed. It's a wonder she's alive."

MacLeod faced the jury. "You're positive the marks are man-made, not from the Devil?"

"Sadly, it seems she lived through hell on earth." Surgeon Johnsson's pale blue eyes rested kindly on Annaliese, the only pity she received all day. "Those 'bites' aren't from animals, let alone hounds from hell. They're burns. You can tell by the puckered skin."

MacLeod said to Annaliese, "Your pa burned you when he was drunk?"

Avoiding everyone's gaze, she said softly, "Yes, sir."

MacLeod raised her arm, hoping his warm touch reassured her. "Here? Here? Here?" He pointed to the circles up and down her forearm. After a few seconds, the jury turned away, unable to look anymore. A few shook their heads, tugging their thumbs across their lips.

Surgeon Johnsson said, "The scar on her hand is from a fire poker. See the outline?"

MacLeod said to Annaliese, "How old were you when your pa first burned you?"

"Five," she barely whispered.

"Five. Years. Old."

MacLeod let the words linger. People shifted awkwardly in their seats, dropping their gaze to the ground. MacLeod kissed her hand and gently let go.

"I walked in on Annaliese burning her doll, not to make a spell, but because that's what she thought parents do to their children." Holding the doll's burned hand next to Annaliese's, he stared down the jury. "Is it starting to make sense?"

"Captain Adams, I'd like to submit this letter from the child's mother as evidence of her cruel treatment. Surgeon Johnsson, please read it aloud."

"'My Dearest George, I know I'm not supposed to write you, but I must. You have a daughter, Annaliese. I fear my husband will kill us. I beg your mercy and forgiveness. If you ever loved me, please save our daughter.' It's signed Eleanor."

MacLeod faced the jury. "The marks on the girl's body are indeed the work of the Devil. The devil's name was Rob Birch."

Visibly shaken, Mrs. Mercer made a *tsk* sound, then covered her mouth with her hand.

A bell rang three times, signaling the change in shifts. A third of the crew went up the hatches as new crew members came to watch, their clothes soaked with ocean spray and skin flushed pink from the blustery weather. Mr. Grubb returned with a satchel and a smug look and sat next to his friends.

TO RESCUE A WITCH

MacLeod didna like Grubb's expression but focused on his witness. "Surgeon Johnsson, in your profession, have you ever treated anyone for nightmares?"

Jurors tilted their bodies forward. Passengers hushed each other, straining to hear.

"Ja, I have, sir. In fact, I've given Annaliese some teas, but only when I saw her wounds did her nightmares make sense. I've had patients—soldiers and slaves—confide they have vivid dreams where they believe they are reliving some terrible event and they wake screaming. There's no cure, I'm sorry to say."

"In your expert opinion, do you think someone with sustained injuries, like this wee bairn, might have similar vivid dreams?"

"I cannot speak to the contents of her dreams, but ja, it's a reasonable assumption," said the doctor.

Reverend Mercer stood. "African slaves? Soldiers fearing battle? This is the so-called expert's theory to explain her nightly wails?" His lip curled into a snarl.

"I speak honestly, sir. A doctor neither chooses nor judges his patients. I'm here to heal."

"And I, sir," the reverend said, "am trying to save this ship from disaster."

Grubb and his cronies clapped their calloused hands together.

"Who anointed you the next savior?" MacLeod said.

Gentlemen in wigs and fine coats pounded their canes on the ground to support MacLeod. Women flitted their gaze around the room, marking the constant shift in power.

Captain Adams asked, "Do you have any more witnesses, Mr. MacLeod?"

He nodded. "I call Ahanu."

Reverend Mercer faced the crowd, outraged. "Objection. In what English court of law is a heathen allowed to testify?"

People perked up, shushing others as they listened.

MacLeod faced Captain Adams. "Ahanu isn't a heathen, he's baptized. And he's not testifying against anyone white, he's merely serving as a translator."

"I'll allow it."

Drifting into the wind, the ship rattled. Ahanu laughed nervously as he came forward, pushing his braids behind his shoulders.

MacLeod said, "Ahanu, please tell us what languages you speak."

"English, Powhatan, from my mother's people, and Algonquin, from my father's people."

"Thank you, sir. Do you remember the first time you met Annaliese? I believe you were climbing from the orlop, aye?"

Ahanu nodded. "Someone called my name, and Annaliese said, 'He Laughs.' That's what my name means."

"You're saying she speaks Algonquin?"

"I wouldn't say she's part of the tribe, but she knows a few words." Two jurors chuckled.

Reverend Mercer said, "Objection. Relevance?"

MacLeod spun to Annaliese. "What curse did you say?"

Rebecca buried her face in her mother's bosom as the court gasped.

"Objection," Reverend Mercer shouted. "Do you attempt to let her utter the curse again?"

Annaliese said loudly, "*Nimatew Maheegan Attemous Keshowse.*"

Rebecca swooned. A frigid blast pitched the hull again, making the ground shake. "Did she curse us now?" Mr. Grubb asked.

"Order," Captain Adams called.

Passengers looked visibly shaken as they settled back in their seats.

MacLeod asked, "Ahanu, what do those words mean?"

Ahanu bit back a smile. "Man, wolf, dog, sun."

Gentlemen in the jury raised their eyebrows. A sunray shone through the open hatch onto Annaliese, making her appear very young.

Reverend Mercer said, "The heathen's lying to protect her, creating innocuous words."

MacLeod held out a book. "Ahanu, can you read?" He nodded. "Please turn to page forty-seven in *The Travel Journal of Thomas Patterson* and tell us what it says."

Ahanu flipped through, then read, "Common words from Chesapeake Bay tribes."

"And do the words *nimatew, maheegan, attemous, keshowse* mean man, wolf, dog, sun?"

"Yes, sir." Ahanu chuckled, pointing them out to the captain.

Captain Adams addressed Annaliese. "You told the preacher's daughter you put a hex on her, and then used Indian words? Man, wolf, dog, sun? That was your curse?"

Annaliese shrugged. "I reckon it was a stupid thing to do."

Men of the jury shook their heads, trying hard not to chuckle.

Captain Adams said to Reverend Mercer, "I should be overseeing my crew and you're wasting my time with childish taunts about man, wolf, dog, sun?"

Reverend Mercer looked flustered. "But the evidence—" Mrs. Mercer rested her hand on her heart, glancing between her daughter and Annaliese.

Captain Adams said, "And you, Mr. MacLeod, should have shared the girl's past with at least some of us instead of allowing the situation to fester."

"Aye, I should have done." MacLeod faced the Mercers. "The girl was treated cruelly her whole life and is misbehaving. Cannae we settle things as fathers rather than involving judge and jury?" He moved closer to the reverend. "We are speaking of executing a child based on the unreliable testimony of Mr. Grubb, a bitter drunk who cannae admit to his own incompetence. Heaven knows the lass was wrong for scaring Rebecca, but teasing isna witchcraft. Reverend, is that justice?"

Captain Adams said to the jury, "What say you? Is she guilty or innocent?"

Gentlemen of the jury whispered among themselves. "Innocent," the foreman said.

Passengers stretched their arms, rolling their shoulders as if a burden had been lifted. A few even joked in light conversation.

Mr. Grubb stood and complained, "This is bollocks. Did you know MacLeod's wife is a witch?" He grabbed Eleanor's journal from his satchel and held it high above his head.

Oh, shite. The crowd erupted. Something bumped into the ship, making a muffled thud, perhaps sharks smelling blood. MacLeod lunged for it, but Grubb's men held him back.

"Order," Captain Adams said. He looked at the skinny, nervous sailor and Mr. Grubb. "Explain yourselves."

Fidgeting with his hip-length gray coat over his checked linen shirt, the sailor said, "Mr. MacLeod threw it overboard when I was scraping barnacles, but I fished it out, sir. At first, I thought it was the Devil's black book, but it's a diary. There's lots of dirty bits in it," he said with a giggle, but flushed red at the captain's serious expression. "There's talk of witchcraft, too. I just showed it to Mr. Grubb now and he said it's evidence."

Annaliese looked like she had been punched in the gut. "You had Ma's book all along?"

MacLeod's heartbeat raced as he pleaded with Captain Adams. "Annaliese's mother has been dead for half a decade. There's no relevance about her musings on my wife."

Grubb said, "The girl confessed her mother, Eleanor, was a witch and taught her spells. Let the jury hear what Eleanor wrote about MacLeod's wife."

MacLeod's fingers and chest tingled. Papers slid across the table as the gales blew louder. Captain Adams stared at MacLeod in dismay.

Grubb opened the earmarked book. "Here's a conversation MacLeod had with Annaliese's mother, Eleanor, in March 1724. They were *drunk*," he said with a sneer, "and talking about his wife, Fiona. Mr. MacLeod said, 'Fiona thinks she has second sight.' Eleanor said, 'Your wife sees the future?' He confessed, 'One day I came home early with the local preacher. Fiona had made a salt circle around herself in the garden.' Eleanor said, 'Your wife's a witch?'"

Passengers and sailors alike began to panic.

"Witch."

"The Devil owns him."

"Order," Captain Adams shouted.

Grubb said to the jury, "He's married to a witch. William MacLeod is the guilty one. He's making the girl a hellbride for his wife's coven."

A third of the crowd stood behind Grubb. Reverend Mercer kept shifting focus between faces, flustered. The veneer of civilization abandoned the crew. Grubb's friends dragged MacLeod above deck, with the entire crowd following.

"Whip him until he confesses," Mr. Grubb said, eyes gleaming, eager to exact revenge.

Sailors bound MacLeod's wrists and ankles to the rigging and ripped away his shirt, exposing the sachet around his neck.

Grubb raised the bag of seaweed and mugwort high above his head. "It's an ill wish."

MacLeod shouted, "That's not an ill wish, it's an amulet for a safe journey, no different than the horseshoe nailed above your bed or the hag stones I see around crew mates' necks."

Sailors instinctively clutched their talismans.

Grubb said, "Hang him and the girl before it's too late."

Jacqueline and her mother hugged Annaliese close, backing away from the crowd. Jacqueline said to Reverend Mercer, "The jury found her innocent. You can't hang her."

Annaliese's hands balled into fists and the wind swelled, rocking the ship leeward as people argued. An eerie sound of water caught in the bilge rolled beneath them as a peal of thunder rumbled above.

Chapter Forty-Six

FIONA

Scotland

    A letter arrived from Lady Margaret with a black seal. A bad omen.

    Fiona's green plaid skirt blew in the wind as she raced her stallion until he foamed with sweat. At the cliff's edge, she dismounted, ripping open the letter as brown buzzards circled the crumbling castle.

> My dearest Fiona,
>
> I've uncovered much since your visit. First, I send you an urgent warning about Lord Percy Monroe, whom we've previously discussed. He was Alexander's friend, so I believed him honorable, but I've come to realize he is a fraud and completely untrustworthy. I've discovered he is the mastermind behind the robbery of your husband's law office. While I don't know his plans, I've heard he left for Scotland with dangerous companions. Fortify your homestead. Sadly, I must also disclose a treachery closer to your heart. We both knew Lord Hallewell takes liberties with his marital vows, but I never thought your husband did. Until now.

Enclosed is a sworn statement from a former scullery maid. Ten years ago, your husband was tasked with teaching my husband's mistress, Eleanor Cameron, to read. Didn't he teach you to read? Perhaps it's his unique form of courting? The maid said he once made all the servants leave for an hour during a terrible snow. When she returned, he was gone, and the harlot was drunk and half naked in bed. While circumstantial, I'm sure a barrister's wife is interested in learning all the evidence and judging the merits herself.

Apparently, there is a by-blow, named Annaliese. Your husband wrote to my lord he would be home in October, yet December approaches. Curious he contacted my lord, but not his wife. Perhaps a guilty hand cannot write?

I'm sure he can explain it to you should he decide to reappear. Then again, you need not be Oxford-educated to put two and two together. Maybe he stayed in Williamsburg with his other family?

I write this not to be cruel but to reveal the true man you married. I'm sorry to be the bearer of bad tidings, but above all, you have my honesty.

Your most humble servant

Lady Margaret Hallewell

P.S.—I've enclosed twelve pounds for the bracelet.

Fiona read the signed and witnessed statement from the maid, then crumpled both letters. *This isna right. Not William.*

But the child's name—Annaliese. William's mother was named Elise. *Coincidence?* Fiona thought back a decade, to when Broderick was four. They fought constantly over the boy. No wonder William stayed in London more frequently and for longer stretches. Fiona remembered that spring blizzard, the worst in a century. She even said a protection spell for his safe return, then felt guilty for using magic.

William said the snow delayed him ... Eleanor Cameron—*his lover*—delayed him.

Fiona pulled her tartan shawl over her head, but it couldn't warm her from the falling rain. Waves battered the rocks. Her knuckles grew white from their grip on the crumpled letter. Collapsing to her knees, hands in the dirt, the vomit came swiftly.

My visions foretold his journey. Didna the fairy girl call me Mama? I thought it might be our daughter who died in childbirth and was now a changeling. I never expected it to be his bastard. She wiped her mouth, feeling empty. *Can I trust Lady Margaret? But this isna insinuation, there's a bloody signed and witnessed deposition. And that note in William's desk from Eleanor, calling him a strict headmaster ...*

Broken shells blew over the rocky cliff. Her anger gathered like a shock in the sky.

Everybody ken but me. Servants. Lady Margaret. What a fool they must think I am. Edijit. I can foresee the future but cannae tell when my husband has an affair?

William had left them in ruins to flee to some whore in the colonies. *I ken he was lying—keeping secrets.* Eleanor wasn't just a mistress; she was *his* mistress.

Fiona screamed a banshee wail at the sky. "Was Eleanor pretty, William? Did you tell her you loved her? Laugh at how stupid your wife was trusting you alone in London?"

William is cruel to Broderick, born through no fault of his own, yet sires his own wee bastard? William promised he would defend me but never did. He left me to be raped and never fought to defend me from the Church; he just allowed them to punish me and paid to keep them quiet to protect his stupid pride.

He's so selfish. All these men were so selfish. William, Lord Hallewell, Colonel Wilkes, Lord Percy. They cause such pain then leave it to women to pick up the shattered pieces.

Fiona rose to confront the sea and held her right hand high over the troubled waters.

Eisd rium a Dhia. William MacLeod, I curse you. Feel abandoned, like you abandoned me to chase after the English nobility. Feel humiliated the way you humiliate Broderick. Hurt until you repent in your heart for the damage you caused our family. So it be done.

A thunderclap shook the earth. Waves exploded into white froth over the jagged rocks as seagulls squawked and staggered in the sky. Strange winds blew such that the sand left the beach to crawl up the ramparts and the sun's fiery orb was swallowed by the darkness.

Fiona opened her fist, and the letter blew out to sea.

Chapter Forty-Seven

WILLIAM MACLEOD

Lightning splintered across the pregnant sky. A storm unlike anything he ever witnessed before rumbled toward the cursed ship from the northeast. Black clouds rose taller than mountains as blue sparks bounced inside.

"I'm innocent!" William MacLeod shouted.

"Try to save yourself now without your charm," Grubb said, throwing Fiona's sachet into the sea. Grubb found a cat-o'-nine-tails and slashed MacLeod's back with the ferocity of a younger man, as thunder boomed. One sailor readied a noose while Annaliese stood stunned beside Jacqueline and her mother.

Captain Adams ordered, "Lower the sails. Steer clear from the storm."

"No, I'm giving the orders now," Mr. Grubb said, gripping the whip and pointing it at him. "Mark my words, once we throw MacLeod overboard, the storm will pass."

Half the crew obeyed the captain, moving to pull down the sails. Mr. Grubb's mutinous men stopped them, holding out their knives, ready for battle. Wind swelled.

"I'm not a witch, you damned fool. Read the rest of Eleanor's diary. My wife was punished by the Church for her sins. She paid her debt to society fifteen years ago. Am I to be murdered for sins already paid for?"

He looked at the Mercers. "Do you not believe in redemption? Were your sermons nothing but lies?"

Reverend Mercer froze, staring at the men ready to do battle on his command.

Captain Adams said to the reverend, "Do you want blood on your hands? If we don't lower the sails now, we'll all be lost. The storm is minutes away."

Reverend Mercer finally found his voice. He held the rail as the gales grew stronger. "God smites the wicked. The girl can be redeemed but throw MacLeod overboard. Let God decide if he should live."

"No!" cried Annaliese, running toward him.

"Gardez-la en sécurité," MacLeod called to Jacqueline's mother. She dragged Annaliese away with Jacqueline following, racing down the hatch to safety. Sailors staggered forward to furl the sails, preparing the ship to weather the tempest.

As the storm rolled closer, the pungent odor of the atmosphere burned his nostrils, and the humidity crushed him. Grubb cast a noose over MacLeod's neck, then cut the ropes at MacLeod's feet and one hand. It allowed enough freedom for MacLeod to punch Grubb's gut as sailors swarmed.

In a shocking instant, the storm howled at a volume MacLeod didna know existed. Terrified passengers were thrown about like cannonballs in a battle. Hail pummeled the mob cramming the ladders to the 'tween deck, fighting each other to reach safety. They battened down the hatches, leaving MacLeod alone with Grubb.

Loose crates transformed into projectiles aimed at them as the ship tilted and Grubb's knife slipped from his hand and slid across the deck. While Grubb chased after it, MacLeod tried to wrench his left hand loose from the rigging, but the more he struggled, the tighter the rope pulled, till he was afraid his hand might sever.

Freezing ocean spray and salt licked MacLeod's open wounds. Coughing up sand, he trembled at the colossal wave forming in the distance, knowing in thirty seconds he might be dead. His life passed before him as the ship began to climb the mountainous surge. Time slowed and he saw Fiona before him.

Fiona, I'm sorry. You were right. I should have believed in your magic and heeded your warnings, instead of always putting my ambition first. I was so busy chasing English nobility, I lost your love. I lost myself. I was cruel to Broderick and created a situation that allowed Annaliese to be harmed.

Grubb lifted the knife from the icy deck and lumbered toward him for the kill as a wave grew insurmountable.

Please forgive me. Oh, God, let me live to make it up to everyone.

Grubb thrust forward with his knife as MacLeod twisted into the rigging to avoid the blade. The wave crashed over them. A blue bolt splintered across the sky and the spark of electricity revealed Mr. Grubb's shocked expression as he got dragged overboard by the hand of an angry God.

MacLeod held his breath as his body was thrown back behind him, but the rope binding his wrist kept him aboard.

∞

Sunshine glistened off the snow, nearly blinding him as he awoke. *Am I dead?* MacLeod found himself slumped to the ground, coughing; his left arm still bound high above him. Pain stabbed every muscle of his beaten body. *How long was I unconscious?*

A hatch opened. Annaliese ran to him, sliding on the snow and hugging him tight. His body burned with fever.

"Annaliese," he said, hoarsely.

Reverend Mercer led his congregation of curious onlookers to check for survivors. People worshiped Reverend Mercer like a king, kneeling and kissing his ring. "It's a miracle. You saved our ship from the storm."

"Where's Grubb?" asked Captain Adams.

"Overboard," said MacLeod weakly. His shivers grew to shaking.

A sailor asked, "Should we lock MacLeod in the brig until we arrive at port?"

Annaliese looked directly at Reverend Mercer. "You said, 'God would smite the wicked.' Well, Grubb's gone and Mr. MacLeod's still here. Seems like God spoke pretty clear."

MacLeod couldn't help but smile. *Wee brave Annaliese is defending me now.*

Glancing between the passengers and crew, the reverend nodded.

"I never liked Mr. Grubb," a woman said.

Ahanu pulled out his knife and sliced the rope to free his wrist. MacLeod rubbed his wrist, raw and stinging from salt.

Mrs. Mercer held Eleanor's journal. "We read the diary. Regardless of what your wife did, I know you don't support witchcraft, Mr. MacLeod. I suppose I should return this to you," she said, handing it to him, but Annaliese grabbed it instead.

"Naw, ma'am. This was my ma's book. It ain't his."

MacLeod lowered his aching head. Someday he'd have a long conversation with her, but right now he could barely keep his eyes open.

Surgeon Johnsson checked his forehead. "I don't like your fever. We need to expulse your waste retention, ja? I'll make you elixir vitriol. Let's help you to the sick berth."

Chapter Forty-Eight

ELEANOR

London, March 1729

"Leave us," Mr. MacLeod ordered the servants, walking into my fashionable London tenement, "for an hour at least."

Snowflakes fell behind him. He took off his overcoat, draping it over the chair. Cold clung to his clothes and heat rose to my face.

"What's the meaning of this?" He waved my letter. "I'm not your damned servant, Eleanor. Why are you sending me notes? You want to get servants gossiping?"

"Stop scowling at me, Mr. MacLeod." My lip quivered.

"Jesus, Joseph and Mary, a weepy mistress. Why are you crying?"

"Lord Hallewell dinna love me."

"So?"

"So? He says he loves me, but is it a trick? He says he wants a bairn with me, but what if he stops being attracted? Even learning to read didna help. He's too talented and worldly for me. I stay in bed for the money, thinking it'll be enough, but I feel dirty because I ken he'll leave."

MacLeod brought a whiskey bottle and two glasses from the cabinet. "Ah, Eleanor, you're young. Do you want my advice? Keep lying with him, and if you feel dirty, take a bath." He uncorked it. We were committed to finishing the bottle now.

He continued, "Lord Hallewell adores you. If you play your cards right, you'll be his proper mistress for a long time and stay in this nice tenement. But dinna get with child, no matter what he says." He handed me a dram. "*Slàinte Mhath.*" We drank.

"What if I already am?"

MacLeod stiffened. "Are you?" His tone disconcerted me.

"No. I was just joking." I traced the glass rim.

Methodically untwisting the cork from the corkscrew, he said, "If you become with child, I'll place the bairn in a suitable home. The bastards are always cared for."

"Bastards? How many are there? I winnae care for my child?"

He stopped twisting. "I shouldnae have mentioned it." Tugging the cork, he stopped again, putting it down. "You're in a delicate condition, aren't you?" MacLeod grabbed my breasts and squeezed. "If you're with child, I'll know in a month when your tits get full."

I smacked his hands away. "Get off me. What the hell are you doing?"

It was such an awkward moment we both started laughing. There was an undeniable spark between us, even though he didna want it. Lord Hallewell was fickle as the moon, but MacLeod would make an excellent Plan B. I needed someone loyal to me and MacLeod had a great arse.

"Perhaps you'd like to examine my diddeys further?" I untied my bodice, freeing them from their confines. His shocked expression was priceless. I enjoyed the constant tension during my reading lessons, him fighting his attraction for me, pretending it wasna there. Headmaster, indeed.

"Eleanor, you take things too far." Tossing a nearby shawl over me, he pitched the cork in the fire. "Keep Lord Hallewell happy because he'll ruin you if you cross him. Rather, I'll be the one to do it, and I dinna want to hurt you, lass."

Outside, snowflakes blew in the wind, sticking to the tall windows. "I have to get home or Fiona will bite my head off. A month from now, I'll be sure to squeeze your tits," he said, putting on his overcoat, buttoning it deliberately.

"I dinna understand you. You say you love her but make her sound like a hag."

His hand rested on the door. "It's complicated."

I poured two more drams. "I'm talking with my lover's solicitor about whether I should stay in the affair for the money. I think I understand complicated."

I held out the drink. Obviously, he came back inside. Men always love to talk about their wives with an understanding mistress. Dropping his coat on the chair, he took the glass, brushing his fingers against mine and letting the touch linger.

"Sometimes people grow apart, even when they dinna mean to." Emptying his glass, he moved to a stiff-backed armchair with the fireplace burning behind him.

Whiskey warmed me. His closeness warmed me. I laid back on the couch. "What's your full name?"

"William George Henri Alasdair MacLeod."

"George is so boring. I like fancy names. French people have the best-sounding names."

My shawl slipped ever so slightly to expose my right nipple. MacLeod looked. He pretended not to, but he ogled before speaking. "Enough whiskey, lass," he said, sliding the glass away. "My mother, God rest her soul, was French."

Speak of your mother to end the flirting. Well played, sir. "Oh? What was her name?" I took back my glass and finished it.

"Elise."

"Now, there's a fancy name." I turned the glass upside down on the table.

"What was your mother's name?" he asked, amused.

"Anna. Not nearly as fancy as your mam."

He chuckled. I started removing the pins from my hair. "I hope you dinna mind if I let my hair down. Can I do that? Let my hair down with you?"

His eyes held mischief. "I'm not the king of you," he said in a lazy, masculine way.

My blonde hair cascaded down my back, soft on my skin. Joining me on the couch, he poured another dram for us. Even big as he was, the whiskey was working its magic. Alcohol provides a delightfully simple excuse for stolen kisses. And more.

"My fair maiden," he said, moving some strands behind my ear, before clearing his throat. "My wife has brown hair."

"Does she? Why does she avoid London? Tell me about your complicated relationship, William George, six other names MacLeod."

I laughed. He laughed, then studied me. "I think you're oot yer tree," he said, his true burr escaping.

I hold my liquor quite well, but he didna need to ken. "Ack, I've nowhere to be, and I sorely need good conversation."

"I think you sorely need more than that," he said, with a dimple in his cheek.

Finishing his dram, he pushed the whiskey aside and sat forward. "I've told no one this, so I trust you to hold your tongue."

"Now, that's how to start a complicated conversation."

"My wife, she's the opposite of you."

"Oh, she's ugly and stupid?"

"Shy." MacLeod adjusted my shawl, covering me more. He really wanted to speak about his wife, poor sot. "I arranged Lord Hallewell's marriage. My reputation as a valuable barrister was growing. Nobles expected to meet my wife, so I forced her to come to London, even when her visions warned her to stay home."

"Your wife sees the future?"

"She thinks she has second sight." He turned away with a haunted look. "I forced her to come to London, then left her to the wolves. I should have been dancing with my wife, but instead I left her alone while I negotiated a deal. Fiona danced with another man."

"Colonel Wilkes."

MacLeod went slack-jawed.

"All the servants gossiped your wife cast a love spell to make you jealous. They said Fiona and Colonel Wilkes were playing at rantum-scantum during Hallewell's wedding."

MacLeod sat stunned, shaking his head, then drank directly from the bottle. "Bloody servants. I'm sure Lady Margaret promoted those rumors, too, bitch that she is. Colonel Wilkes was *her* lover. Lady Margaret lusted for another man at her own wedding." He stared forward, staring into the past. "I quizzed everyone, 'Have you seen Fiona?' 'Dancing with the colonel,' Lady Margaret said. Fiona's not in the ballroom. 'Have you seen my wife?' 'Drinking with the colonel.' 'Walking with the colonel.' There were a hundred rooms. 'Where is my wife?'"

"Where was she?"

"Colonel Wilkes had raped her. Left her bleeding on the library floor like a lamb at slaughter. I snuck her out before anyone discovered her state."

His eyes welled, and it frightened me.

"The bruises between her legs—I'll never forget them. It was all my fault. I forced her to come to London. She warned me, and I—"

"William, I'm so sorry—"

"I dinna need your pity," he said bitterly. "The cowardly colonel went missing before I could run a sword through him. Rumors spread I must have killed him. Wilkes' powerful friends closed in to have me arrested, and there wasn't even a body. Now Lord Hallewell had to fix something for me. He saved me from the hangman's noose, but he's reminded me about it ever since. So now whenever something illicit needs to be done, I fix it. He'll let me do a little side work here and there for his friends, but he keeps a tight leash."

Slouching, he rested his chin in his large hands. I sat up, wrapping the shawl tighter.

"You're a barrister. Why didna you clear your name? Even if you killed Wilkes, no one would blame you. Raping a man's wife is a capital offense, no?"

He took another swig. Now I moved the bottle away. His eyes were glassy, and he spoke with a slur. "Oh, you dinna ken the half. God laughed by making Fiona with child. Can you imagine my wife at the Old Bailey with a bulging belly? Hearing the Lord Mayor say, 'Truly forcible violations don't result in impregnation'? Put her through public shame? Never."

"I dinna understand. Why didna she take pennyroyal?"

"She tried … One day I came home early with the preacher, thinking we might pray together for comfort. We found her crying like a banshee in the garden, holding the pennyroyal." His eyes welled. "Fiona had made a salt circle around herself."

I covered my mouth. "Your wife really is a witch?"

"Fiona's not a witch. She's—her aunt was a wise woman—taught her Druid traditions." He slammed his glass upside down. A brown drip wet the table. "How was I to ken she'd be doing that? I made matters even worse for her. Reverend MacDonald accused her of witchcraft. She never worshipped Satan; she just prays differently. He said God was punishing her and we must raise the bastard as our own, as penance for witchcraft and the rape."

"How is rape your wife's sin?"

"Why else would she be in a delicate condition? She must have wanted it." MacLeod ran his fingers through his thick hair. "And by God did he make us repent to keep things quiet. Took my best land, made her do the most degrading penance each Monday in a burlap sack for a year. Trust me, any lingering desire to follow Druid traditions was stomped out of her soul. We named the bastard Broderick." He bit the boy's name as though it tasted of vinegar and ash. "What a puny, pathetic excuse for a lad. Looks exactly like his rapist father. Dark hair, mud eyes, a complete coward. Always sniveling and crying. I couldn't wait to send him away to school, so I didna have to stare at the bastard's face."

"William, it's no' his fault. What's the Bible say? Sins of the father?"

"I'm done with bastards, and witchcraft, and bloody Lord George Hallewell, holding it all over my head. If someone had raped his wife, I would have fixed things out of friendship, out of honor. The man has no honor, so he has no friends. No real ones. I'm the closest he's got, and God, I hate him and his bitch wife."

MacLeod stood, glancing out the window for a long minute, letting the falling snow cool his temper. I'd never beheld him truly upset before. Rubbing the back of his neck, he muttered, "I shouldnae have spoken."

"Stay till the storm's passed." I stood and deliberately stumbled. "I'm dizzy," I lied.

"You're blottered." Lifting me like I weighed nothing, he laid me on the bed, bumping my nightstand. "Those are Lady Margaret's earrings. Lord Hallewell gave them to you?"

"No." I smiled, naughtily. "When Lady Margaret was out of town, I snuck in her bedchamber and wore her gowns and jewelry. I kept one souvenir. She'll never notice." My fingers stroked my throat. "See? Now we both have secrets about each other."

My fingers trailed toward my cleavage, and I let my shift fall off my shoulders as he swallowed. My breath quickened as my gaze was drawn to his lips.

"I'm married," he said, as much to himself as me. His body stilled.

I laughed. "So is Lord Hallewell. He mentioned how he was on the brink of poverty, and you were laird of a manor when you met. You were the smart one, the successful one, on track to be King's Attorney. You could have married a rich widow with connections yourself. Bought your way into the aristocracy and then Lord Hallewell might be working for you instead. I might be your mistress."

His eyes threatened violence. "Shut it, Eleanor—"

"But you married the wrong woman, didna you?"

I kissed him. Felt his rough whiskers, tasted the whiskey off his tongue, felt him at war with his desires. He kissed me back hard. Putting a possessive grip on my breast, he squeezed as his tongue explored my mouth in a deepening kiss. He climbed on top of me. I didna care if he was fucking me or was fucking over Lord Hallewell, as long as I made him my own pawn.

McLeod pulled away, panting. "I cannae do this with you."

"Why are you stopping?"

Breaking his gaze, he said, "I love my wife more than I hate George."

A flush crept over my cheeks, and I ground my teeth, seething. *Sod him then.* "Fine. Go home to your witch wife and her bastard son. You better hope I won't accidentally call George by your name next time we hump."

MacLeod looked at me with raised eyebrows, then away, then back with utter disbelief, as though I had betrayed him somehow, the arsehole. Standing with ramrod posture, he traced his fingers over Lady Margaret's earrings on my nightstand and left.

Chapter Forty-Nine

ANNALIESE

In the flickering light of the sick berth's hanging lantern, Annaliese squinted at the fat black blobs Surgeon Johnsson tugged off Mac's chest while Reverend Mercer prayed. Hiding in the shadows, she wanted to scream at the reverend, "*You're the reason he's sick*," but she stayed silent so they wouldn't make her leave.

"There's not much more I can do for him beyond leeching," Surgeon Johnsson said, as Reverend Mercer finished his prayer.

Annaliese darted glances between the good doctor and the bad preacher, and her breath grew shallow. Blood trickled into pools on the hammock and her own muscles trembled. *How can someone so big become so helpless?*

Quiet as death, she stayed hidden until the men finally left. Annaliese kissed MacLeod's burning forehead. *Ma, if you're in heaven, ask God to make him better.*

He moaned.

"I'm right here, Mac. Tell me what to do."

"Fiona," he mumbled, his breathing rough.

His body stilled with only a faint rise and fall of his chest, looking just like Ma did before she passed. "Ah, hell, you're gonna die, ain't you?"

His head moved back and forth like he was upset. His gasps were shallow.

Annaliese punched his shoulder. "You promised to protect me and deliver me to my father. Well, you ain't finished the job. I ain't—I don't even know where he lives or how to find him."

A sailor called down the hatch, "We'll port at Glasgow in the morn'." Everyone cheered. Someone played a fife in the distance while dancing feet happily stomped. While Mac was dying.

"Fiona is standing right next to me, and she wants you to wake the hell up." He opened his eyes but got confused and closed them as the ocean hit the ship in cross-currents.

"Sorry, Eleanor," he mumbled.

"Now I know why you hid Ma's book. Jacqueline read all of it to me. You made Ma an indentured convict." She blew out air. "I'm pretty mad at you. I wish you'd get better so we can fight about it."

Mac's eyes fluttered open as his breathing slowed.

A drum joined the fife. Hands clapped and men sang a bawdy song. Not even Reverend Mercer interrupted the celebration.

Mac likes things clean. Mopping his bloodstained wounds with a nearby rag, she took a fresh sheet from another bed and tucked him in, like he did to her every night. He stayed quiet, but she sensed him listening.

"I wish my ma had been a better person. Jacqueline said she was just trying to survive." Annaliese laced her fingers through his. "I wish Ma had lived longer. I wish her life had been easier."

He closed his eyes in pain. Annaliese climbed in the hammock and rested her head on his shoulder. The swing soon slowed to mimic the movement of the ship crossing its final passage.

"When I was four, I told Ma, 'I hate you.' She said, 'One day I'm going to be gone and you'll regret you said that.' Before Ma died, her skin felt hot, too. I was lying in bed with her, with Sam on the other side. Pa was drunk in the corner. She called out to George." Suddenly aware, Annaliese glanced up. "I reckon George is my London father."

Her cheek grew warm resting against his chest, burning with fever.

"Ma said, 'Protect Sam.' There was a rattle in her ribs. When I woke, her skin was gray, and her jaw was stuck open. She wasn't asleep, she was dead. I don't know where Pa was. Gone. I carried Sam outside, so he didn't have to see her like that, and we sat on the chopping stump and waited. It was dark when Pa finally came home. He screamed, 'No.' I never knew if he loved her or hated her."

Mac squeezed her hand, seeming aware.

"Pa dug a hole under the tree. I watched him shovel the dirt on her. She wouldn't have wanted to be in the dirt. Ma liked things clean, too. That's when I remembered the mean things I said to her."

Annaliese peered up at him, eyes welling. "Who says they hate their own mother? I ain't mean it. That's all I do. Say hateful things. You're right, I am wicked. All you ever did was show me the sun and all I ever did was fight to stay in a cave. Mac, I'm so sorry you're dying in a room with me, and not with your wife and sons. I'm sorry for everything. Guess you and Ma will have both died trying to save me. I wish I was worth it."

Mac squeezed her hand hard. "Annaliese." His breathing was rough. "You're good."

Tears streamed down her face.

"You're good."

***

Annaliese jolted awake in the sick berth. MacLeod was gone and Surgeon Johnsson put his hand to her head. "No fever. You're a fool for sneaking in here."

Happy passengers thumped their belongings past the berth onto the deck. A lady said, "I'm going to kiss the beach and never set foot on a ship again."

Her throat sounded scratchy as she asked Surgeon Johnsson, "Did you throw his body overboard while I was sleeping?"

"You trying to rush me to my grave, lass?" MacLeod asked, coming inside.

"Mac!" Annaliese spun off the hammock, sprinting to hug him, almost knocking him over. He felt so thin.

"I thought you was dead. You were shaking and called Fiona all night."

Surgeon Johnsson said to him, "You're lucky. Not everyone survives the fever. Stick to my sweet wort today. You'll enjoy your wife's cooking soon."

MacLeod pinned his clan brooch to his tartan, then grabbed Annaliese's hand. "Come on. We're almost at port." Slogging forward, he held onto the sideboards for support as they climbed above deck.

Other ships with giant masts approached the harbor. Sailors called across the bows at each other, waiting for their chance to dock. Gentlemen lined the deck with their battered trunks, while ladies washed their faces with beer to give them some color. Captain Adams immediately came to MacLeod to discuss business. Everything smelled salty and fishy.

Annaliese approached Seamus as he carried a trunk from below. "You gonna visit your parents now?"

Seamus frowned. "Ireland's far, and my family's sold off. You wouldn't understand." Adjusting the trunk on his shoulder, he forced a good-natured smile. "Have a safe trip to London, Miss Cameron. I hope you get on well with your father," he said, pivoting to leave.

Annaliese swallowed and tapped his shoulder. "I'm sorry I was such a—"

"Witch?" he whispered with a devilish grin.

Her eyes popped open. "I'm glad I punched you so many times, Seamus," she said, punching his arm once more. He laughed, then dashed toward the rowboats with the trunk on his shoulder, as squawking seagulls flew over warehouses with peeling paint.

The fizz of activity reminded Annaliese of delivery days on the James River. Behind the Big House, the sailors would unload supplies from London, and the slaves would roll tobacco barrels onto the ships, singing spirituals. She started humming "Wade in the Water."

Jacqueline ran up and kissed both her cheeks. "Such wonderful news Monsieur MacLeod is well again." Snow flurries fell. "Catch them on your eyelashes for good luck, ma chère."

They leaned back their heads and smiled as the ice crystals stuck.

A shadow fell as the Mercers arrived on deck with their belongings. Jacqueline nudged Annaliese to follow the plan. It was risky.

"Can I—may I talk with you? Alone?" she said to Rebecca.

Mrs. Mercer arched an eyebrow. Rebecca took a few hesitant steps away from her parents' earshot. Both girls pulled their cloaks tighter.

Annaliese said, "I've been thinkin'. You said pretty mean things, but I feel bad for hurting your arm. My pa would of done that, and I ain't never want to be like him. I'm sorry."

Rebecca looked to Jacqueline, who gave an encouraging nod. Rebecca tilted her head, considering, then gave a faint nod.

That weren't too bad.

Jacqueline put an arm around each girl's shoulder. They gazed over the rail at the harbor. "We finally made it," Jacqueline said.

Annaliese hummed again, staring at the men working on the dock, blowing on their hands to warm themselves.

"What song is that?" Jacqueline asked.

"They used to sing it on the plantation. The last part says, 'God's gonna trouble the water.' That happened to us, huh?"

Rebecca thought for a moment. "It's based on John 5 verse 4. I think you're misunderstanding. Troubling the waters is a good thing. An angel went down to a pool and troubled the water. Anyone who was brave enough to go into the troubled waters left healed."

Are you brave enough to be Annaliese Cameron? She peeked at Jacqueline, who offered a supportive smile. *Here goes.* Taking a deep breath, she pulled her jar of shells from her pocket and dug out Rebecca's cross. "Sorry I took it."

Rebecca gasped wide-eyed with the joyful surprise of finding something precious lost, then grew serious. "Why are you giving this to me? I could have you arrested."

I knew this was a bad idea. Old Rebecca was back and out for revenge. An icy wind blew as the crew dropped anchor, and the ship floated backwards.

"For what crime, ma chère? Borrowing a necklace? She returned it."

"After she stole it. You're unbelievable, Annaliese. You put a hex on me! And you're a thief and a liar even if you aren't a witch. You didn't even get whipped because the storm came, and Father said I had to be nice to you." Her breath came out in cold puffs.

A seagull dropped an oyster shell on the deck near them, cracking it open, pecking the flesh then flying off. Annaliese and Rebecca were locked in an intense stare.

Rebecca's lips thinned. "Mother, Father, Annaliese stole my necklace!"

Shit. Rebecca's parents met her halfway as she ran to them, holding the golden necklace and gloating. Annaliese's hands trembled as she put the jar on a crate. Jacqueline held her hand to steady her as the Mercers came. MacLeod leaned against the ratline stone-faced with his arms crossed. Her head lowered as the ship tugged to an abrupt stop. *Double shit shit.*

Reverend Mercer held the cross and looked down at her. "You stole this?"

A nod.

"And now you've returned it." The reverend smiled and patted her cheek.

Rebecca's grin shifted into angry confusion. "She's a wicked girl and should be punished."

Mrs. Mercer said, "Jesus commands us to turn the other cheek." Mrs. Mercer had a peaceful expression as she clasped the cross necklace around her daughter's neck. "I hoped God would touch your heart one day, Annaliese. Rebecca, say thank you and goodbye to your friends."

Reverend and Mrs. Mercer nodded at MacLeod then strolled off, leaving the girls alone to sort things. Seamus passed them again with another trunk. Sweat dripped down his face beneath his wool cap.

Large snowflakes fell and glistened on Jacqueline's fur-lined cloak. She said, "Annaliese returned the cross, confessed and is truly sorry."

Rebecca remained unmoved.

Jacqueline put her hands on her hips. "You are not a complete innocent, ma chère."

Stroking the cross with her cold, red fingers, Rebecca said, "Fine. Truce."

"Rebecca," called Mrs. Mercer, lining up to leave.

After hugging Jacqueline goodbye, Rebecca shot a cold look at Annaliese then skipped back to her family.

Annaliese glanced at Jacqueline. "I still hate her."

Passengers walked the gangplanks to leave. Jacqueline handed Annaliese the address for her school, gave a giant hug and left with her mother into the snow.

Mac approached Annaliese at last, putting his arm over her shivering shoulders, looking relieved. "I'm proud of you, Annaliese Cameron."

She bit her lip, feeling taller. No one had ever been proud of her before.

Dusting the snow off her cloak, he said, "Welcome to Scottish weather. My home is only a few hours north from here. We'll stop there first to rest, then travel to London in a day or two."

"What if my father don't ... doesn't like me? Will he send me back to Pa?"

"You're never going back to Rob Birch. I promise."

Her eyes narrowed at the tone of his voice. "You shot him dead, didn't you?"

MacLeod paused before looking her in the eye. "What makes you think that?"

Annaliese shrugged. "He came to me in a dream one night with a bullet in his brain and a ball and chain around his ankle."

A fixed look of concentration fell over MacLeod's face. "Aye. I shot him." Rubbing his beard, he had a faraway gaze. "You should speak to my wife about your dreams."

Annaliese's fingers tapped the cold rail as she stared into the brown water for a long while, feeling numb. Praying for Pa's death was different from finding out it had happened. "Why didn't you tell me?"

"I reveal information on a need-to-know basis."

Annaliese glared at him with anger and pain. "Why do *you* get to decide what everybody needs to know? You should of told me 'bout Pa, and it was *my* ma's book you stole. I understand why you tried to get rid of it, I guess, but it was still a shitty thing to do."

"Aye. Not my finest moment." He took a deep breath. "Would you have preferred not learning about your pa?"

"I ain't want to talk right now," she said, shifting away. They stood in silence as the snow fell faster around them. "Sorry for cussing." Tightening her hood against the cold flurries, she looked down. "How come the truth's so confusing?"

"Because people are complex and flawed."

Annaliese wanted to punch him while simultaneously craving for his hug. Mostly she wanted to move on. MacLeod squeezed her shoulder. "Everything will get easier now, lass."

"For you."

Chapter Fifty

LADY MARGARET

London

Sunshine streamed through the elongated windows of the domed music room. Lady Margaret's ten-year-old daughter, Elizabeth, pounded the harpsichord keys. Her twelve-year-old son, Thomas, home from Eton, scratched out notes on a violin sounding less music and more screeching cat. Her eight-year-old, Gregory, watched with Lord Hallewell. Only the twinkle of Fiona's bracelet mitigated the children's headache-inducing concert.

Lord Hallewell seemed genuinely impressed with the performance. "Smashing, children. Thomas, you should be a musician, and Beth, you've improved so much. Brava."

Thomas rested his polished violin next to a wide assortment of other recently purchased instruments. Apparently, Lord Hallewell's passion for music had been rekindled.

Did Eleanor like to listen to you play, George? Do you envision your second family gathered around the piano singing merry little tunes?

"Thank you, Papa." Elizabeth stood and curtsied, her pink petticoats swaying merrily. "I love Christmastime. I'm so happy our whole family is together—well, except for Alexander."

Lady Margaret soothed herself with the thought that Alexander's absence would give her plenty of time to plan Lord Hallewell's demise. "Yes, well, your dear papa will spend less time at home, too, Elizabeth."

Lord Hallewell's eyes widened. "No need to discuss such things now, Margaret." His eyes threw daggers at her.

"Whatever do you mean, Mother?" the girl asked, while the boys leaned in.

"Nothing to trouble your little minds over. I want to visit Grimbly Manor more," he said, distracting the children with biscuits.

Lady Margaret sauntered to the round table and began playing solitaire.

George was the children's favorite parent, a distinction he didn't deserve. She needed his esteem ripped from their little hearts. "Don't you think your legitimate children might be curious why their father doesn't want to spend time at the family home? And stop feeding her biscuits. Elizabeth is plain as it is, do you want her plump as well?"

Elizabeth lowered her head, returning the biscuit to the plate.

Lord Hallewell raised the girl's chin. "Oh, I don't know. Plumpness didn't seem to prevent Lord Percy from marrying Lady Catherine. I suppose she's Countess Catherine now."

Lady Margaret snapped down a card. A suicidal Jack. Lord Percy would soon discover there was a cost to betraying her, as her husband was finding now.

A nanny collected the children, and they were alone again.

Lord Hallewell poured port. "No need to ruin the children's holiday, Margaret," he scolded. "You should have held your tongue."

"Then don't abandon us to live with your whore, darling." Flipping her cards, she internally smiled at the turmoil he must be experiencing right now. In truth, Lord Hallewell was a kind and loving father, which made his desertion even worse.

Staggering to the overstuffed couch next to her, he said, "I've heard interesting news." He swirled his glass of port.

Lady Margaret held the card midair. "Oh?"

"Apparently, a special visitor came here while I was in Oxford."

Continuing her game, she said, "People call daily. Who piqued your interest?"

"Mr. MacLeod's wife ... More secrets, Margaret? Belmont informed me."

Of course he did. Damned butler. "You know Fiona. Pleasant, but simple. I didn't deem it necessary to trouble you with the details, since apparently she'd written you three times."

George sipped his drink, thinking. "Sent multiple correspondences, did she? How can I trust I received them all? You seem to have a knack for intercepting letters."

"Well, did you receive them?"

"Yes."

Obviously, Lady Margaret had read all the letters from Fiona first, but they were innocuous enough to reseal and let him receive them. 'Where is my husband?' and so forth. Fiona had too much pride to mention her mysteriously growing debt or anything about Colonel Wilkes. Fiona was a non-threat. *Such a letdown for a witch. She didn't even read my tea leaves.*

Placing her aces at the top, she said, "You should have replied. Spared her a trip. You know Fiona detests leaving Scotland. She must truly love that man to travel here for answers. You should tell her about William's affair."

Taking his drink to the harpsichord, he rested it on top. "Not everybody is preoccupied with settling old grievances." Cracking his knuckles, he pounded the notes of a concerto by Bach. "Besides, in hurting William, I'd be devastating poor Fiona, and she's done nothing to deserve such cruelty."

Lady Margaret frowned at the brittle, rattling notes, flipping a useless deuce. "You men all stick together, don't you? Even when you double-cross each other."

That's why I told her MacLeod was as adulterous as Lord Hallewell. Fiona thought she had the perfect little marriage. Sod her happiness. Let the truth devastate.

Lord Hallewell pressed, "What did Fiona say when she visited?"

"She came—unannounced, mind—looking for her husband and money. I sent her off with neither, as I'm sure you would have done."

His breath fogged the windows behind him. "She needs money?"

Lady Margaret completed a row. "Something about a famine in Scotland. She should do a water spell." Fiona's bracelet looked divine on her wrist. It sparkled as she flipped over the kings and queens. *Everything's a game, isn't it?*

Belmont entered, seeming concerned. "The afternoon paper's arrived, my lord."

"Thank you, Belmont." Lord Hallewell sat by the fireplace and read. "Oh, my God. There was a hurricane. They suspect the *Icarus* was lost at sea."

"Shipwrecked?" Joining him, she scoured the paper for the deceased list.

Lord Hallewell reread it. "MacLeod, Annaliese ... Eleanor's name isn't there. I don't understand. My family, my—everyone is lost?"

A smirk flew from her lips before she flattened them.

Lord Hallewell scratched his face. His complexion mottled so easily these days. "Does that tickle your heart, Margaret? The thought of my family dying?"

Lady Margaret caressed Fiona's bracelet. *Yes.*

Chapter Fifty-One

FIONA

Scotland

Fiona quietly suffocated as she visited her brother's overcrowded croft house. Her three younger sons huddled near the fire with their bowls. Six months ago, they ate salmon prepared by a chef. Now a dozen of them vied for grubbed sheep's turnips boiled with some barley and salt.

Lachlan grumbled, "I hate famine food. It looks like paste."

Malcolm snapped, "If you want something better, laddie, join the navy and collect the king's coin." Facing her, he looked worried. "Are you unwell?"

Fiona stared blankly. "I'm sorry, I'm a wee bit lost."

Sitting beneath a cross nailed to the wall, Malcolm was ready to render judgment against his absent brother-in-law. "Well, it's because you married that damned fool. Everyone was so impressed by his wit and his land, but I always ken there was something about him I didna trust."

Fiona watched her boys bite their tongues.

Mary said, "Dinna berate her, she's worried."

Everyone picked uncomfortably at their meager meals.

"I'm no' berating her, I'm mad at him. How is it he can send Lord Hallewell a letter but no' his own wife? What did Lady Margaret say again?"

"William was supposed to arrive late October. Lady Margaret sent some money."

"Aye, you mean she sent you a pittance of what she should have paid for your fancy bracelet. Fifteen years in service to that so-called nobleman," Malcolm groused. "Your family is in dire need and his lordship sends the salary of a scullery maid? Unbelievable. And what about your other son and William's brother? Can they help?"

"I've written to both David and Cam but haven't heard yet." Eating a spoonful, her wedding ring spun so loosely it almost fell off.

Fiona spoke in a daze. "If we can just hold on until spring, we'll have a better harvest—"

Malcolm was having none of it. "You had to marry the great William damned MacLeod." He waved his hands in mockery. "He takes off to London with the blasted lords and ladies and politicians who don't give a rat's arse about Scots, then takes off to the colonies. I swear his nose must be dark brown with as much fart sucking as he does. All the good it's done you. Soon I'll have to cram your family in here so you're not homeless."

"Malcolm, perhaps not in front of the children?" Mary said.

"They ken the truth. You think they dinna ken their father left? You think they aren't lying awake at night thinking about their mother being thrown in debtors' prison, and themselves sold off? Wasted money sending them to Lottington Hall. They can conjugate Latin but cannae plow a field worth a damn."

"You're selling us, Mam?" Broderick's coloring faded stark white.

"Never," Fiona roared at her brother. "Stop scaring them."

"The lads need to face reality. You all do. James told us selling the farm and all those expensive law books won't be enough to pay the loans, so, aye, the creditors might force the bairns to be indentured. The colonies are overflowing with convicts and debtors' sons."

Lachlan said, "I'm not being sold. I'll join the navy tomorrow."

"No. William is alive and is coming home," Fiona said, voice cracking.

"Is he?" Malcolm tossed his napkin on the chair. "I'm going to smoke my pipe. I've lost my appetite."

Fiona scratched through her ever-graying hair.

Mary said, "Let's take a jaunter."

Outside, Fiona wrapped her shawl tighter beneath her chin as millions of stars blinked above. They walked arm in arm, like they used to as girls.

"He'll be home soon," Mary said.

"Mary, I did something awful," Fiona whispered. Malcolm puffed away on his pipe, petting his horse as he did. Tobacco lingered in the cold air, mixing with the smell of the chimney fire. "You can't tell anyone, especially Malcolm."

"What did you do?"

They walked further, beyond earshot. "Lady Margaret's letter said more. She thinks William went to Virginia to claim his bastard daughter." The words caught in her throat.

"Whose bastard? William's? The man worships you. I cannae ever see him as the adulterous type. It dinna make sense."

"It makes perfect sense. The timing is right. We weren't—I wasna performing my wifely duties." Fiona hung her head.

"All married couples go through difficulties, especially when the bairns are young."

"He stopped asking and started working more often in London. I ken he'd grow bored with me. He always longed to live the life of an aristocrat. Of course he had a mistress, and I was too stupid to notice. I told him to marry an English noble. He's ashamed of me and my Celtic ways."

They came to the woodlands where Auntie used to teach the stories of Beira, Queen of Winter. A fat water vole flopped into the stream as they approached.

Auntie, give me strength to confess my sins and make things right. "I predicted this, Mary. I warned him the journey would be dangerous, not realizing my own hand in the matter." She took a shaky breath. "I cursed him, Mary."

"What?" Mary covered her mouth. "God in heaven, forgive her."

"I read the letter by the sea, and my rage manifested into a storm. I didna mean for it to happen, but suddenly I was saying the words Auntie taught me, and the letter blew in the wind. The spirits took it from me." Clasping her hands over her mouth, tears spilled over her fingers. "Mary, I fear I killed him. That's why all this is happening. When you do an unjust curse, it haunts you three times. I lost my husband, my wealth and now my sons will be sold. Oh, God have mercy on my soul, what have I done?"

Mary checked over her shoulder, then shook her head. "No, Fiona. I dinna think you could do an actual curse. It's not your nature. The storm was a coincidence, not a curse."

"Was it? William told Lord Hallewell he would be home by Samhain. It's December. His ship left Virginia but never arrived in London. There must have been a storm. My storm. Oh, my God, Mary, I've killed my husband."

"Did you sign your name in blood?" Mary was trying to fathom it.

"No, it dinna work like that. You ken I only do potions for love or healing, never for harm, but he made me so angry." Fiona balled her fists. "He throws his seed about, making a bastard, and yet Broderick ..."

Mary bit her lip. A knowing look crossed her face.

Fiona barely whispered, "I feel like I dinna even ken him anymore. I only wanted William to repent for how he hurt us. Hurt *me*."

Mary exhaled. "Well, there you have it. You didna wish death, you wished redemption."

"Mary, what if he dinna want to be redeemed? What's the only other option?"

༄

Fiona and the boys walked home in silence. Seeing James' horse in the open barn and a candle in the window made her sigh in relief. Inside, her face fell. Nelly's eyes were red from crying. James sat by the hearth with his head in his hands and a newspaper at his feet.

Fiona touched Nelly's belly. "Is the baby all right?"

"Nelly's fine. Mam, sit down," James said, wiping his eyes.

Fiona blinked.

Lachlan grabbed for the newspaper, but James pulled it away. "Mam, please sit."

Her fingertips tingled as she sat in William's chair and read as her sons crowded around her.

TRAGIC MYSTERY AT SEA

The *Icarus*, Owned by Lord George Hallewell, is Feared to Have Met with a Dreadful Accident While on its Voyage Across the Atlantic— Reliable sources claim ship formerly owned by Lord Percy Monroe, Sixth Earl of Cheshire, was CURSED by African slave. Burnt remains of ship found off coast of stormy Newfoundland. Several broken tobacco barrels stamped *Icarus* found on shore near dozens of shallow graves. Hope of Lives Saved Grows Faint.
Passengers LOST: William MacLeod, solicitor for Lord George Hallewell ...

Wind kept howling, howling, howling. *I killed my husband and dozens of innocent souls? I prayed for redemption not death! Please let this be wrong. Eisd rium a Dhia. Come home to me, William.*

Chapter Fifty-Two

Lord Percy Monroe

Scotland

Lord Percy pounded on the manor door with his iron fist, savoring the moment.

"MacLeods hold fast," Fiona said as she opened the door, drawing her shawl tight against the raw cold.

How did MacLeod end up with someone as divine as her? Lord Percy impulsively attempted to kiss her hand, but she snatched it away.

"May I help you, sir?" Fiona asked. A dark-haired youth and a little redheaded brat hid behind her skirts. A blonde woman in a delicate condition waddled over.

Lord Percy grinned. "You certainly may. I'd love to tour my house."

"You dinna look like William MacLeod," Fiona said.

Feisty little enchantress. "My dear lady, your husband's in debt. The soldiers will enforce the transition." Percy flashed the pistol strapped across his jade waistcoat to intimidate her.

"My oldest son is resolving the matter in court. Your name, sir?"

"Lord Percy Monroe, sixth Earl of Cheshire." Glancing at his mechanical hand, he said, "Your husband and I have been acquainted."

Fiona averted her eyes. "My lord, William is …" She took a breath as the other woman squeezed her shoulder. "Lost at sea. It's my understanding you and he were not on good terms, but perhaps we can settle a payment plan? Surely you have charity for a widow and her children at yuletide."

Large snowflakes blew chaotically into their mostly vacant home as Lord Percy grinned. "Surely, I do not. I'd love nothing more than to watch MacLeod's family sold off bit by bit to the workhouses."

The little ginger hugged his mother tightly. Fiona said, "May I review your paperwork, my lord?"

"Paperwork?" Lord Percy feigned confusion, toying with her.

Fiona stood taller. "You expect our entire family to leave based on your say-so? You dinna frighten me."

Lord Percy held a document. "Well, this warrant of possession says the manor and all attached lands are mine effective immediately, and it's signed by the sheriff. You know how I know?" he asked, hardly containing his mirth. "Because the sheriff is my cousin."

Snatching the paper, the dark-haired youth pored over it, with the expecting woman reading over his shoulder. Clopping horse hooves made them glance up. Black carriages with gold accents rattled as they trudged the icy path to the country estate. A dozen mercenaries rode behind the coaches.

"Who are all these people?" asked Fiona.

"They've come for the auction. I'm going to sell all your worldly possessions, and if it's not enough—and it won't be enough—we'll force the sale of your sons. I think we'll start with this little bugger who resembles MacLeod."

Fiona spat in his face. Lord Percy raised his left hand to cuff her, but the dark-haired boy blocked him.

"Dinna lay a finger on my mother," Broderick said. "This warrant means nothing. It's signed by a sheriff in the wrong jurisdiction. But you ken that, otherwise you'd be standing with a bailiff, not three soldiers. I dinna ken what's going on, but I ken this is bollocks. Get inside, Mam."

Lord Percy whistled. Soldiers dismounted and approached. Wiping the spittle off with a handkerchief, he volleyed his gaze between Broderick and a soldier. "Hey, Wilkes, this boy could be your twin."

Fiona's hands quavered at the name. "Get off my property."

Lord Percy shoved her.

Broderick muttered, "Hold fast," let loose a primal scream, tackled Lord Percy to the snow, drew back his fist and delivered a punch to Percy's jaw.

"Broderick, watch out," Fiona called.

Soldiers wrenched Broderick off, arresting him.

Lord Percy tasted copper as he sat in the snowdrift. Jumping to his feet, he spit blood. *The boy startled me, that's all.* His hired swords averted their laughing eyes as the soldiers tied the insolent boy to an alder tree.

"You'll be dangling by your neck from it later." Lord Percy slapped the snow from his expensive coat.

Snow fell faster, and the soldiers held MacLeod's family hostage. Lieutenant Wilkes seemed visibly shaken as he looked between the dark-haired boy and Fiona.

Lord Percy chuckled. "My, my, Mrs. MacLeod. What naughty things have you gotten into?" *No wonder MacLeod killed Wilkes' father.*

Mercenaries piled MacLeod's belongings in a heap on the muddy ice. *Not much left.* Lord Percy walked through the contents of MacLeod's life: an oversized chair, a cross necklace, worn law books. His merchant friends picked through MacLeod's home like an open market.

Percy's gaze hovered over a crude drawing of a smiling family with "I love you Da" scrawled in a child's chicken scratch. Ink ran as wet snowflakes fell, making the picture seem to cry. Fiona hugged her little boy.

Am I a disappointment now, Father? I restored honor to our family name. People used to laugh at me. Now, men fear me.

MacLeod's thatched roof manor appeared so peaceful in the snowfall.

"Burn it," Lord Percy said.

"No, please," Fiona cried.

Soldiers sparked their flints against fallen branches, then set fire inside the house as the family shouted helplessly. Lord Percy closed his eyes, inhaling the glorious scent of justice. Rebuilding a manor would be expensive, but watching the children cry as their home burned was priceless.

Percy wished Lady Margaret had witnessed this. Ever since he had married Countess Catherine, Margaret refused to dally with him. Well, what did she expect? Why would he pursue Margaret for a wife when her husband needed to be murdered first? Nevertheless, they had such fun together. That needn't change.

White plumes from the house grew thicker, passing in a wave over the roof. Lord Percy collected cash from the merchants, storing it in MacLeod's own strongbox. *Nice touch.*

Lord Percy tucked his iron hand into his waistcoat, keeping his secret weapon dry, though he didn't need it now, with MacLeod in a watery grave. *What a pity.* He should have liked to kill MacLeod personally, but his family would suffice.

Villagers with walking sticks and hay picks trickled down the road. *Ah, how sentimental.* Percy had an army with muskets. Flames curled around the roof like fingers grabbing hold. The commoners shuddered at the soldiers and the blaze.

Staring down his broken nose on them, he said, "They call me Lord Percy of the Iron Hand, sixth Earl of Cheshire. I own these lands now. You'll pay your rent to me today, or your families will experience the same fate as your former laird, William MacLeod." Switching from stunned stares to his own men, he said, "Have their possessions been sold? Is the debt covered?"

"Not enough, my lord," said one of the soldiers.

Orange flames danced up the window curtains.

Lord Percy enjoyed taunting Fiona. "Madam, as your noble creditor, I demand full payment. My business associates need indentured servants to do hard labor in the West Indies." Lord Percy faced the little redheaded boy. "Do you love your father?"

Tears rolled down the boy's face as he nodded.

"You shouldn't."

Plumes transformed into charcoal clouds circling the house. A soldier grabbed the boy.

"No, please, my lord, not my bairns," Fiona begged. "Sell me instead."

"Madam, I'd love nothing more than to sell you first." Lord Percy dragged the wife and stood her on an abandoned trunk as townspeople stood gaping in obvious shock. Old men and womenfolk from the village kept arriving in small groups.

"Who will give me thirty pounds for this fine enchantress?"

MacLeod's sons begged for their mother to be saved. The little one looked scared enough to piss himself, and the older boy was bound to a tree with his head slumped. *Pathetic scions. Didn't MacLeod have five boys? Where were the rest?*

The village idiots spoke among themselves. "We cannae let the laird's wife be sold."

They discussed pooling their money to purchase her freedom. What would they pay with? Turnips? Percy noticed a few men leered at Fiona with decidedly calculating expressions, perhaps wondering how much fun it might be to work their mistress to the bone.

Lieutenant Wilkes said, "Don't sell her. Tie her to a stake and burn her." He growled, "What spell did you cast on my father, witch?"

The villagers muttered among themselves.

"I'm not a witch," she said. "I'm a wise woman. Your father was the devilish one."

A carriage came at a full gallop. A Highlander jumped out, roaring, "What the hell is going on?! Release my wife. Put out the fire."

As if awakened from a trance, the tenant farmers reached for buckets, but the soldiers guarded the well with their bayonets.

Lord Percy swung his face into the wind, blinking hard. *It can't be.*

"William!" Fiona and the little boy broke free and ran to him, squeezing him in a hug. "My spell worked."

Spell?

"You're alive?" Lieutenant Wilkes said, his expression inscrutable.

MacLeod gaped at the tree. "Broderick? Untie my son."

Air constricted in Lord Percy's lungs. *I read the newspapers myself. William MacLeod was lost at sea. Why is he dressed in plaid?* MacLeod certainly resembled a ghost—weak, a graying beard and two stone lighter. MacLeod kissed his wife's head quickly, then pulled his sword, *Justice*. A phantom pain stabbed where Percy's hand had once been.

Lord Percy's men surrounded MacLeod with weapons drawn. MacLeod observed the legion guns and swords trained on his throat. Lord Percy had rehearsed this in his mind for so long. *Should I shoot MacLeod? No. Draw it out. Humiliate him.*

MacLeod asked, "Who are these people?"

Lieutenant Wilkes stepped forward. "I think you knew my father. Colonel Wilkes."

MacLeod's face lost all color. A little girl exited the coach, clutching her doll. Skinny little thing. Her tresses glistened like fire against the snow.

Fiona covered her gasp. "She has your hair."

"*My* hair?" MacLeod asked, bewildered.

Lord Percy scrutinized the girl. *This must be the child Lady Margaret wanted strangled. Beautiful girl. No wonder Margaret envied the mother. Maybe I'll send the little brat's eyeballs to her as a peace offering. Margaret will absolutely suck my cock in gratitude.* He snickered. This day was becoming better than he ever imagined.

"Surely you remember me, MacLeod?" Lord Percy revealed his iron fist.

"You?" MacLeod said, blinking.

Lord Percy stood taller. "Did you think I wouldn't find your weak spots?"

"What do you want?" MacLeod stubbornly gripped his own sword. "Money? Your ship? It's at the port. Take it."

"You think all this was over a ship? Did you think I would slink off for eternity? Forget the dishonor done to my reputation?"

As the heat grew oppressive, windows on the top floor burst with a pop, shattering glass to the ground as townspeople blocked their faces.

"The boy's escaped," a soldier shouted. A dirk and a doll lay in the snow where the boy had been tied. Two sets of footprints led down the road.

Lieutenant Wilkes said, "Find him. Are there any tracks?"

"About ten thousand on the road, sir," the soldier shouted over the wind.

It sounded like more horses coming in the distance, but the noisy fire and the chattering villagers made it difficult to decipher.

Lieutenant Wilkes scanned the farm. "There they are."

The children raced across the field. In the distance, beyond the Scots pines, sat a decrepit castle overlooking the sea. Lieutenant Wilkes mounted his horse. "My lord, I entreat you to keep MacLeod and his wife alive until I come back with the boy. I'd like to question them about my father's murder. Please, my lord."

Lord Percy sighed. "You're lucky I'm in a generous mood, Wilkes."

"Don't hurt my children. You want me," MacLeod called, as Wilkes rode off.

"Shut your jaw," said the mercenary with the eye patch, disarming MacLeod and tossing *Justice* to the ground.

Lord Percy said, "If you want mercy for your family, you must kneel."

MacLeod sank to the snow, never taking his eyes off him. The distinct sound of approaching hooves amplified. *Are more soldiers on their way? Wilkes never mentioned it.*

"I, Lord Percy Monroe of the Iron Hand, sixth Earl of Cheshire, shall deliver justice today. I claim your house for my ship. Your life for my hand. Your wife for my honor."

"Touch my wife and I'll fucking murder you," MacLeod grunted, with his head lowered and shoulders hunched. Breath from his nostrils seemed like smoke in the frigid air. A bull threatening to charge.

"Do it, my lord," the mercenaries jeered. As anticipation grew, the merchants stopped loading MacLeod's wares to enjoy the spectacle. Lord Percy would give them a show to remember.

Brandishing his five-shot flintlock pistol with his left hand, he aimed at MacLeod's unblinking face. Villagers pulled their checkered brechans tighter against the wind and watched behind their fingers as clopping hooves grew louder.

"Lachlan!" Fiona called.

From the south, a teenager holding a burning standard led dozens of farmers with raised axes and sickles into the fray.

The haunting screech of bagpipes rained down from the hilltops. The little redhead boy waved frantically, shouting, "James, David, Uncle Cam!"

Guttural screams pierced through the wind as fifty Highlanders galloped from the north brandishing claymores and spiked targes. A bearded man leading the charge had a pair of steel pistols he pulled and shot.

Fiona called out, "Now!"

Womenfolk pulled woolen hose from their pockets, tucked rocks inside and pelted the merchants. They fled on whinnying horses, leaving MacLeod's belongings in the ice.

Lord Percy lowered his pistol, glancing in all directions.

"Protect me," Lord Percy demanded. His mercenaries encircled him as he tried to fathom the three-sided siege. *Who are these barbarians? How did they know to come?* Cracking pistol fire mixed with women's screams and the hacking of his men getting cleaved by battleaxes. He'd trained for a duel, not a bloody rebellion.

After a moment, he came to his senses and put his pistol over his right forearm. His finger wrapped around the trigger, but the little redheaded boy came from nowhere and swung a long stick at his kneecaps, making him buckle. Percy's bullet shot an armchair in the snow, splintering the wood at the top as the little bugger ran off.

In the chaos, MacLeod grabbed his claymore and sliced the eye-patched mercenary diagonally from his ribs to his hip with a single blow of *Justice*. The ruffian's torso landed by Percy's feet, his slimy red guts steaming in the snow. Percy gazed up, locking eyes with MacLeod. *Fuck. He'll kill me.*

Percy broke into a cold sweat and sprinted toward the burning house.

"Block him, James," shouted MacLeod.

James pursued Lord Percy with a targe covered in cowhide and a death spike in the middle. Lord Percy tripped over the threshold beneath a gigantic chandelier twenty feet high. Orange-red blazes rolled above it and it rained burning plaster.

Aim your gun, fool. Lord Percy fired a shot from the ground, but he was off balance and missed.

James charged screaming when an ear-shattering crack startled them as the chandelier crashed down, spewing flames and filling the air with smoke. Cinders blew into James' face. Blood filled the whites of James' eyes as he staggered back and covered his face, writhing in pain as MacLeod ran to his son.

Percy tucked his flintlock back in his chest holster and crawled blindly, choking on the noxious fumes. Seeing a light at the end of a long hall, he realized it was a busted window. Smoke billowed out like it too desired escape. Lord Percy hoisted himself over and fell into a snowdrift, wheezing. Metal on metal screeched around him in a swirl of blue-green plaids destroying his mercenary force. This wasn't a fair fight. In the distance, he saw Wilkes' horse approach the castle ruins. Taking a deep inhale, Lord Percy pushed himself from the ground and staggered to a horse. *If I can't kill MacLeod, I'll slaughter his children.*

Chapter Fifty-Three

Fiona

Fiona spied Lord Percy galloping toward the castle. Grabbing William as he excited their burning manor, she said, "We have to find the weans before they do."

They rode her black stallion toward the castle ruins, Fiona's green tartan dress snapping in the snowy wind. Embracing his warm body, she wished to wake from this horrid dream as the sun set over the scattered ruins on the edge of the Firth of Clyde.

Where would the bairns hide? Nether Bailey to the north, or the Upper Bailey to the south? Lord Percy's silhouette blended with the shadows to the south, where the gatekeep and scant remains of medieval buildings lay. They rode in the opposite direction.

Dismounting, MacLeod gripped his claymore, straining under its weight.

Fiona followed her husband inside the Nether Bailey into a medieval kitchen and froze. Lieutenant Wilkes had captured Broderick.

"Your hour has come, MacLeod," Wilkes said, raising his imposing Brown Bess.

William said, "Take my life, not the boy's. I killed your father in a duel."

A hitched gasp escaped Broderick as he stared at William. Fiona pinned her arms against her stomach as the final rays of sunlight streamed from the collapsed roof onto her face.

Lieutenant Wilkes snorted. "Still lying? There was no proper duel—my father would have won. I know your witch wife seduced him so you could murder him. I saw your wife's blood-soaked shawl. All these years you made us suffer."

"I killed him," Fiona whispered.

"Fiona, no—"

Slowly, she emerged from her husband's shadow. "I've held this secret for fifteen years, like a poison killing me from the inside."

"Mam?" Broderick's eyes opened wide.

William's hands kept clenching the hilt, each muscle in his body tightening. "It was me."

Placing her hand on William's arm to quiet him, she faced the young soldier. An eagle flew from its nest in the rafters outside the collapsed roof.

"I killed Colonel Wilkes at Lord Hallewell's wedding." Fiona exhaled a cleansing breath, as though confessing lifted a weight from her shoulders. "He asked me to read his palm. I was excited to believe someone so well respected honored the ancient ways of magic as well. Blinded by this false connection, I thought nothing of it when he gave me a drink. I dinna ken what he put in it, but I could barely move."

Wind whistled through the ruins. Wilkes said, "No. My father was honorable—"

"He brought me to a room in the back of the estate—"

"Fiona, you dinna need to say anything—" William said, his voice thick with emotion.

"William, I do. The lad needs to ken the truth. Colonel Wilkes pulled me into a library away from the reception. I kept saying 'no.' God knows it to be true. He was angry at William for stopping his affair with Lady Margaret, so he used me to send a message, I suppose."

William expelled a pained breath.

Lieutenant Wilkes gripped his musket tighter. "No. You, you're a whore—" His lips formed a tight line. "My father was a hero."

"The colonel climbed on top of me. He was choking me. I clawed at him, tearing off his Saint George emblem and ripping off my fingernail." Her voice broke. "I found my dirk and, oh Jesus Christ, forgive me, I stabbed him till he stopped moving. William found me covered in blood, the colonel dead on top of me."

Lowering his Brown Bess, young Wilkes stared into the distance.

Fiona stared at her hands. "Every day, I relive that moment. Why did I take a drink from him? He wore the Order of the Garter for valor and honor. Why did I believe a medal told the entire story?"

Broderick's slowly shaking head swung wider and faster as his eyes filled with tears. Fiona broke at the sight of him. "I never wanted you to ken."

Facing Wilkes, she said, "Your father took away everything from me. My sense of safety, my honor, my peaceful marriage. Well, today I'm reclaiming myself. The truth is I did nothing wrong. I defended myself and I refuse to hide or be his victim forever."

Lieutenant Wilkes rubbed his ear, as though her words unlocked a memory. His voice became subdued. "When I was a boy, maybe eight, we were at a crowded ball. I didn't understand it at the time—I saw my father dragging a semi-conscious woman into a room—then heard the door bolt lock." Lieutenant Wilkes' eyes welled. "We never spoke of it."

Fiona placed her hands on Broderick's shoulders and turned him toward the lieutenant. "This is your brother."

The moment was shattered by a scream in the distance. *Annaliese's* scream.

William sprinted, slipping down a hill of dirt and stone leading to another decaying tower's base, with everyone panting to keep up.

Lord Percy called from a window dripping with icicles. "MacLeod, I've got your girl."

Moonlight made the snowy courtyard glow blue. Fiona saw the terror in her husband's and Annaliese's eyes. Snow blew through the window opening.

William bellowed, "Let her go."

"As you wish," Lord Percy said with a smile, then shoved her over the ledge.

Annaliese fell, shrieking, as MacLeod watched in horror. The girl reached out for help, just like in Fiona's vision, but grabbed nothing but wind through brittle branches.

Fiona lifted her hands to the sky. "*Eisd rium a Dhia.* Protect the changeling girl."

All sense of time dissolved as the child flew backwards, swept into a churning whiteness.

A loud pop followed a flash as Wilkes aimed his Brown Bess at Lord Percy, but the bullet hit stone instead. William charged like a bull into the castle with *Justice* drawn as Wilkes rammed the rod to reload.

Lord Percy said, "You bloody traitor." A blast leveled Wilkes into a snowdrift, soon colored red with blood.

Not stopping to think, Fiona ran inside the tower, but the ruins were disorienting, a tangle of crumbling stone and snow blowing through open spaces. Fiona moved silently, scanning the shadows as she entered a cavernous ancient dining hall, which led to the parapet overlooking the Firth of Clyde.

Laughter rolled somewhere beyond her. The slow, metallic *click-clack* of Lord Percy's pistol cock echoed in the domed room. Fiona froze. *Where's William?*

Lord Percy said, "I still have two bullets, MacLeod. One for you, and one for your lovely witch wife."

Every hair on her arms stood upend. Creeping beneath wooden rafters of a middle ceiling that had splintered and fallen long ago, she spotted William gripping his broadsword tighter, studying the shifting shapes floating along the walls.

"Come out and fight me, then, Lord Percy of the Iron Fist," William mocked, circling.

"I should thank you. You made me," came the voice from the shadows.

MacLeod wheeled around. "I didna make you. You chose who you wanted to become."

Bang.

Justice clattered as it landed, making sparks against the rocks it hit as William fell to his knees, gripping his side.

"William!" Fiona knelt beside him, pressing the wound to stop the bleeding.

"Run," MacLeod gasped, trying to rise.

Lord Percy appeared from his hiding spot and aimed for her head. Fiona backed away with the harried feel of a trapped animal. The pistol jammed, and Percy dropped it in frustration. He tugged a leather strap on his right arm, releasing a ten-inch dagger from his iron hand. "Who needs a gun?"

Fiona bolted onto the crumbling parapet, but Percy caught her hair, yanking her back into his control. He held the blade against her soft neck, drawing her into his chest, close enough to kiss, as William watched helplessly through the door opening.

"And I thought all witches were ugly. Do you have a magical cunt? I'll find out."

Fiona's whole body shook with tremors passing like waves through her limbs until the atmosphere changed. She spun to face Lord Percy. Her movement and the odd sky startled him, and he retreated a step on the icy rampart, letting his knife dip lower.

Fiona raised her arm, spreading all five fingers. "*Eisd rium a Dhia.* I call forth the Merry Dancers of Skye to curse you."

Lord Percy blinked rapidly. "What?"

Green clouds spiraled across the heavens, glowing over the violent sea. "*Eisd rium a Dhia.* I curse you Lord Percy to claim the fate you wished on us."

"You're truly a witch? With powers?" Lord Percy stumbled backwards onto the uneven battlements marked with blasts from previous invaders.

MacLeod panted, slowly rising, pressing his left hand against his bleeding wound. "Aye, my wife's a witch. And I'm a better shot than you."

Bang.

Percy squealed like a pig as he fell over the ramparts until a spiked rock impaled him. A shocked expression etched over Percy's dying face as his guts spilled into the dark waters.

Fiona ran into William's arms, and he sagged against her. Catching his breath, he kissed her hard and she savored the scratch of his whiskers against her lips. Green waves of the Northern Lights flashed purple then faded, leaving them again in the darkness.

A slow smile crept over Fiona's mouth. "You see the merits of magic?"

He let out a shaky laugh. "Aye. Only when you practice it."

They heard sobs and looked down. Annaliese had fallen into a snowbank in the inner courtyard. Broderick rocked her in his arms.

Annaliese was crying. Crying means life.

Chapter Fifty-Four

WILLIAM MACLEOD

William MacLeod cradled Annaliese while Fiona dressed her wounds. Her arm was hurt, and her chin needed a stitch, but remarkably she lived. Fallen leaves covered in a deep snowdrift cushioned her fall just enough to permit survival.

Fiona always carried a satchel of herbs and supplies on her horse, and her foresight paid dividends. William glanced at his side, now tightly wrapped. The bullet had gone straight through his waist and out his back.

Fiona said to Broderick, "Check Lord Percy's pack. See if he has bandages. I've run out."

As Broderick went to the horse, Fiona checked Lieutenant Wilkes, who rested against a pillow of snow. Lord Percy's bullet was lodged in his shoulder. After Fiona dug out the round, she stitched up the wound.

"Mam, Da, look," Broderick said, with a fistful of letters.

William said, "What the devil? These are the letters I sent to you and Lord Hallewell. How did Percy get them?"

Fiona held a letter. She looked at William and then averted her gaze. She muttered, "How could I have doubted you? Of course you wrote to me."

Lieutenant Wilkes scanned a half-written letter. "Mr. MacLeod, you should see this."

As William read, his facial muscles went slack.

Broderick asked, "What happens now?"

"Let the buzzards pick at Lord Percy's brains," Lieutenant Wilkes said.

Fiona said, "And what of me?"

Wilkes thought for a moment, then spoke in a lower-pitched voice. "Beyond my mother, no one needs to know how my father died ... I've no interest in involving the law." To William, "You have my word our dispute is settled." He shared a pained glance with Fiona. "I'm sorry ... for what my father did to you."

William said, "Broderick, help Lieutenant Wilkes onto his horse."

The half-brothers walked off, speaking quietly. Wilkes gave a nod, a final glimpse at Broderick, then rode off.

As Fiona gathered her things and mounted her stallion, William gingerly approached with Annaliese. "You haven't properly met, have you? This is Annaliese Cameron."

They nodded at each other.

"Mam, why don't you ride ahead?" Broderick held her stare, making it apparent he wanted to speak with William alone.

Fiona nodded and the boy lifted Annaliese in front of her. They rode toward home.

A falling star fell over the snowy field as MacLeod and Broderick walked side by side. Snow crunched beneath their brogues as they entered the forest. It appeared enchanted, sparkling with snow on each branch. When they reached the creek by the old tree, MacLeod washed the blood from his hands in the water trickling around the rocks. "I'm sure you have questions."

Broderick ran his fingers through his dark hair, exhaling. "Where to begin? I never ken why you hated me, what I had done. It makes sense now, beyond my cowardice."

MacLeod inhaled before facing his son. The lad's cheeks grew red from the cold. "Whenever I looked at you, it reminded me of my failings, and no man wants to be reminded of that. I still feel guilty—I should have never left your mother's side."

Broderick sighed. "All I ever wanted was to be like you." Picking up stones amongst the ice and the twigs, he threw one into the creek. It landed with a plop. "And all you ever wished was that I'd never been born."

Shite. That came out wrong. "I wish a lot of things. I wish your mother had never been raped, I wish the reverend hadn't inserted himself into our private decisions, I wish I'd been kinder to you. I'm saying my anger's been misdirected. I've been angry with you when I should have been angry with myself all these years."

Broderick skipped the last stone before speaking. "Wouldn't it make more sense to be angry with Colonel Wilkes? He was the rapist."

Why hadn't I ever realized that before? Swallowing the lump in his throat, he nodded. "Aye."

Broderick moved toward the alder tree, glancing at Fiona chatting with Annaliese beneath the moonlight. "My mother murdered my father."

MacLeod shifted foot to foot.

An inch of snow rested on the swing. Broderick brushed it off and sat. Tall trees creaked in the wind. "I guess—I guess I should be grateful you raised me. Not all men would have, even if the Church forced them." He kept rubbing his head, never quite sure where to land his gaze.

All MacLeod's nagging worries about how he treated Broderick were confirmed. Didna Rob Birch treat Annaliese monstrously and think she should be grateful for getting scraps from his table?

MacLeod leaned his throbbing side against the thick tree, its bark scratching him. The scent of pinecones and his house smoldering in the distance filled his nostrils. *I have to make it up to him. Show him the same patience—the same love—I do with Annaliese, no matter how hard it gets.* MacLeod grew flustered, curling his hands inward. "I couldna see past my pain to love you, even though you did nothing wrong." He lightly touched his son's shoulder. "Broderick, I'm sorry. For everything."

Broderick stared at his feet before lifting his eyes. "Do you think I'll become like Colonel Wilkes? Are criminal traits inherited?"

"I dinna ken about traits, but I ken you. You care too much to hurt other people for fun. I'm proud to call you my son, Broderick MacLeod."

Broderick nodded carefully, then rose. "We should get back."

Small animals rustled in the underbrush as they walked toward the path. MacLeod said, "Why did they tie you to a tree?"

A shy grin crept across Broderick's face. "They tried to hurt Mam, so I tackled Lord Percy and beat his face until two soldiers pulled me off."

MacLeod laughed out loud. "Broderick? Fighting armed ruffians three to one? No wonder they bound you."

Broderick grinned. "MacLeods hold fast." His face fell. "Though I suppose I'm a Wilkes. I look like my half-brother." Tilting his head, he mused aloud, "How many siblings do you think I have? I have an entire second family."

"I dinna ken, but I doubt they'll be interested in having dinner with you."

Broderick snickered. "Dinner would be awkward, wouldnae it?"

Slow grins spread across their faces and they both began to laugh at the absurdity. MacLeod hugged Broderick for the first time in his life.

When they reached home, William and Fiona stood bloody and battered in front of their clan and smoldering house. Their sons joined them, visibly shaken. Holding Fiona's hand, William finally felt at peace.

"We'll rebuild stronger," he said. "These are things. We all have each other, aye?"

It felt so good to be a family again. Annaliese stood outside their circle until Fiona reached out and pulled her into their fold. Their own clan.

That night, they had a celebration with the whole village. They huddled in the barn, catching each other up on the last half year of turmoil and triumph. Somehow, they found whiskey. Their second son, David, played his bagpipes, and everyone danced reels until the wee hours. Horses snorted and whinnied as the villagers and Malcolm said goodnight and went home with their picks and axes and new stories to tell.

William sat on his favorite chair, now with a bullet hole, inside the barn. His brother, Cam, sat next to him on Annaliese's trunk, eating some mutton stew the village women had scraped together. William put his hand on Cam's shoulder. "Thank you."

"You really shagged the sheep, didna you, wee brother?"

He cringed. "Aye."

"It's going to be a cold winter. You should move your family home." Cam bit into his steaming stew. "We could use a barrister in the clan who kens English laws. You can always rent a croft house on Skye from The Wolf, or you can come with me to Raasay and help with my shipping business."

"Ack, I'm done with ships."

"I'm being serious. Change is coming." Cam passed his whiskey flask over a bucket of water. "To the true king. The time is coming. Not now, but it's coming. You'll need to choose a side."

Chaff floated in the moonlit air, landing on sweet-smelling hay bales. Fiona's cat, Pooka, curled around his leg then left to pursue a mouse.

"I've no interest in clan disputes, nor who sits on the throne."

Cam snorted. "No interest? How about duty?"

William thought a long moment, then slowly nodded. "Aye. When my house was burning and Englishmen were tossing coins to purchase my wife and sons, it was our clan who saved us. It's time to stop chasing British aristocracy and come home. I see that now."

"Good," Cam said, smiling. "You look better in plaid anyway. And get a proper bonnet, for Christ sake." Cam chewed on his meat as Annaliese's laughter rang out. William's sons joined in, ribbing each other. "Now, what about the lass?"

William had never seen Annaliese at such ease before. "What about her?"

"Is she yours?"

The cat chased a mouse across the floor. "Absolutely not. Eleanor's diary proves it."

Cam nodded, biting into a turnip. "You're sure there're no pages missing?"

William's jaw clenched. "Positive."

"Fiona's about to read it now. The girl handed it to her." Cam nodded to Fiona, climbing the wooden ladder into the loft.

Shite. William blushed. *Will she forgive me?*

Cam said, "I can take the lass back with us. Clan Cameron's on the way. She should be raised by her mother's people."

William shook his head. "She belongs to Lord Hallewell. You ken the law."

"There's the law and there's what's right. Fiona might forgive you, but do you think Lord Hallewell will?"

"I didna—"

"I ken. I'm sure he'll welcome you and the bairn with open arms. English nobles are famous for their compassion."

Hamish tapped on William's back. "Excuse me, Da."

"What?"

"Did Annaliese really climb a mast a hundred feet high? Lachlan and Broderick say it's bollocks, but she swears she did, and to ask you. Did she?"

"I'll be over in a minute. And watch your mouth." Hamish ran back to the children.

Cam drank from his flask. "Interesting lass."

MacLeod took a long sip as well. "You've no idea, brother."

Lantern light flickered on the loft ceiling. *How far into the diary was Fiona now?*

"My family will leave with you in the morning. I'll come to Skye after I settle the girl in London."

"It's for the best," Cam said.

"Aye."

William headed over to his family. Broderick and Lachlan rested on their arms around a small fire. Fiona's sister and Nelly had already fallen asleep near the children. William tucked in Hamish, then Annaliese—with her arm in a sling—under an old blanket.

Fiona glanced over the rail, closing Eleanor's diary. He gulped.

Annaliese tugged his sleeve. "Tell her you're on a new trajectory."

A half-smile played on his lips. "Aye." He kissed her forehead goodnight.

Climbing the ladder, he sat next to his wife, inhaling the sweet hay, grateful their ordeal had ended and that he was home.

Fiona slapped him hard across his face.

MacLeod lowered his eyes and nodded. "I didna plan on it to happen."

She slapped him again.

"I'm sorry." It would be stupid to say it was only one kiss or that it happened long ago. Everything was new and raw for Fiona. "Can you forgive me?"

"I've a confession, too," she whispered, not quite able to hold his gaze. "I sent the storm."

A sudden feeling of coldness expanded in his core. "What?"

"I placed a curse on you." She added quickly, "I didna wish you death, only redemption."

They blinked at each other.

"You cursed me?" He scratched the back of his neck in disbelief.

"I didna plan on it to happen," she said, with the same tone he had used. Fiona's words gushed from her mouth. "In fairness, my redemption curse worked. You're home. You're yourself again. And you've finally reconciled with Broderick. I probably should have held my tongue about it, but after so many lies revealed and secrets spilled today, what's one more confession?"

Heat rose to his face as he breathed through his nostrils. But then it struck him. "What does it say about me that I drove the kindest, most peace-loving woman on the planet to lay a curse on my head? I suppose I deserved a redemption spell. I'm sorry for all I've put you through."

Fiona hugged him. "All this time I thought my second sight was a curse, but it's a blessing, a gift from God."

"We still need to hide your powers from most of the world, but I promise you'll never have to hide who you are from me. Now let me try some sorcery on you." Pointing his finger at her forehead, he said sternly, "Man. Wolf. Dog. Sun."

"Ack, no more curses, please. Every time a spell is cast, we end up with another bastard."

A smile crept across her face. MacLeod kissed her deeply, tasting the sweetness of her mouth, smelling the earthy scent of mugwort on her clothes. He stroked her cheek, happy to see her smiling again.

"Fiona, you always could hold my attention."

Chapter Fifty-Five

ANNALIESE

"Time to meet your father."

MacLeod rented a black post-chaise with four brown horses on Lord Hallewell's credit. A handsome postillion sporting a tricorn hat helped Annaliese hobble inside, her arm still throbbing in a sling. She bounced excitedly on the red-and-white-striped cushions.

"Behave," Mac said, tilting his wool bonnet the proper Scottish way before climbing in.

It was a tight fit, even for two. Fluffing her petticoats, she flattened her blue cloak with her palm, then caressed the velvet seats. "Ain't never felt nothing so soft."

"Annaliese, your grammar. We pause your lessons for three days and you're back in the wilderness."

The postillion clicked his tongue, and they left. Everything looked different from home—the stone houses with thatched roofs, the ancient churches and crumbling castles dotting each village, even the cows looked different. Snow melted from the branches in the forest they passed.

"This where the Powhatans live?"

"No, love, this isn't Virginia. Enough chatter. Let's use this time wisely. What are you to do when we arrive?"

"Curtsey and say, 'Good afternoon, Father.'"

"It's a formality, but you're not his legitimate bairn. Say, 'Good afternoon, *my lord*.'"

Annaliese frowned. "Good afternoon, *my lord*," she muttered.

"And if he asks you something?"

We practiced this a million times already. "Answer politely. Hold his eyes. Boy, do I got some questions for him."

"No."

"I traveled across the ocean and cain't ask him one question?"

"Annaliese, I dinna like your tone. You're blessed Lord Hallewell rescued you. His only duty is to pay for your care, not sit for an inquisition."

"I only want to know him, is all. I won't say nuthin'. I'll be good."

Roasting lamb chops scented the air. A young couple kissed near a haystack then went inside a stone cottage. Last night, she saw MacLeod give his wife a long kiss in the barn, away from everyone's eyes. Annaliese reckoned she shouldn't have stared at them, but she'd never seen married people in love.

A city crammed with towering buildings with mismatched stone came into view. Some shops had pointed roofs and weathervanes spinning in the wind. Older boys carried a finely dressed lady seated in a chair up a steep alleyway as people lugging bundles shoved past. Annaliese gaped at hundreds of people walking at the speed of running.

"Edinburgh has grown," he said, craning his neck out the window. "They're draining the north loch to build a new town. No one wants to live in the medieval part anymore."

"Is that a castle?"

"No, the castle is on the hill. That's the University of Edinburgh."

"Will I go to school there?"

"No, lass." MacLeod rubbed his thumb across his lips, staring out the window.

Scullery maids in upper balconies called, "Gardyloo," then emptied chamber pots to the street as people dodged the filth. Urine mixed with the fish market stench. *In a few days, I'll be alone and unwanted. Everything stinks here.*

Ten days of traveling later, they left the final inn and headed to London on the road from Greenwich. Wiggling her fingers, she was happy to no longer need her sling.

"How many tolls until we arrive, lad?"

"Three, sir," the postillion said, holding his hand over his eyes to block the snow flurries.

MacLeod nodded, climbing inside. His head scraped the roof. "Today's the day."

"Good afternoon, *my* lord. Good afternoon, my *lord*."

Fried eggs and blood pudding from the taverns scented the air. Shops unraveled before her from a never-ending spool. Apothecary. Law Office. Wig Shop. In a blink, the landscape changed. MacLeod pointed out the Thames River, which appeared and disappeared as they wound through another forest. They stopped at the first turnpike and the postillion paid some copper coins.

Bouncing her leg unconsciously, she was startled when MacLeod tapped her knee and said, "Dinna fash. Just be a polite version of yourself."

Wish I was anyone but me.

Another town appeared. Ladies with big hair and exquisite hats strolled past broad-faced men on horseback. They stopped at the second turnpike. One toll left.

"Am I ever gonna see you again?"

"Annaliese, look at me. After all we've been through? Certainly, we'll meet again."

She inhaled deeply to calm herself, then crinkled her nose. "It smells like a stale fart."

"Welcome to London. That's why the postillion wears a nosegay."

Curiosity replaced her nervous thoughts. They snaked through the congested streets. "There're so many buildings. Cain't hardly see the tops, though."

"London's foggy. There's the Monument," he said, pointing. "To remember the Great Fire of 1666."

Twisting, she gawked at the column grasping for the sky.

Further down the road, he pointed out the Tower. "Do you know what the first Norman king's name was before he became William the Conqueror?"

"William MacLeod?" she guessed.

"William the Bastard," he said. Aye, it's true. His father was a king, his mother was a tanner's daughter."

Annaliese giggled. "There's hope for me." She glanced down and gasped. "My gloves. I left them on the nightstand. We have to go back."

"Dinna fash yourself. You have another pair in your trunk."

"But what if my father sees my hand before I put gloves on?" Her lungs grew tight and the lump in her throat felt painful. Everything began to itch.

The horses drove hard, and the landscape blurred. Merchant signs, townspeople, cottages. Two boys boxed on a corner. A crowd swarmed, throwing pennies. Everything moved too fast.

Mac squeezed her hand, interrupting her thoughts. "Your pa told you this scar marks you as worthless, right?"

Traffic snarled to a halt. She nodded, blinking back tears.

"What do *you* believe it says about you?"

Closing her eyes, she stroked the puckered skin, remembering all the times Pa had hurt her, used her, laughed as she cried. Every day he tried to tear her down, but she was still standing. The tightness in her chest loosened and her breath came a little easier.

"I'm strong."

Mac nodded. "Our pasts make us who we are. Take pride in your wounds."

They paid the final toll and steered onto a private road lined with snow-dusted trees. A three-story stone palace with four gray-white columns came into view. Untouched snow covered the grounds, stretching in every direction for miles. Above the turret, a union flag snapped in the wind under a cloudless sky.

"My father lives here? He a king?"

"He's richer than one, as long as he stays away from card games."

A sculpture of a soldier on a rearing horse overpowered the lawn. "That was General Winston. Your father married his widow, Lady Margaret."

"She's the real rich one, huh?"

"That's one way to describe her."

Dozens of stable boys brushed down stallions in a barn larger than three governor's mansions back in Williamsburg. They crossed an arched bridge over a frozen pond pretty as a painting that led to a mansion with more windows than she could count.

"How many people live here?"

"Only his family and the help, about sixty-five total, but it fluctuates. He often hosts guests. I'll need to have a few private words with your father before you meet him."

Servants in blue uniforms assembled as they approached. She remembered having to line up on the plantation when important men visited Master Crowan.

"Ma would have stood there?"

"Hm? Aye."

They jostled to a stop. Annaliese flashed a smile, a mixture of panic and thrill, guessing at her future. "We made it."

A footman opened the door. MacLeod went out first, then the footman reached for her trembling hand. She leaned her head back to gape all the way to the top of the building.

Servants stared at her and pointed at Mr. MacLeod's tartan, whispering until a man dressed in a black overcoat and powdered wig coughed disapprovingly. Everyone went quiet.

Annaliese curtsied. "Good afternoon, Father."

MacLeod yanked her arm, smiling nervously. "That's the butler. Get up."

"Oh, sorry. He looked important."

The butler bowed politely as the servants exchanged glances. Tugging on Mac's coat, she whispered, "I have to make water."

He crinkled his brows. "Now?"

"I'm nervous. Where's the outhouse?" she asked, searching around.

An older woman dressed in black with an enormous key ring tied to her waist came forward and took Annaliese's hand. "I'll take her." She glanced at Annaliese's scar but said nothing.

I'm not bad, I'm strong.

MacLeod followed. "I need to speak with Lord and Lady Hallewell."

Chapter Fifty-Six

LADY MARGARET

London

Lady Margaret swirled the claret in her glass as her lady's maid scooped a dollop of pig fat and worked it into her hair, pressing and pinning it into curls crowning her face.

"Too tight." Lady Margaret winced, shooting a grimace that made the girl quake.

"Sorry, my lady." The maid took a thin brush in trembling hands, stroking powder over each tress, finishing quickly.

Lady Margaret thought MacLeod's shipwreck would make her happier, but it caused more problems. Now aware that his mistress and bastard were dead, Lord Hallewell had no impetus to move to Oxford and thus stayed home in constant inebriation. She couldn't even escape into the joys of high society. Attending balls lost their fun since Plump Catherine was now Pregnant Catherine. Lord Percy's betrayal made her mood bleak as the English weather.

Lady Margaret waved off the servant and stared out the window. A carriage with four horses traveled up their private road. *Lord Percy?* Who else would come in the snow?

Squealing with delight, she left the window. *Why does he come directly? Did he discover my double-cross warning to Fiona? Good ... Yet*, she hoped he would attempt to woo her back.

Adding rouge to her cheeks, she grew giddy. With MacLeod's family destroyed, Percy would finally challenge her husband to a duel and end her misery. *Even if I'll never be Percy's wife, at least I can be George's widow.*

Lady Margaret smiled at her reflection, enjoying the sensation of being a master puppeteer, then descended the stairs. Servants fled at her footfall.

"My lady, a guest ..."

Pushing past the butler, she plopped on the couch, gracefully fluffed out her petticoats and stroked Fiona's bracelet, giddy to see Percy. Directing her gaze to the crackling fire at the other end of the study, she gasped. "You're alive?"

MacLeod said, "Nice to see you, too." His damp hair still held snow.

"Are Eleanor and my daughter alive?" Lord Hallewell asked, bursting into the room with his drink in hand.

"Just the girl."

Lord Hallewell collapsed ashen-faced on a chair, lowering his drink to a table.

MacLeod glanced at Lady Margaret. "Lieutenant Wilkes came to call on me. Nice lad. I allowed him to leave breathing."

Lady Margaret shrunk in her seat. *How can this be happening?*

MacLeod stood stone-faced with his legs in the stance of a warrior. "Lord Percy paid me a visit as well." MacLeod unearthed an iron fist from his pocket and dropped it, chipping the hardwood floor.

"Oh my God," she said, covering her mouth, feeling her eyes bulging. She tried to plan her next steps, but her mind fogged.

MacLeod said to Lord Hallewell, "I think Lord Percy wanted to pit us against each other. I found intercepted letters from me to you in his pack, and this correspondence with a mercenary plotting your murder."

Lord Hallewell rose, sobered, then read the letter, trying to comprehend it. MacLeod glanced between the two.

Taking quick, shallow breaths, her mind raced. *Percy must not have mentioned me in the assassination plot, otherwise the constable would be here, too.* All was not lost. Seizing her opportunity, she gripped Lord Hallewell's trembling hands. "I was right to warn Fiona of my suspicions about Lord Percy. I never trusted the man. Thank God she took heed and found help."

Lord Hallewell retreated a step. "While you were warning Fiona, you might have warned me." He stared at Percy's iron fist. "He plotted my murder?"

Lady Margaret said, "You suspected already. Weren't you hiding from him to avoid a duel? It was only a matter of time before he came for you." Her heart pounded in her ears. *Shift allegiances. Act the thankful wife.* Hugging Lord Hallewell tightly, she tried to force tears from an empty well. "Thank God MacLeod stopped Lord Percy, or it could have been you dead on the floor." Now actual tears fell.

Lord Hallewell tentatively hugged her back, then faced MacLeod. "We should speak privately."

"Aye."

Trembling, Lord Hallewell poured himself a drink, then picked up Lord Percy's mechanical hand. Lady Margaret stared as the iron fist, and the death of her hopes and plans, disappeared inside her husband's desk drawer. *What have I done?*

Barely making it three steps into the hall, MacLeod followed and grabbed her forearm. "Now that the Wilkes matter is settled, I consider all bribery payments completed. Fiona will be pleased at the safe return of her bracelet."

Lady Margaret swallowed. "Of course." Unhooking it, she handed it over.

MacLeod spoke in a hushed tone. "I suppose I should thank you, for warning Fiona about Lord Percy's plan. I'm curious why you did."

A hint of a smile crossed her face. "Keep the girl away from me, MacLeod," she whispered. "We'll fight another day." She turned her back to him.

Servants peeked from behind doors and around the corners. Her own hands went limp, and her chin sank into her chest. *Eleanor's bastard lives. Percy is dead by my own actions. Plump Catherine is the rich widow—not me. I've lost at everything.*

Chapter Fifty-Seven

WILLIAM MACLEOD

William MacLeod returned to the study. Much as he wanted to cleave off Lord Hallewell's head, there was Annaliese to consider.

Lord Hallewell sat behind his solid walnut desk guzzling port. "You brought the girl?"

"Aye. She's using the water closet."

"I had you expunged from Alexander's trust."

MacLeod nodded. "We'll settle on Annaliese's schooling, and we'll never have to cross paths again."

Lord Hallewell poured another glass, frowning at MacLeod's outfit. "Is she even mine? I hear women are drawn to men in Highlander garb."

MacLeod's cheeks grew hot. "She is. I have proof." He dropped Eleanor's diary on the desk with a thud.

Lord Hallewell crossed his arms. "No, I want to hear from you. Tell me about your affair with my mistress. All the servants knew. They were laughing at me. *You* were laughing at me."

"It wasn't an affair; it was one drunken kiss. Read Eleanor's diary since you dinna believe me. I've marked the section."

Lord Hallewell said, "Always the solicitor. I found my own evidence. I went to the Old Bailey and spoke with the Lord Mayor. Why would you betray me? I loved her. I bloody loved *you* as a brother."

"Eleanor stole from you. She would have cheated and dragged me down with her. I was protecting you, like I always do. Like you neglected to do for me."

Lord Hallewell's voice rose. "I don't protect you? Didn't I save you from the Wilkes situation?"

"You blackmailed me for the Wilkes situation."

"I never blackmailed you," Lord Hallewell said, leaving the safety of his desk.

"Not for money, but you certainly held it over my head." MacLeod scowled in disgust.

Lord Hallewell spoke full of righteous indignation. "I made you. I gave you your career, made you rich. I buried a body for you!"

"You made me? I made you. I found you a wife to gain back your status, and you transformed me from a friend into a prisoner." MacLeod's chest rose and fell, every muscle tightened. "You fucking bastard. I'm off for months to rescue your by-blow, and you send Wilkes after my wife?"

"Does it hurt to be betrayed, William?" Lord Hallewell asked with mock sympathy.

MacLeod drew his sword, ready to cut him in two, but stopped as his friend raised his hands and cowered.

Dropping to his knees, Lord Hallewell said on the verge of tears, "Kill me. I've nothing to live for."

MacLeod curled his lip and lowered his sword. "Aye, you do. Her name's Annaliese." Returning *Justice* to her sheath, he said, "And you've other bairns besides, you selfish shite."

Lord Hallewell tugged at his jabot. "It's shameful, isn't it? How utterly weak I am. The people I love don't love me back, the people I trust betray me. Am I really so reprehensible, William?"

"Aye."

Lord Hallewell's eyes bulged, and he itched his neck.

MacLeod said, "How is it your wife, who hates me, does more to protect my family than you? She warned Fiona about Percy. You never answered my wife's cries for help. She killed Colonel Wilkes in self-defense during a rape—Jesus Christ, you helped me bury him—yet you sent Wilkes' son after her?"

A rash spread across Lord Hallewell's neck, creeping up his cheeks as he rose, grasping MacLeod's arm. "No, William, I told Wilkes *you* killed the colonel. I was furious you shipped away the woman I loved. I was hoping he'd duel you when you returned. You have to believe I would never put Fiona in danger, never. I didn't know Wilkes had joined forces with Percy, or I would have sent her protection. On my honor, it's the truth." Lord Hallewell walked a few steps away, pulling the jabot from his neck, wheezing.

MacLeod studied Lord Hallewell's slumping frame and knew him to be telling the truth. "What's wrong? Are you well?"

Hives spread to Lord Hallewell's face. "No, I'm not bloody well," he panted. "I haven't had rashes like this since I was a little boy, but now they come constantly." He tore at his skin. "Could this day become more humiliating?"

"My lord, breathe." MacLeod put his hand on Lord Hallewell's shoulder. "George, breathe. This flustering and the hives happen to Annaliese as well." MacLeod helped him onto a chair.

Lord Hallewell glanced up, eyes welling. "She gets rashes, too?"

"Aye. Whenever she gets upset."

Lord Hallewell inhaled deeper. "She's really mine?"

"That's what I've been telling you."

Lord Hallewell slumped in his chair, elbows resting on his knees. It took several minutes to compose himself. "Well. How horribly embarrassing," he said, laughing nervously.

MacLeod sat beside him. "I never meant to betray anyone. Not my wife. Not you. Shite, not even Eleanor. I thought sending her away solved things, for me at least." He beheld his friend's eyes. "I should never have done so."

They sat in silence for a long moment.

"I suppose we've both done horrible things," Lord Hallewell conceded.

MacLeod said, "If you were ever truly my friend, we'll call a truce. I'll stay in Scotland, you stay here."

Lord Hallewell nodded, and the hives slowly receded from his cheeks. "Thank you—for bringing my daughter home. How did Eleanor die? When?"

"In childbirth, after she sent you the letter."

"I wish she were here. There was so much left unsaid."

MacLeod picked up Eleanor's diary and flipped to a well-worn page. "You'll want to read about the day Annaliese was born. It may comfort you."

Chapter Fifty-Eight

Eleanor

Virginia Colony, December 25, 1730

My dearest George,

Today, I held our daughter for the first time. She's perfect.

Our baby had the good sense to wait until Christmas afternoon to arrive, a half day off for slaves and indentured. From three o'clock in the afternoon until eleven at night, the cook, bless her, helped to midwife me between roasting Christmas goose for the Crowans. Wiping the sweat from my brow, she rubbed my aching back, and gave me chamomile tea for my stomach, but nothing would stop the hiccups. You'd think I was drunk.

Labor pains. Yet another hazard of being a daughter of Eve. Adam's descendants have it easier. You're in your mansion, probably playing at rantum-scantum with a new servant, while your bitch wife buys jewels she never wears. Then there's Mr. MacLeod. He warned me he'd be the one to lower the ax. In my stupid naivety, I didna believe him.

I scribbled his name from the journal's inscription. I almost ripped it out completely, except his advice was good. *Reflect.* My choices led me to be exiled in the wilderness, didna they? George, I'm sorry. You were always good to me. I stole and cheated and now here I am in hell. A piece of me loved you, but it frightened me. It doesna matter now, I suppose.

Gripping the birthing stool, I prayed to Jesus to let this bairn come out. The pain was excruciating, a burning that ripped me to shreds. I cried out for my mother, long dead and in the dirt of Inverness. No husband, no sisters to guide me. Barely nineteen. A violent push later, and the cook pulled out our daughter, slimy and wet.

In comes the mistress with the reverend to take my baby to the orphanage. I haven't even held her, George. "No, please," I begged.

Master Crowan hears my cries. He inspects the babe, petting her fuzzy red hair.

"MacLeod, you Scottish bastard," he mumbled. "I knew there was a reason he negotiated such good freedom dues." My master sighed. "You may keep the bastard on the plantation. But mind, I own her indentured contract now. Since the reverend is here, let's baptize her. What's her name?"

I remembered a conversation with Mr. MacLeod. My mother was named Anna. His mother was named Elise. Mr. MacLeod's friendship with my master saved our child from the orphanage. I hope you won't mind her name. It was the right thing to do.

Finally, I held her.

"She's beautiful," I said, tears rolling down my cheeks. "My little Annaliese, you're going to make the world a better place."

Chapter Fifty-Nine

ANNALIESE

Annaliese left the water closet and the maid tapped Annaliese's nose with her finger. "Sweet child. You're Eleanor's girl."

"You knew Ma?"

"Shh, dear."

In the gallery, they bumped into a woman in a blood-red dress snapping orders at a thin man and a girl about ten. *Is this ...?* Annaliese curtsied at the man. "Good afternoon, Father."

Yanking her up, the maid said, "No, dear. This is Lady Margaret Hallewell and the tutor."

Annaliese scratched her head.

Lady Margaret gripped Annaliese's face in her icy fingers and lifted her chin toward the light of the chandelier. "You don't belong here."

The lady's brown eyes pierced her, making Annaliese squirm.

Releasing her tight grip on Annaliese, the lady said to the other girl, "Come along, Elizabeth." Scanning Annaliese up and down, the other girl said nothing. They disappeared into a room lined with books.

"Sweetheart, stop bowing to every man, thinking he's your father," whispered the maid.

"Sorry. I ain't known—don't know what a lord looks like. Please don't tell Mr. MacLeod on me."

"You've survived meeting her ladyship. There's no need to be nervous now."

Back at the grand entrance, Annaliese gazed up and realized the angels painted on the ceiling were completely naked, and she giggled uncontrollably all the way into an enormous study where Mac sat next to a medium-sized servant with a powdered wig catching his breath on a chair.

The maid curtsied, closing the thick doors as she left. Annaliese tried really hard to stop thinking about the angels' behinds, but she kept snickering.

"Annaliese." MacLeod rose, giving his evil eye, but she couldn't stop her giggles.

Covering her mouth made her laugh even harder.

"What are you twittering about?" the fancy servant asked, smiling.

"Them angels on the ceiling are naked! You can see their butts!" Tears rolled down, she laughed so hard. "Don't be mad, Mac. I won't do this in front of my father."

"Miss Annaliese, this is Lord Hallewell."

"Oh, bugger! I mean—I'm sorry! I'm so sorry! I ain't known—good afternoon, my lord." Her face burned as she curtsied, keeping her head bowed as her whole body trembled. *His lordship is really gonna kick me out now.*

"Stand up, child, I'm not the king."

Annaliese stood and stared at … her *father*. She panted like she'd run a mile.

Lord Hallewell held his hand over his mouth, slowly shaking his head. "William, she's a living portrait of Eleanor."

"Aye."

Lord Hallewell spoke to Annaliese. "I'll tell you a little secret. Many children laugh at those naked cherubs. Well, let's have a look. Spin around. Let me see you."

Lord Hallewell flicked his hand at her. Mac nodded. Annaliese spun around, maybe too fast. *I ain't known the right speed to present myself to a lord.*

Annaliese stared at his nose, his teeth, his blotchy red face. "You get rashes like me?"

He blushed. "I suppose I'm nervous meeting you, too."

"I hate hives. People think you're bewitched, too?"

Lord Hallewell scrunched his face. MacLeod gave her a subtle head shake.

"Have a seat." Lord Hallewell pointed to the chair he was sitting on and moved behind his desk. He offered her a small plate from a nearby table. "Would you like a biscuit?"

"Yes, please, my lord. I mean—" she heeded MacLeod. "Am I allowed?"

Lord Hallewell laughed. "You have her reasonably terrified of you. Good job, MacLeod. Yes, darling, it's allowed. I wouldn't have offered it to you otherwise."

"Thank you, my lord." Annaliese sat primly as she took the biscuit, the sweetest, most buttery thing she had ever tasted. "I ain't scared of Mac," she muttered, swinging her legs.

Mac's jaw went tight. He always acted a little nervous when she spoke to adults.

Lord Hallewell steepled his hands together and kept staring at her face while crumbs fell on her dress. "My condolences for your mother."

"Did you love her?" Annaliese moved her tongue over her teeth to get the crumbs out.

"That's not an appropriate question, Miss Annaliese," MacLeod gently scolded.

"Yes," Lord Hallewell said. "I loved her very much." Her father pulled a golden locket from his desk drawer. "See? You look exactly like her, except for your hair."

Annaliese took the locket. "A real painting of Ma? It's tiny." Running her finger over it, she said, "Ma looks so young. Ain't remembered how pretty she was." Annaliese smiled. "Ma loved you, too."

Lord Hallewell perked up. "Why do you say that?"

"'Cause she called out 'George' when she was dying. Pa's name was Rob."

"She said my name?" His voice hitched. He strode to the window to collect himself.

After several minutes, MacLeod tapped her shoulder. "Time to go."

Lord Hallewell sniffed and wiped his eyes. "Go? Why, she's only arrived."

Annaliese beamed and sat on the chair's edge. *My father wants me.*

Lord Hallewell seemed to take in everything about her. His brows knitted when his eyes rested on her burned hand. "What happened?"

MacLeod said, "Miss Annaliese, go explore the study."

Her face dropped. Sliding from her chair, she let them talk about her behind her back. MacLeod said to her father, "I need to tell you about Rob Birch."

Her heels clicked on the hardwood floors. Stunning red paisley rugs rested beneath carved furniture, prettier than anything at Sweetwater Plantation. There were shelves of books, a giant split stone with purple crystals inside, and trays of butterflies with their wings pinned open. A fiddle rested on a table. Annaliese plucked a string, and a loud *ping* came out, vibrating against her fingers.

"He did what?" Lord Hallewell shouted.

Annaliese backed away, fearing he was mad she had broken his fiddle, but then overheard MacLeod say, "My lord, she has no diseases, but it's too risky for her to go out in London society yet. God kens what she might say—"

Oh. That. Why'd Mac have to tell the truth and spoil the day? Couldn't he let my father believe I'm still a virgin?

The men spoke in low voices. It started getting dark. Servants came with long sticks to light the chandelier and the candles around the room. It looked bright as day.

Lord Hallewell called, "Come here, darling."

Annaliese raced over and he held her hands in his own. She gazed into his brown eyes.

He said, "How would you like to visit with me again this summer? I'll show you London. Sound appealing?"

My father wants to see me again? Annaliese covered her mouth. "This a trick?"

Her father laughed and said to Mac, "Her sense of humor positively tickles me."

Annaliese didn't realize she'd made a joke but was happy her father liked her.

"No trick, darling. I'm completely sincere. You are delightful, and I should very much like to take you to the theater. Eleanor loved the theater." Her father patted her cheek. "My children visit Oxford every summer, so we'll have an entire month together before they return."

Her face dropped. *Don't cry, Annaliese Cameron. What was you expecting? That he'd say, "Come live with my legitimate family?"*

Lord Hallewell drifted behind his enormous desk, its polished wood separating them, then pressed money into Mac's hand. "I believe this should cover all the expenses, not as your employer, but as your friend once again."

Mac's eyes grew wide. "Aye. See you in July, George."

"You can leave from the back entrance, so my wife and children don't see the girl. I'm resolved to get on good terms with Margaret. Why rile the beast?"

Annaliese forced a frozen smile and curtsied. Glancing once more at her mother's picture, she returned Lord Hallewell's locket to his desk and headed outside, hugging Ma's diary to her chest. *Ain't no one gonna take this from me again.* Beautiful shades of pink cast from the setting sun, but she only noticed the looming darkness as she climbed inside the coach.

MacLeod said, "That meeting went better than I thought. You dinna seem happy."

Annaliese shrugged. "Ditch me and be done. My brain hurts."

The postillion clicked his tongue, and the horses lurched forward.

"I should give you fair warning, lass. Your new tutor is extremely strict."

Slumping in her seat, she said, "Of course she is."

Sensing being watched, she saw the lady in red glowering at her from a third-floor window with the *legitimate* daughter next to her. *Is Lord Hallewell dumb enough to think his wife wouldn't know a bastard came to visit, even if we hadn't bumped into each other?*

"He is."

Annaliese glanced up. "Sorry, what?"

"Your tutor. You're looking at him."

She blinked. "What?"

"Fiona and I discussed it, and your father agreed just now. We're going to foster you on the Isle of Skye. How could I possibly leave you alone in London?"

"Really, Mac?" Annaliese threw her arms around his neck, not even minding the whiskers from his beard tickling her cheek.

"Aye."

Isle of Skye, Scotland

Annaliese sat in her nightgown by the hearth, playing with her doll while Fiona brushed her hair. Feeling toasty wrapped in a woolen plaid, she inhaled the salty-pine scent of the peat moss fire in MacLeod's croft house by the sea.

How noisy the house sounded! But the good noise of her five new brothers laughing and teasing while Nelly rocked the baby in her arms. Her face hurt from smiling so much. MacLeod affectionately squeezed Broderick's shoulder as he came over to adjust the peat with the fire poker.

Annaliese whispered to her doll and tipped her head back, laughing.

Mac knelt. "What's your doll saying, Annaliese?"

Flinging her arms around his neck, she felt the tickle of his whiskers on her cheek and whispered, "She says, 'I love you, Da.'"

Mac took his resolute bull broach and pinned it to her shawl, then squeezed her hand and said, "Now everyone will know you're part of our family."

Warmth spread throughout her body and a tear rolled down her cheek. That was the moment she knew she was home.

Acknowledgments

During the spring of 2020, both my favorite uncle and father-in-law died during lockdown and the world felt chaotic and dangerous. I remembered my own father, long past, and missed the power of his hug to soothe. Suddenly, this story spilled out of me. While editing, Roe v. Wade guaranteeing a woman's bodily autonomy was overturned and Fiona's plight felt visceral in a way it hadn't before. Even though this story is set in the past, it felt immediate.

Writing historical fiction is a labor of love and I'd like to thank the figurative midwives who helped along the way. Many thanks to the historians and re-enactors at Colonial Williamsburg for sharing their knowledge, especially Lindsey Foster. Thank you, Judy from Shirley Plantation, for the historical documents you sent me, and thank you history professor Dennis Johnson for checking my facts. Thank you, Anne Daly, for your guidance through Scottish history while showing me Glasgow, Edinburgh, the Highlands, and the Isle of Skye, and for pointing out secret passages in castle ruins. Thanks to therapists Nicole Richardson and Shawn Wood LCSW, CYC-P, who helped put my characters on the proverbial couch and, in Shawn's case, told me about Newfoundland. I'm grateful to have found the Jerry Jenkins Writers Guild and to have received amazing feedback from Jerry and my mentor, David Loy.

TO RESCUE A WITCH

The History Quill not only helped with valuable resources and peer-to-peer feedback, but also helped me figure out how a mechanical hand in the 18th century worked. Special thanks to Kahina Necaise for editing and helping me unearth MacLeod's original sin. Sydney Young, thank you for outstanding guidance, friendship and helping me rename the book! Thanks to my beta readers Meghan Montague, Deirdre Ryan, Amanda Wright, Shauna McIntyre and Gwen Langley. Your feedback was invaluable.

Finally, if you want a lesson in humility, ask your fifteen-year-old to read your first draft. Thank you, Rylee, for being my toughest editor and for all your fashion research. Little Henry—thanks for making me keep in the cuss word section and the funny parts. Big Henri—thanks for telling me that a whale is bigger than a shark (long story). I love all of you!

The books I read included:

Hudson, Jr., Carson O., *Witchcraft in Colonial Virginia*

Meiklejohn-Free, Barbara, *Scottish Witchcraft, A Complete Guide to Authentic Folklore, Spells, and Magickal Tools*

DK London, *A History of Magic, Witchcraft & The Occult*

Dr. Flamstead's and Mr. Patridge's New Fortune-book, Second Edition

Morse Earle, Alice, *Child Life in Colonial Times*

Grose, Captain Francis, *A Pocket Dictionary of the Vulgar Tongue*

Miley Theobald, Mary, *Death by Petticoat, American History Myths Debunked*

Olsen, Kirstin, *Daily Life in 18th-Century England*, Second Edition

Hagist, Don N., *Wives, Slaves, And Servant Girls, Advertisements for Female Runaways in American Newspapers, 1770-1783*

Gibson, John, Mayor and Fisher, William, Mayor, *Record of Indentures of Individuals Bound Out as Apprentices, Servants, Etc., in Philadelphia, Pennsylvania 1771-1773*

Eddy, Bill, *5 Types of People Who Can Ruin Your Life, Identifying and Dealing with Narcissists, Sociopaths, and Other High-Conflict Personalities*

Foyster, Elizabeth, *Marital Violence, An English Family History, 1660-1857*

Dana, Richard Henry, *Two Years Before the Mast*

LISA A. TRAUGOTT

Bowen, Ashley, *The Autobiography of Ashley Bowne 1728-1813*
Rees, Siân, *The Floating Brothel, The Extraordinary True Story of An Eighteenth-Century Ship and Its Cargo of Female Convicts*

A Note About the Author

Lisa A. Traugott lives in Austin, Texas with her husband, kids and English bulldog, Bruno.

Her memoir, *She's Losing It!* led to her being cast on John Cena's reality TV show *American Grit* where she managed to last five episodes. Who knew? She also wrote and illustrated *Mind Your Manners Minnie Monster*, which won a silver Mom's Choice Award. Fun fact: she spoke five lines on *Buffy the Vampire Slayer*.

If you're looking for fun content, head over to her websites:
LisaTraugott.com (Author blog)
ShesLosingIt.com (Fitness blog)
Instagram: @lisa__traugott.

Printed in Great Britain
by Amazon